On the Rim of Mexico

On the Rim of Mexico

*Encounters of the
Rich and Poor*

Ramón Eduardo Ruiz

Westview
PRESS

A Member of the Perseus Books Group

Copyright © 1998 by Westview Press, A Member of the Perseus Books Group

Published in 1998 in the United States of America by Westview Press, 5500 Central Avenue, Boulder, Colorado 80301-2877, and in the United Kingdom by Westview Press, 12 Hid's Copse Road, Cumnor Hill, Oxford OX2 9JJ

Library of Congress Cataloging-in-Publication Data
Ruiz, Ramón Eduardo.
    On the rim of Mexico : encounters of the rich and poor / Ramón Eduardo Ruiz.
        p. cm.
    Includes index.
    ISBN 0-8133-3499-3
    1. United States—Relations—Mexico.   2. Mexico—Relations—United States.   3. Mexican-American Border Region—Social conditions.
    4. Mexican-American Border Region—Economic conditions.
    5. Mexicans—Mexican-American Border Region—Ethnic identity.
    6. Mexicans—Mexican-American Border Region—Social conditions.
    7. Mexicans—Mexican- American Border Region—Economic conditions.
    I. Title.
    E183.8.M6R83   1998
    303.48'273072—dc21   98-23319
                                                                                                                    CIP

The paper used in this publication meets the requirements of the American National Standard for Permanence of Paper for Printed Library Materials Z39.48-1984.

PERSEUS
POD
ON DEMAND   10   9   8   7   6   5   4   3

He compuesto este estudio con viejos recuerdos de mi madre, de nombre Dolores Urueta, quien fué hija de un ranchero de Chihuahua y, gracias a la providencia, vivió años fortuitos en ambos lados de la frontera norte.

Se que es muy decente ser un escritor bien, pero estimo de mayor decencia ser un escritor honrado. . . . Y por ese motivo escribo lo que pienso y lo que siento, sin preocuparme porque mis opiniones coincidan o difieran de las comúnmente aceptadas.

—Mariano Azuela

Contents

Poor Mexico, so far from God and so near to the United States.

—Porfirio Díaz

Preface

This is a book about the people who live on the other side of the southern border of the United States—a sprawling landscape of mostly arid lands and deserts that stretches from the Mexican city of Tijuana, cheek by jowl with the Pacific Ocean, to Matamoros, in the neighborhood of the Gulf of Mexico—and their links to the other side, where Americans make their homes from Brownsville to San Ysidro. It is one of the longest international boundaries in the world, setting apart two entirely different countries for more than two thousand miles. Nowhere else does a poor, Third World country like Mexico share a common border with a wealthy, powerful neighbor.

As any reading of American journals readily informs, the borderlands, to employ a term coined by the historian Herbert E. Bolton, are headline news: Witness the hullabaloo attached to the North American Free Trade Agreement (NAFTA) and the global economy, the pundits who label assembly plants the saviors of the Mexican poor, the accounts applauding the capture of Mexican drug lords, and column upon column devoted to stories about illegal immigration, to call to mind just four topics of the day. For Mexico and the United States alike, border relations should be a matter of special interest. Both California and Texas, two of the biggest and richest states of the American union, front on Mexico, as do Arizona and New Mexico. Every day, more and more people inhabit both sides of the international line. A huge majority of Mexicans depend for their livelihood, either directly or indirectly, on the United States, but just the same, American border cities would slumber were it not for cheap labor and customers hungry for American goods. The exchange of goods and services underlies the dynamics of border economics.

The subject of the Mexican border brings back memories of my youth and forebears. My mother, her father and mother, and her grandparents, as well as patriarchs before them, were born and matured on the outskirts of Parral, a mining town in the border province of Chihuahua that dates from the early seventeenth century, where most of them were also overtaken by death. My mother and two of her sisters were the exceptions; they married, migrated north, and then succumbed on this side of the border. One of the sisters, who dwelled for decades in Ciudad Juárez, is buried there. Her oldest daughter, after divorcing a captain in the Mexican army, married a fat, and probably corrupt, policeman in Ciudad Juárez. For my part, excluding time spent flying aircraft in the army air force during World War II and memorable years in Massachusetts, I have spent most of my life within hailing distance of the Mexican border, at one time or another calling Texas, New Mexico, Arizona, and California home. El Paso and Ciudad Juárez, as well as the two Nogales, I know from my youth—a long, long while ago—when my parents decided that I should study at the National Autonomous University of Mexico; those were the days of train travel to Mexico City by way of those ports of entry, lonely journeys for someone young and away from home for the first time. In the 1960s, when my family and I had a home in northern Mexico, we passed through Nuevo Laredo countless times, as well as Piedras Negras, Ciudad Acuña, and Brownsville.

My memory of Tijuana goes back to the early 1930s, when my father, whose idea of a Sunday was to visit Mexican friends, would drive his family there. On the way home, he stopped at the Long Bar, the longest in the world, as the sign over its doors proclaimed, to drink a bottle of Mexicali beer and decry, one foot on the copper railing, the injustice of Prohibition. My wife—who is also of Mexican stock and speaks Spanish as I do—and I have lived all over Mexico and in the border states, in Hermosillo, the capital of Sonora, on a ranch in the municipality of Arteaga, Coahuila, and in the industrial citadel of Monterrey, Nuevo León. I grew up in a small town on the outskirts of San Diego, which had no more than 250 thousand inhabitants, and I recall Tijuana, the home of our eldest daughter, now an anthropologist at the Colegio de la Frontera Norte, when it was a "typical" border town, as Americans were wont to say. The saloons on Avenida Revolución outnumbered respectable places of business, but it was also a place to meet girls at the Sunday-evening dances at the *palacio municipal*, where mothers kept a watchful eye on their daughters' virtue. Much of what I write about comes from people I met during my visits and travels, men and women ready to share anecdotes and eager to explain why they would not live anywhere else.

The *hilo conductor*, or theme, of this book is the borderlands themselves—what they are, how they came to be, and the salient aspects of life in this region of the world. The focus, as outlined earlier, is on Mexicans and their neighbors, but with Part Two, which begins with the chapter on unwelcome strangers, it shifts more and more into binational themes. All the same, for Mexicans who live and die next door to the almighty Uncle Sam, nearly everything, as we shall see, has a binational ring, even the matter of personal identity, not infrequently at the center of intellectual discourse.

I am indebted to multitudes of scholars, writers, and travelers, whose books and articles did the spadework for me, as well as to the countless border Mexicans whom I have known over the years and to residents of the other side I meet from time to time. This book is richer for their help. I am grateful especially to John Hart, who read the entire manuscript, as did Samuel Schmidt and Rodolfo Acuña; I also thank Jorge Bustamante, who placed at my disposal the resources of the Colegio de la Frontera Norte and, for hours on end, shared his knowledge of border affairs with me. I thank, too, my daughter Olivia Teresa Ruiz, an anthropologist and expert on border life, who read chapters and set me straight when I strayed from the facts. I am also grateful to my friends and former colleagues at the Colegio de la Frontera Norte in Tijuana, particularly Humberto Felix Berumen, its librarian and an authority on all things literary along the border; I thank as well the Colegio staff and the women of special collections of the libraries at the University of Texas at El Paso and the University of Texas at Brownsville, who were always ready to find what I was looking for.

Ramón Eduardo Ruiz

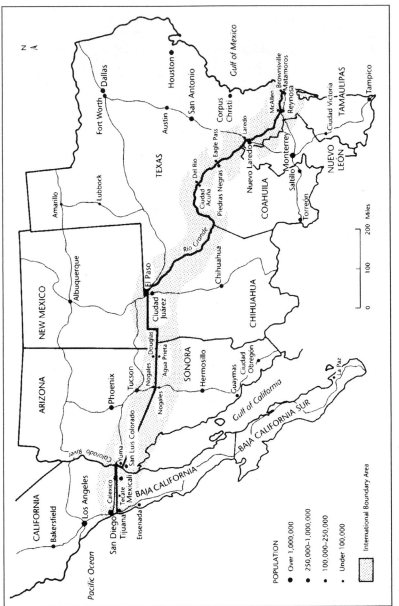

Map of the U.S.-Mexican Border

Source: Reprinted, by permission, from Lawrence A. Herzog, *Where North Meets South: Cities, Space, and Politics on the U.S.-Mexican Border* (Austin: Center for Mexican American Studies, University of Texas at Austin, 1990), 34.

Part One

Mexicans and Their Neighbors

1

The Shifty Peso

To cite a bit of wisdom from Mexico, when Mexican shoppers fill the stores of American border cities, something is dreadfully wrong with the economy. As the editor of *El Zocalo,* a newspaper in Piedras Negras, a small city on the edge of Texas, puts it, if Mexicans can buy food at cheaper prices in Eagle Pass, where the dollar wears the crown, then "you know that the peso's value is inflated." By the same token, peso devaluations spell trouble, and this is true not just for Mexicans who shop across the border but also for American merchants who stake their fortune on sales to them.

These axioms, my father lectured us time and again, were the gospel truth. In his day, Mexicans spoke of pesos as *plata,* or silver, and of dollars as *oro,* or gold, the latter worth more. Those days are gone, like my father, but the dollar still calls the tune. The devaluation of the peso in December 1994 brought this asymmetry, which my father lamented, home to me with startling clarity and spelled out in detail the unvarnished truth of this unequal relationship between a poor Mexico and its wealthy neighbor.

On that terrible day for Mexicans, I had been in Tijuana for nearly a year, collecting material for a book, fully aware of the inequality along the border. Even though I had anticipated the peso's pratfall, I was unprepared for the humpty-dumpty behavior that started just before Christmas in December 1994, when the newly enshrined regime of Ernesto Zedillo decided to deflate the peso's value. A few days later, Eliseo Mendoza Berrueto, until recently the governor of the state of Coahuila, invited me on a fact-finding trip that Jorge Bustamante, the president of the Colegio de la Frontera Norte, a Mexican-government think tank, had entrusted him with at the behest of Zedillo's economic czars. The goal of this survey of public opinion was to ascertain how the peso's plunge had affected key sectors of border society. Mendoza Berrueto was formerly a senator and leader of the Partido Revolucionario Institucional (PRI) majority in the Chamber of Deputies. I was, therefore, in the company of a man most people believed had the ear of bigwigs in Mexico City. They would, I learned quickly, therefore be willing to unburden their souls while I listened and asked questions. In the course of these discussions, and hours of others with Mendoza Berrueto, I also gained insights into the twists and turns of Mexican politics.

In late January 1995, we set out by automobile from Tijuana for Matamoros, on a journey that took us more than two thousand miles in just over two weeks. Traveling on Mexican roads whenever possible, we stopped at every city and interviewed each *presidente municipal* (mayor), almost all of the newspaper editors, merchant groups (CANACO), organizations of industrialists (CANACINTRA), campesino leaders, and, on occasion, women of stature in their communities. Except for the women and the mayor of Ciudad Juárez, all of them swore undying loyalty to the PRI, which, under an array of acronyms, has run Mexican politics since 1929. The only people who spoke flatteringly of Priistas (members of the PRI) in Mexico City were the mayors, with the exception of Francisco Villarreal in Ciudad Juárez, a member of the opposition party, the Partido Acción Nacional (PAN). The loyalists, beholden to Mexico City for their jobs, could not speak ill of the hand that fed them.

Yet even among Priistas, notorious for their unwillingness to see, hear, or speak evil about their fellow bedmates, we encountered anger with politicos in Mexico City, anxiety over the future, and fear of economic turmoil. The devaluation, they all agreed, was a disaster for Mexicans. Although most of them declared this a propitious time for Mexican exports, few had anything to sell to their American neighbors. When we crossed the border at such places as Nogales (Arizona), El Paso, Del Rio, Eagle Pass, and Brownsville—all Texas citadels—to check on the effects of the peso's downfall, we encountered ghost towns, empty shopping malls, and worried store proprietors. Mexican buyers were conspicuous in their absence; with only weak pesos in their pockets, they stayed home. Along the U.S.-Mexican border, clearly, the peso's nosedive posed an international crisis.

o o o 🏵 o o o

The economic disarray of 1994 was merely the latest chapter in what one critic calls the drama of Mexico's "permanently devaluating currency," a situation encouraged on this occasion by NAFTA, the North American Free Trade Agreement. True, as most scholars believe, NAFTA alone did not give life to the Mexican economic crisis of December 1994; but it is equally certain that NAFTA is integral to the austerity formula that has been foisted on Mexico since the early 1980s by the International Monetary Fund and the World Bank, an economic package that has added millions of Mexicans to the poverty rolls and has gutted national industry, while opening the country to the influx of highly volatile speculative capital from the United States.

The peso's problems, as indicated earlier, are hardly new. The earliest of its flip-flops occurred in 1890, when its worth dropped to half that of the dollar because of the decline in the value of silver, then the cornerstone of Mexican currency. Those were the days when Mexicans, such as my father, bought and sold *plata* for *oro*. In 1931, the peso's worth in relation to the dollar fell to 2.91, then to 5.3 by 1940, a decline that pushed the cost of living sky-high in places such as Ciudad Juárez, because Mexican currency purchased far less in stores in El Paso. During the late 1940s, its value plunged again to over 8 to the dollar and stood at 12.5 from 1954 to 1976. Despite that, the peso was soon "overvalued," leading, in that age of Mexican tariff walls, to higher and higher levels of inflation. Oddly, the inflated peso was, in actuality, a subsidy to Mexican consumers of American goods. Unable to sustain the peso's illusory worth, the government devaluated it twice in one year. When border Mexicans stopped shopping across the border and merchants on the U.S. side went broke, American cities that relied on Mexican commerce for their well-being applied for federal economic disaster relief. When the bottom fell out of the petroleum market in 1982, the peso shrank once more. Until then, oil-rich Mexico had enjoyed a bonanza; on the border, petroleum pesos, as Mexico's currency was labeled, allowed the Mexican middle class to squander vast sums on costly imports from all over the world. The peso's pratfall of 1982 put an end to that shopping spree.

Mexican border cities quaff the bitter cup because virtually all of their transactions are in dollars. They are Mexican urban hubs, but their economy revolves around dollars. One can always pay with dollars but, ironically, not always with pesos, particularly in Tijuana, where restaurants and stores are known to write up sales slips in dollars. After the plunge of the peso, in the words of one Tijuanense who earned pesos but purchased consumer goods in American stores and paid his financial obligations in dollars, "There won't be so many shopping trips to San Diego."

These theatrics of the peso outline dramatically the nature of the border Mexican's relationship with the powerful and wealthy neighbor *del otro lado* (on the other side). The currency ups and downs reveal the asymmetrical nature of the dependency that binds together Mexicans and not a few Americans along the nation's southern flank. What affects one affects the other, although obviously not in an identical manner. Average citizens in San Diego or El Paso seldom take note of the misfortunes on the other side, but their business, banking, and commercial colleagues surely do, since many of them have Mexican clients.

Border Mexicans, conversely, rarely escape unscathed, unless they stash dollars away in some bank account. Most of them shop on the other side, buying everything from clothes to food, while others augment their family income by finding jobs in the United States. Mexican merchants who import American goods for resale as well as industrialists who buy their machinery and supplies across the border must pay in dollars; cheap pesos translate into expensive dollars, which, unless purchases in the United States are paid for in cash, leads to debt accumulation or, in the worst scenario, to bankruptcy when dollar debts balloon beyond the ability to repay. A Mexican agency that resells used automobiles acquired with dollars in El Paso cannot survive a peso devaluation if customers in Ciudad Juárez stop buying, and the owner will find that the agency's dollar debt has skyrocketed. However, other Mexican hallmarks usually fare less badly: The ubiquitous curio shops, restaurants, discotheques, bars, and other enterprises that live off American tourists see these visitors come in bigger numbers because their dollars go farther in Mexico. They are the bargain hunters in the wake of the devaluations, even buying groceries.

All of this goes to the heart of what is tenuous and distorted in the Mexican border economy and, clearly, in the national economy. The reasons for this lamentable instability, which brings untold hardships to Mexicans, are numerous and complex. The inflated peso is the tip of the iceberg. What led to the latest devaluation of 1994 was the growing Mexican trade deficit, caused by the inability of industrialists to compete with American manufacturers, not only in the export market but also on the home front. To keep prices in check, the economists of the Carlos Salinas regime (Salinistas), which left office under a cloud of accusations of corruption in December 1994, used the inflated peso to permit foreign imports into Mexico. The overvalued currency gave the wealthy and the affluent middle class access to these goodies, kept them loyal and content, and, ironically, kept inflation at home in check. Mexican economists and neoliberals in Washington boasted about the single-digit inflation rate. Had age-old tariffs remained in place, the competition for scanty goods would have led to higher prices.

The enactment of NAFTA in January 1994 opened wide the gates to foreign, mostly American, imports. Since Mexico had little to sell abroad, the national deficit grew by leaps and bounds. A story in the *Los Angeles Times*, which speaks approvingly of freight trains rumbling through Nuevo Laredo "funneling auto parts, grains and plywood into Mexico's heartland," documents this growing trade imbalance. The Mexican market, reported a president of the Southern Pacific Railroad, "is the fastest growing one we have." The volume of trucks traveling into Mexico, at the same time, overwhelmed the highways and bridges to Nuevo Laredo; "we have trucks lined up for a mile and a half—two miles some afternoons—waiting to cross the bridge," declared a city official. At the Otay Mesa crossing east of San Ysidro, a suburb of San Diego, California, an average of 1,100 American trucks enter Tijuana daily. To keep Mexico's trade deficit in check, the Salinistas sold *tesobonos*, or short-term treasury bonds, that paid exorbitant interest rates to American speculators. When the juggling act collapsed, so did the peso, particularly since wealthy Mexicans, some undoubtedly forewarned of the imminent financial disaster by friends in the higher echelons of the administration, took their millions of dollars out of Mexico. The loss of faith in the government, which spurred on the wholesale flight of capital, was particularly acute in the border states. The house of cards, known as the "Salinista miracle," which Wall Street fervently eulogized, became simply a bad dream.

The bloated peso spawned other negative effects. Mexican consumers, seldom renowned for their frugality, flocked to buy what they coveted in stores across the border. In 1987, according to one study, 93 percent of American teenage girls described shopping as their favorite activity; if that question were posed to Mexican women of the middle and upper classes, an equal number of them would surely confess that they were similarly addicted to the shop-till-you-drop mentality. The peso's precipitous fall put a stop to that pastime and discouraged the expansion and sales of Mexican manufacturers, as well as the growth of jobs on the Mexican side, particularly in commerce. That consumer frailty made Mexicans on the border more dependent on the United States. With bloated pesos at their command, Mexican consumers did not buy what they labeled "inferior" Mexican goods—a belief that led the wife of one former official of the Baja California State Police to buy eggs in San Diego supermarkets because their "shells are cleaner." The inflated peso also held back Mexican investments in industry, further retarding the development of a native edifice. Flaunting their money, Mexican middle-class families in cities such as Ciudad Juárez and Matamoros took to dining out in the United States, eating sushi delicacies in Japanese restaurants in El Paso or broiled steaks at the Fort Brown Hotel in Brownsville and spending millions in Disneyland or Las Vegas.

∘ ∘ ∘ 🏵 ∘ ∘ ∘

Pundits in the United States who study the border talk about "interdependency," a term that seems to imply a certain equality in the binational relationship. Closer scrutiny leads to results that contradict that interpretation. Take the interrelated questions of peso devaluations and border commerce: Proximity to a U.S. city actually hurts Mexican merchants because their American rivals, offering better prices and better goods, entice Mexicans to buy in their stores. For sundry reasons, starting with the fact that their country belongs to the Third World of "underdevelopment," Mexican storekeepers can seldom compete; sales in the United States hurt them. Unless the peso is deflated, Mexicans buy what they can elsewhere. Cut off from their own potential customers, Mexican business owners must woo U.S. tourists, opening cantinas for the thirsty and serving them "Mexican delicacies" such as enchiladas, tamales, and tacos in "quaint restaurants" and selling them arts and crafts and *ropa típica* (native or regional dresses for women), which vary in quality and design from the grotesque to the simple and beautiful. Of late, too, a gamut of auto body repair and upholstery shops, not to mention drugstores, also beckons to Americans across the border. In 1995, Tijuana alone had 700 pharmacies, double the number of five years earlier, and received 250,000 visits to pharmacies and physicians by Americans from across the border who stocked up on antibiotics, vitamins, and geriatric medicines, mainly because they cost less and require no prescriptions. To quote a Mexican in the business, "Everyone with money opens a pharmacy."

Net benefits, for all that, go to American merchants, whose sales to Mexican customers buying food, clothing, stoves, refrigerators, television sets, home entertainment sets, and used autos—just to name a few products—easily outweigh in value what is sold south of the border. Stores such as Neiman Marcus, Saks Fifth Avenue, Nordstrom, and even Dillard's that cater to the wealthy have no counterparts on the Mexican side, not even in Monterrey, the big city two hundred miles south of Laredo, Texas. The bloated peso exacerbates Mexican dependency because it encourages sales in the United States, at the expense of local commerce. In addition, because of the higher dollar value, farmers in places such as Nogales, Sonora, try to sell in the United States, which leaves their neighbors at home facing higher prices for scarce vegetables and fruits.

The devaluations of late 1994–1995 temporarily ameliorated the commercial imbalance but merely postponed Mexican spending across the border. True, money once again flows into Mexican coffers, saving many small Mexican border enterprises from bankruptcy, such as restaurants in the city of Reynosa; but thousands of other businesses in the interior of Mexico have closed their doors for lack of customers. Americans hungry for a cheap Mexican meal kept the border businesses open. Yet that balancing act is partly make-believe. Mexican restaurants and curio shops operate on the dollar market; they not only rely on supplies and equipment purchased across the border but, most likely, pay their rents in dollars. When asked to assess the impact of the 1995 currency changes, an official of the Tourist and Convention Committee of Tijuana confirmed that devaluations are hardly lifesavers for these businesses. Nor does devaluation always result in enlarged columns of American tourists everywhere along the border. The interdependence of local economies plays a role as well. In cities such as Piedras Negras, according to the editor of *El Zocalo*, the local newspaper, tourism does not increase because the inhabitants of Eagle Pass, which is just across the border and whose livelihood depends mainly on Mexican consumers, do not prosper because Mexicans stay home. When American merchants cannot sell, and their suppliers and employees cannot work, none of them travel to Piedras Negras to eat in its restaurants or patronize its curio shops. At the same time, the sale of used cars ends immediately and their owners go bankrupt, half of them, in the case of Ciudad Juárez, in one month. It is a vicious circle: Hard times in Mexico add up to hard times north of the border. Every U.S. economic malady is felt in Mexico, which means that the entire Mexican border economy fluctuates according to what transpires on the other side. To quote chapter and verse, when the California economy collapsed in the early 1990s, one-third of the merchants on Avenida Revolución in Tijuana went out of business.

Nor do devaluations necessarily help the few Mexican border enterprises that might be expected to profit from exports. To quote an article in the *Los Angeles Times*, which dealt with the L.A. Cetto wine barons, an enterprise just south of Tijuana and Mexico's largest and perhaps best winery, "From the corporate trenches . . . the peso crisis looks like bad news for everyone." Decrying the idea of benefits from the recent crisis, Luis Alberto Cetto, one of the owners, maintains that economic benefits are ephemeral. Any price advantage in exports, he explains, "will be offset over the next year with higher domestic and foreign costs." For Cetto, whose company exports one-fifth of its wines, the international marketplace offers no advantages. Although some Mexican exporters might profit by making their products cheaper overseas, the devaluation has disrupted and damaged business operations that relied on foreign supplies or sold products on the domestic market. Cetto emphasizes that over three-fourths of his expenses were in dollars, used to purchase wine casks and young vines from France, wood stakes from across the border, presses from Italy, and Japanese fermenting vats. Moreover, the inevitable inflationary spiral that accompanies every peso downturn raises the price on everything the Cettos buy.

Devaluation, on top of all that, means unemployment on both sides of the border. The California economy offers a vivid illustration of this. Mexico is one of California's major trading partners, buying chemicals, electronic components, and lumber, among a long list of items, while exporting leather, vegetables from San Quintín and the Mexicali Valley, and textiles. When the peso weakens, Mexicans must pay more for U.S. goods, which curtails their purchases, hurting manufacturers and exporters and ultimately causing layoffs of American workers. The 1982 peso fiasco had a dramatic effect on McAllen and Laredo, Texas border enclaves that rely on Mexican trade; by December 1984, they had the two highest unemployment rates in the United States. In Laredo, where retail trade virtually collapsed, the jobless rate went from 11 percent to over 27 percent, and the increase in McAllen jumped from 9.2 percent to 13.3 percent. Even El Paso, which suffered least, had an unemployment rate of 13.3 percent by 1984, compared to 9.2 percent two years before. In 1995, the *Diario de Juárez* reported that Texas stood to lose over one hundred thousand jobs tied to exports to Mexico because of the latest devaluations; Texas exports represented almost half of all exports to Mexico from the United States.

During the 1980s, the unemployed from Matamoros to Tijuana, legally or otherwise, began to dream of work across the border, given that jobs had dried up on the Mexican side and wages had declined; workers felt the heaviest blows of the devaluations. At that time, currency deflations, according to some experts, depressed real wages in the manufacturing sector by over 50 percent. In Tijuana, to give an example, the minimum wage in 1983 had only 63 percent of its buying power of 1981 and merely 43 percent that of 1976. The cycle had similar repercussions in 1995.

Inflationary spirals, like the earlier ones as well as those that kept company with the devaluation of 1994, are felt more strongly along the border. Just hours after news of the peso's fall reached merchants, they began to "adjust" their prices upward ("reticketing"), despite appeals as well as threats of retaliation from Mexico City if they did so. The cost of meat, tortillas, and sugar, basics of the diet, shot up. In a matter of a few days, prices had risen by nearly 5 percent in the largest border cities, Tijuana and Ciudad Juárez. It was a circus, with tortilla makers in Tijuana threatening to close their doors unless federal authorities gave them the green light to hike prices, while they negotiated to pay their rents in pesos. At the other end of the tug-of-war, state employees demanded price controls on food, clothing, and rents.

Businessmen, perhaps, were the most caught off guard. Since almost all of them had been through the scenario of 1982, they should have known better. Still, as in prior devaluations, the explosion of 1994 caught them napping, with many of them heavily in debt to creditors on the other side. Soft-drink makers owed money to syrup companies in California, as did newspaper moguls who purchased their supplies from American retailers. Meanwhile, Mexican banks, among the worst-run in the world, offered potential borrowers no respite because they were charging interest rates beyond the ability of small business owners to pay. Devaluation, declared the *Diario de Juárez*, exacerbated the problem of the *cartera vencida*, the overdue and unpaid debts, in this case dollars to banks and other creditors across the border. Schoolteachers and other white-collar professionals, who had credit accounts in American department stores, found that their dollar debts had multiplied manyfold overnight, and their salaries lost buying power. For example, stores in El Paso, once eager to accept payment in pesos, from one day to the next told their Mexican customers to pay in dollars.

As if that were not enough, workers now found themselves competing for scarce jobs with migrants from the interior of Mexico. Especially since the 1960s, migrants have been a feature of border society, many of whom are simply temporary residents awaiting the opportunity to cross the border in order to find jobs. The peso devaluation of 1994, however, coincided with the determination of U.S. authorities not to permit more of them onto their soil. When the migrants arrived in Tijuana and Ciudad Juárez, they found a beefed-up border patrol standing in their way. In time, jobless men began to appear on the streets of border towns, and when they decided to settle in the popular sites of Matamoros, Ciudad Juárez, or Tijuana, they added to the drain on city coffers. Many of the migrants were first-time crossers, a sure sign of a national peso crisis. A significant number were failed merchants, professionals, middle-class entrepreneurs, and young men, and according to the *Los Angeles Times,* all of them were "particularly vulnerable to the swirling economic currents buffeting the nation."

An analysis of the catastrophe of 1994 also reveals its staggering ramifications on the U.S. side. At San Ysidro and other South Bay shopping haunts of Mexicans, retail trade dropped by 50 percent and more. *Casas de cambio* (currency houses) that speculate in dollars and pesos appeared everywhere. In San Diego, merchants lost millions of dollars in sales that never occurred; one company selling computers went out of business because its Tijuana customers went bankrupt. Store owners in Nogales, Arizona, explaining that four out of five of their customers were from Mexico, claimed the devaluation reduced their sales by 80 percent. El Paso, where residents of Ciudad Juárez purchase about 40 percent of all locally produced goods and services, felt the economic pinch immediately; a headline in the *El Paso Times* announced that the crisis closed doors, shriveling sales that "normally drive the downtown economy." Property owners gave their store tenants discounts on their rents so that they might stay afloat, yet some still could not collect them. As Mexican buying power shrank, so did El Paso businesses, as complaints of gasoline station owners testify.

The devaluations devastated the economy of the Rio Grande Valley of Texas, which runs from Laredo to Brownsville. According to the *Brownsville Herald,* the decline of the peso caused a 72 percent drop in sales in a twenty-four-block area of downtown, which added up to a $31.5 million loss;

nearly three out of four shoppers came from Mexico. The city fathers reported a $1.2 million loss of revenue from declining sales taxes. There were fewer pedestrian and truck crossings at the international bridge that joined Brownsville to Matamoros. Mexican customers in the stores of McAllen, Texas, were rare. "We have been off about 70 to 80 percent," said one store owner in the downtown area, which is almost exclusively dependent on Mexican customers. It became a ghost town after the devaluations of the early 1980s; but Roger Tolley, general manager of the bigger La Plaza shopping mall, where only one-third of the customers are Mexican, was less pessimistic, predicting that Mexicans would soon return, since they could save up to 50 percent on purchases. Tolley could speak optimistically because suburban malls in border towns are seldom hurt as much as downtown businesses, as they sell little to poor Mexicans. Their customers are wealthier types who drive automobiles and continue to buy even with weakened pesos. Conversely, as a vice president of the International Bank of Commerce acknowledges, in Laredo, where the health of the local economy depends upon Mexico, a decline in sales was inevitable. Pawnshops, meanwhile, sprang up throughout Rio Grande Valley towns, offering dollars to cash-strapped Mexican customers.

As the effects of the disaster spread, city managers scrutinized budgets, curtailed travel requests, and rejected employee insurance claims. They began to lay off workers. Business, particularly commerce, followed suit, and rates of unemployment climbed upward; this was especially true for Texas border towns, because some are almost wholly dependent on Mexican retail trade. Mexico's tailspin also bode ill on the export front, especially in Texas, where Mexican trade accounts for 3.5 percent of total employment, and in Arizona, twice as dependent as California on southbound commerce.

The adoption of NAFTA did not help matters. To the contrary, the evidence suggests that it hurt both sides of the border. For Mexicans, it curtailed business, which proved unable to compete with its more efficient counterpart in the United States. Wal-Mart, which attracts Mexican customers likes bees to honey, made survival of the Mexican corner store highly problematic; by the same token, the arrival of other chain stores, which sell nearly every article under the sun, has undermined a host of Mexican small businesses. At the same time, downtown sales in El Paso also suffered. Until NAFTA, Mexicans shopped in El Paso, even when times were bad, because they could purchase goods not available at home. After NAFTA, not only did El Paso merchants have to contend with the devaluation but also with a further loss of sales insofar as Mexicans could buy the identical goods in Ciudad Juárez. Among the retail outlets most buffeted by the peso's plunge were those handling U.S. goods: groceries, gifts, perfumes, apparel, furniture, appliances, and autos.

But not all enterprises have endured hardship. Devaluations assure the success of the *maquiladora* industry, foreign assembly plants that dot Mexican border cities and stand to gain from a suddenly cheaper source of labor. In response to labor demands, they granted a perfunctory wage raise, the so-called maximum allowed by Mexican regulations, but still not enough to compensate workers for the rise in the cost of living. The crisis cut two ways. For the two hundred workers at the Aldila plant in Tijuana who spent their days molding sheets of graphite into golf shafts, the devaluation, which translated into a 40 percent loss in dollar wages, reduced incomes already unable to cover the cost of living. But for Aldila owners, lower wages translated into big profits. As the general manager of Aldila de Mexico, acknowledged, "We are saving 60 cents per worker per hour."

o o o 🏮 o o o

The devaluations breathe new life into this lopsided international relationship by reinforcing inequality, cheap labor, profitable imports, and the proclivity of Mexicans, when the peso is strong, to buy in American stores. Over the years, as Mexicans themselves concede, the existence of nearby American stores has helped mold the character of consumer habits. Most consumers want to shop on the other side. When Mexican customs decreed in 1992 that shoppers could bring back no more than $50 worth of U.S. goods, outraged citizens of Nuevo Laredo tore down its offices. The president of the Chamber of Commerce of Tijuana, who sympathized with the protesters in Nuevo Laredo, demanded a limit of $300 for each car. When customs installed radar lights to detect smuggling at San Ysidro, the head of the local CTM, the Confederación de Trabajadores de Mexico, complained that the measure hurt workers because it denied them access to cheaper products.

In the evolution of this behavior, American merchants have not sat on their hands. To dig up a bit of history, since before the turn of the century, merchants in Nogales, Arizona, have paid for ads in Hermosillo newspapers. Merchants in Brownsville, Texas, started advertising after World War II, attracting customers from as far away as San Luis Potosí and Veracruz. Newspapers in Ciudad Juárez carry the *Juárez Shopper*, replete with commercials from El Paso merchants, a practice typical of the entire border. The Broadway, a chain store, pays for a twelve-page advertisement in the Tijuana edition of *El Mexicano*. At the same time, radio stations broadcast similar messages, and American businesses pay up to $10,000 for thirty seconds of television time, not infrequently with Mexican shoppers in mind. This custom of buying what the northern neighbor sells has been around for more than a century; history buffs claim that Francisco I.

Madero, Pancho Villa, and Pascual Orozco, heroes of the nationalistic Revolution of 1910, purchased their clothes in El Paso.

Nothing signals the demise of this addiction. Quite the contrary: It fattens on the customs of yesteryear. In *Where North Meets South*, Lawrence A. Herzog refers to the burgeoning consumer markets along the border as one of the leading retail developments in both countries. The evidence partly supports this conclusion. Up to 90 percent of Mexico's imports originates in the United States, but only three-fourths of Mexico's exports travel north. Mexico ranks among the leading trading partners of the United States. Still, a word of caution is needed here, lest we exaggerate the importance of this trade relationship. Sales to Mexico amount to less than 1 percent of all goods and services produced annually in the United States. Although on the rise, this exchange accounts for just 3 percent of the total of U.S. international trade.

Most of this trade, all the same, occurs along the border. Nearly 90 percent of exports comes from American border states, and approximately 70 percent of what is imported ends up in these same markets. Scholars claim that in Texas this trade generates hundreds of thousands of jobs. According to an estimate from 1980, the total direct dollar impact on the Arizona economy from Mexican visitors exceeded $500,000. The billions spent yearly in San Diego County by Mexicans generates $120 million in California sales-tax revenue.

The trade-off, for all that, is unequal; Americans more than Mexicans profit from border business. Mexicans spend more than twice as much in the United States as they do at home. They also buy more on the other side than Americans do; Tijuanenses, according to one estimate, annually spend $2.6 billion in the San Diego area, but San Diegans spend no more than $2 billion in Tijuana. The unequal union may be more lopsided. The president of the Greater San Diego Chamber of Commerce put the benefits to San Diego business at a "conservative $3 to $4 billion." Of the 5.8 million crossings at San Ysidro, the newspaper *El Mexicano* reported, 1.4 million were made by Mexican shoppers bound for San Diego County.

A recent publication of the Chamber of Commerce of El Paso states that Mexican commuters—men and women who live in Mexico but work on the other side—spend over half their paychecks in El Paso. There is nothing novel in this. As early as 1926, Juarenses, annually spent $15 million in El Paso but only $1.56 million at home. In 1995, Mexicans accounted for over one-fourth of El Paso's annual retail trade of $4 billion and up to 90 percent of the retail trade in the downtown area. The merchants of Brownsville, Texas, wield the upper hand in the retail commerce of the twin cities. Ironically, Brownsville depends for its economic health on Matamoros, the more powerful and larger of the two economies. One local academic writes that Brownsville merchants treat *chiveras*, Mexican women who come to Brownsville "to purchase items by the lot, such as 600 pairs of pantyhose, . . . as if they were visiting dignitaries."

Statistics demonstrate that Mexicans buy more and more in American stores. Were it not for devaluations, they would spend billions of pesos in American stores. Mexicans are very much aware of this habit, as the stories husbands tell about their wives' shopping sprees in McAllen, Tucson, and San Diego reveal. A day in McAllen is a social event for middle-class women who, in groups of three or more, drive there from Saltillo or Monterrey. Those from Mexicali refer to Highway 8, which runs from Yuma to the California coast, as the "non-toll road" to the malls of San Diego and Los Angeles. On Morley Avenue, the main street of Nogales, Arizona, where up to 80 percent of the shoppers are from Mexico, residents from Hermosillo and Guaymas routinely meet friends from Navajoa, Ciudad Obregón, and Culiacán, cities farther south. To quote one resident of Nuevo Laredo, "We have always purchased our groceries and clothes in Texas."

This habit turns economics on its head. For example, Mexican spending puts the city of Laredo, with one of the lowest wage rates in the nation, among the top cities in per capita retail sales. Just the same, one mayor of the city, as late as 1993, was "trying to get all the streets paved . . . so that outsiders would stop referring to his city as a dusty border town." In Agua Prieta, Sonora, the average person spends over 60 percent of each paycheck in Douglas, mostly on groceries. Business in Eagle Pass relies for survival on Mexican shoppers, and more than half of the merchants in Piedras Negras buy articles for resale in Eagle Pass.

Some aspects of border trade are bizarre. Take the case of Nogales, Sonora, where consumers buy tortillas and frijoles, staples of their cuisine, in Arizona. Residents of Baja California import pinto beans from California. Inhabitants of Mexicali, who live in a city of nearly 1 million, patronize stores in Calexico, a town of no more than thirty-five thousand, where Mexicans make up 85 percent of the trade. Some of the more affluent, by the same token, buy their gasoline in Calexico, preferring to "fill up" in the United States. Nearly all border Mexicans buy their poultry, a favorite with them, from Americans; true, on the eastern end of the international border, they can buy poultry in Monterrey, but at a higher price. Sales of Avon products do well in the working-class *colonias,* or neighborhoods, of Ciudad Juárez, where potential customers organize sales get-togethers in each other's homes.

Mexicans shop on the other side for multiple reasons, among them the prestige of American goods. For the snobbish at heart, the label means a great deal. In this context, it is not unusual to see a Mexican businessman driving a Ford Taurus and listening to rock music on radio or cassette; like his wife, he wears clothes purchased at Nordstrom's. Income determines where Mexicans shop. The poor buy at the cheaper stores nearest the international border; the affluent, who drive autos, as was pointed out earlier, shop in the better stores in suburban malls, as in McAllen, Texas, where their buying habits cushion the shock of peso devaluations. "McAllen is a super place," writes Guadalupe Loaeza in *Las Niñas Bien*; "people are so courteous that for everything they say *thank you, honey*." During the holidays it is a daily occurrence to hear Spanish spoken in the Saks Fifth Avenue and Neiman Marcus stores of San Diego, where some of the sales clerks, young women dressed in the latest fashions, are Hispanic. When a pricey mall opened in San Diego, its marble and glass beckoned to Mexican buyers with opulent stores, valet parking, and a pianist performing under an art nouveau statue of a nymph. One female customer, according to one account, paid cash for $60,000 worth of designer suits.

From the point of view of one official at the chamber of commerce in Chula Vista, a San Diego suburb, retailers could not ask for better customers: "They don't use credit cards, so you don't pay a fee. . . . They don't write bad checks—they buy everything with cash. They don't bring back anything." Chula Vista is part of San Diego's South Bay, the "closest geographically, emotionally and, perhaps, most important, financially to Mexico." An estimated fifteen thousand Mexicans shop daily in Chula Vista.

∘ ∘ ∘ 🏯 ∘ ∘ ∘

Discussions on the impact of peso devaluations, however, must get beyond talk of Mexican buying habits. On the border, everything is relative. Take the matter of automobile ownership. Obviously, most Americans have better and newer cars, as a cursory glance at autos on the streets of border cities confirms. Yet, car ownership along the border is the highest in Mexico. Per capita ownership of autos in Baja California is the highest in the republic. This would not be possible were it not for used-car dealers in the United States. One Mexican businessman calculates that each year 1 million used cars are brought from the United States to Mexican border towns, some of which are *carros chuecos*, or stolen vehicles. According to *El Financiero*, a Mexican version of the *Wall Street Journal*, in 1995, border Mexicans spent $150 million on purchases of used American autos. Those who benefited most were auto dealers in Texas. Auto dealers claim this occurs because the Mexican auto industry cannot keep up with the demand. All of this commerce comes to a virtual halt when the peso falls.

Of utmost importance to United States border communities is the traffic in stolen cars. From California to Texas, bands of thieves steal cars in American cities and sell them in Mexico. Some are taken and sold as they are; others, reports *El Bravo*, a Matamoros newspaper, are dismantled and sold as parts. The parts business results from the demand for repair parts from Mexican owners of old cars; even in good times, when pesos are riding high, few Mexican customers can afford a new car. A good deal of the commerce of Del Rio, Texas, relies on Mexican buyers of used autos, chiefly from Ciudad Acuña.

These autos are one aspect of the secondhand trade, which is ubiquitous because of poverty and weak pesos; another commodity is used tires, providing a lucrative business up and down the border. Countless Mexicans ride on used tires. In 1994, the 1,200 *llanteros* (tire dealers) in Baja California estimated that their customers bought no fewer than 1 million used tires each year. In saying this, they were protesting the decision of authorities in Mexico City to restrict imports to six hundred thousand used tires. Government officials pointed out that there were already more than 7 million junk tires in the state, which represented a growing environmental hazard and, as the National Ecological Institute recognized, competition for the Mexican tire industry. Import restrictions, as well as peso devaluations, have repercussions north of the border, where California dealers consider Baja California a lucrative tire market. So large is the traffic in used tires that in Tijuana an entire rubbish dump is set aside for those no longer usable. No one doubts that they originated in the United States. Some old tires never die, however; residents of poor *colonias* use the rubber shells to shore up their crumbling hillsides.

Impotent pesos compel Mexican consumers to acquire American discards of nearly everything, including ton upon ton of old clothing. Mexican trucks of every conceivable size, loaded with everything from mattresses, furniture, and appliances to lumber, are a common sight on U.S. border highways. Some are so heavily loaded that other drivers surely wonder whether they will ever reach their destination. This is good business for American merchants but not always for Mexico: For instance, using old refrigerators and air conditioners wastes electricity, which taxes municipal supplies, especially in desert cities such as Mexicali.

No less affected by the ups and downs of the shifty peso are banking, real estate, and brokerage firms that thrive on the importation of capital from Mexico. Not only do businessmen use American financial and banking facilities but so do people who simply want to stash dollars away for safekeeping. Rich Mexicans, speculators as well as others, invest in American real estate as a safeguard against currency deflation. Padre Island, just short miles away from Brownsville, is a mecca for well-off home buyers. On the opposite side of the continent on the Baja California peninsula, roughly forty thousand Americans, lured by an exchange rate in the dollar's favor, have moved in from Tijuana to the port of Ensenada. Largely retirees, they dominate a seventy-mile stretch of beachfront settlements that range from cheap trailer parks to tony condominiums and red-tiled homes. Their owners or renters provide jobs for Mexican housemaids and handymen, but these residents also monopolize the beaches, now closed to Mexicans. The contrast between their abodes and the shacks of poor Mexicans who live on hillsides across the way is startling. Current Mexican law forbids foreign ownership near international borders or seacoasts—but loopholes abound. A common way to circumvent the law is to acquire property through bank trusts called *fideicomisos*; the bank holds the title to the property, but the investor has rights to it for thirty years.

📇 2

Asymmetry

At the border, two nations colossally unequal in wealth and military strength face each other in a modern version of David and Goliath. Nowhere else in the world does the asymmetry loom greater, as the huge gap in per capita income and production between the two neighbors verifies. The border is an "open wound," writes Gloria Anzaldua, the Chicana poet, "where the Third World grates against the first and bleeds"; or, in the words of a Mexican, where people fleeing from ubiquitous poverty, the ceaseless search for jobs, and the bane of political thuggery are drawn northward by the mirage of the First World.

Distinct heritages and cultures clash at the border: One, a Catholic and Spanish society resting on Roman law; the other, by language and values, Protestant and, despite its surging minority population, English at heart. South of the Rio Grande lies Latin America, the *Ariel* of Enrique Rodó, the essayist from Uruguay and, to the north, his *Caliban*, Anglo America. America shares one of the world's two longest international borders with Canada, and the other with Mexico, but the differences between the two neighbors of European origin shrink when compared to those that separate mestizo Mexico from Rodó's colossus. For nearly two centuries, the overwhelming presence of the United States has been a sword of Damocles for Mexico; little of importance occurs north of the border that does not intrude upon the life of Mexicans.

Economics dictate this asymmetrical relationship. But without the distorted capitalism of Mexico that confronts the financial and industrial capitalism of the United State, the trade and commerce that joins them together would not exist. The disparity stimulates economic exchange, giving rise to border cities that handle dissimilar exports and imports. The United States provides the finished products and the financial capital, while burgeoning

Mexican populations serve as markets and as reserve pools of cheap labor for factories and farms on the other side. The transnational economy is anything but equal, given Mexican reliance on the United States, due largely to the absence of wealth-creating alternatives.

Unequal development spurs the border economy, which includes the movement of people and capital, the exchange of goods, commercial relations that fluctuate according to the value of the peso, and the pools of cheap Mexican labor waiting to cross the border. At best, Mexican municipalities have only one-fifth the per capita income of their American counterparts, though twice that of their sisters to the south. In 1992, the wage rate for Ford production workers in the United States was $16.50 an hour, but the Ford plant in Hermosillo paid less than one-sixteenth of that.

A story published by the *Los Angeles Times* illustrates well one of the consequences of this asymmetrical reality. In Sunland Park, New Mexico, just a hop, skip, and a jump away from El Paso, Mexican "bandits" were, in the time-honored tradition of the Wild West, plundering the cargoes of Southern Pacific trains. After robbing them, the bandits scurried back to Mexico, which in some spots was just steps away. The Colonia Anapra, their point of emergence, is a squatter's camp of cardboard and wooden shanties, mostly discarded junk from the United States, where forty thousand unemployed and hungry Mexicans live without running water, electricity, sewers, or police. "Its residents," reported the *Times*, "store drinking water in 55-gallon drums encrusted with chemical residue and cook corn tortillas over burning tires." Many of the children had "rotting teeth and gum disease," probably from drinking polluted water. When the border patrol closed down the gates to jobs in El Paso, the Mexicans turned to robbing American trains. Only Los Angeles and Chicago suffer more train robberies. The bandits—poor Mexicans fleeing from Mexico's latest economic crisis—improvise a livelihood by robbing their wealthy neighbors.

Every Mexican city from Tijuana to Matamoros lies next door to the United States, a condition that distorts border society. As Graham Greene once wrote, "The border means more than a custom house, a passport office. . . . Over there everything is going to be different." For years, officials in Mexico City have spoken of the need to integrate the border with the rest of the nation, more so now in these days of a global economy spearheaded by American transnational giants. Research indicates that although Americans along the border are almost always "inflexibly ethnocentric" and don't care much about Mexican culture and language, Mexicans sometimes look to the United States as a source of fresh values and ideas.

The examples are obvious. Border Spanish, for example, incorporates countless English words into its vocabulary, giving them a peculiar spelling and pronunciation. Students of language refer to the results as "Spanglish." Border residents know these words by heart: *lonche* for lunch, *troca* for truck, *breca* for automobile brake, and *quequi* for cake, plus a myriad of others. In all Mexican communities, English language classes are compulsory. San Diego, the city near Tijuana, boasts of well-off Mexican residents, especially after the collapse of the peso sent them fleeing from their country. An expatriate colony dubbed "Taco Towers" by unkindly neighbors monopolizes a part of the Coronado shoreline across the bay; its inhabitants live in San Diego for reasons of social prestige, convenience, and the fear of kidnappings at home. Many children of the border *burguesía* (bourgeoisie) are born on the American side; their parents covet U.S. citizenship for them. In his novel *El Gran Pretender*, Luis Humberto Crosthwaite, one of the best known of border writers, has Johnny, an affluent "junior," living in San Diego with his parents and going to school at Southwestern College. He spends Sundays in Tijuana, visiting his friends and driving his father's Ford LTD.

Crossing the border is anything but an equal experience; it depends on where you come from. Citizens of the United States can enter any Mexican city freely so long as they stay within twelve miles of the border; on the Baja California peninsula, they can travel to Ensenada, sixty miles south of Tijuana. With passport or birth certificate, it takes them just a few minutes to acquire a tourist visa that permits travel and residence in Mexico for up to six months. But Mexicans, who endure long waits by auto at the border, must possess a permanent U.S. residence permit, referred to as a "green card," or must have a visa or other valid documentation obtained in advance. As early as 1903, U.S. immigration officials at El Paso, depending on their whims that day, fumigated people arriving from Mexico. My mother, the daughter of a respected family of Parral, never tired of telling how she feared having her hair disinfected for lice upon entering El Paso. As Alicia Castellanos, a Mexican scholar, says, these inequities come about because of the power of the almighty dollar.

o o o 🔯 o o o

The U.S.-Mexican border has thirty-one ports of entry. How far north and south the border region stretches is a subject of heated debate. Miguel León Portilla, a distinguished Mexican historian, claims it extends out at least sixty miles in both directions. By his calculation, the border region exceeds in square miles the territory of nations such as Spain and France. For Jorge Bustamante, how you define it depends on what you are looking for: The "operational extension north and south of the region," he believes, varies according to the yardstick being used. The spatial definition is not the same if the focus is on economic, as opposed to ecological, concerns. The social and economic expanse of a binational zone is not determined by a geographic boundary but rather by the interaction of the people who live on both sides of it. It makes more sense, argues another Mexican writer, to define the region as the sum total of the forty-nine U.S. border counties and the thirty-nine municipalities on the other side.

Geographic proximity alone, as experts recognize, does not by itself shape the character of a border region; it is clear that other factors such as economics, improvements in communication (the information highway), and transportation also determine the nature of the relationship. Thus, as the American Southwest changes, so does the scope of the border region. Two examples of this interaction, which have drastically altered the nature of Mexican border society since early in the century, stand out: One is the growing need in the American Southwest for cheap Mexican labor; the other is the never-ending American demand for tourist facilities and commercial services south of the border. Both expand, as well as dramatically alter, the scope and character of Mexican borderland society.

No matter what the impact of these transformations, any definition of the border region for Mexicans starts with the recognition that Mexico's location next door to the United States largely determines its historical, economic, and cultural outlines. That fact dates from the War of 1847 and the Gadsden Purchase of 1853, which, by the boundary survey of 1849–1855, gave form to the present demarcation line between Mexico and the United States. Relations between the two countries were initially fleeting; then, with the coming of the railroad, pairs of neighboring cities sprang up. The obvious examples are Ciudad Juárez and El Paso; the two Laredos; both Nogales; and Brownsville and Matamoros. Until then, it was impossible to distinguish on the Texas-Mexican frontier one cowboy from another in this sparsely populated region. The railroads, and changes made possible by them in the early twentieth century, transformed this marginalized territory and its population, resulting in development that came to fruition in the Sunbelt during World War II and its aftermath. Until then, the boundary between the two countries retarded development; as scholars point out, regions on the edge of borders tend to develop at a slower pace compared to similar interior areas.

For those who live next to each other but on opposite sides, the border is both a surreal and a material reality. From one end of the border to the other, to cite the *Brownsville Herald*, two battles go on. "In one, U.S. businessmen are practically begging for more Mexican customers to cross the border; in the other, politicians are demanding that we put up an assortment of fences, walls and human blockades to keep Mexicans out." Reality tends to side with the businessmen: The border is increasingly porous.

That is logical; on the one hand, an international border must be an obstacle that separates two peoples, but it must be porous, on the other hand, in order to allow a relatively free exchange of goods, people, and capital. The emergence of cities, to cite one more opinion, "is a barometer that measures the degree of transformation" of the region's integration. As both sides become more populated and their economies become diversified, the transborder swells in size and complexity. As Carey McWilliams wrote years ago, "From El Paso to Brownsville, the Rio Grande does not separate people; it draws them together." In El Paso, a Mexican American recalled during the 1930s and 1940s: "I can't remember the family not going to Ciudad Juárez every Sunday. I don't remember eating out in a restaurant in El Paso. Ciudad Juárez was our life."

For many Mexicans, both sides of the international border are often adjuncts of each other; they seldom separate them from their kin across the way. Age-old crossings dot the border, joining families of Mexican origin and towns populated by them, many on the shores of the Rio Grande. In the Big Bend country of Texas, Mexicans from San Elena and Boquillas del Carmen, remote villages in the state of Chihuahua, daily cross the Rio Grande to visit relatives, see friends, buy groceries and gasoline, and use the phone. Some even have mailboxes in the American towns of Presidio and Redford, both heavily Mexican. Owners of rowboats who sell their services ferry these people across the river, on a trip that takes just minutes. West of El Paso where the Rio Grande turns north, other Mexicans either walk or drive across the border; in some places there is not even a barbwire fence to separate neighboring communities, largely because no American authorities are around to enforce the law and because that is how it has always been done.

To illustrate what this can lead to, each year in Cochise County, Arizona, officials get together with their counterparts from Sonora for a day of sports and pleasure. They have christened it "A Celebration of Nation to Nation," a day when officials on both sides proclaim mutual goodwill, putting aside daily problems of drugs, pollution, and smuggling. The *abrazo,* or embrace, is the sign of the day, symbolized usually by a game of volleyball with conventional rules. Yet there is something amiss: The net is not a cloth mesh stretched between two poles; the seven-foot chain-link fence separating Mexico from the United States serves in its place. But Tom Miller, who tells this story, asks how you can celebrate the end of a game with a handshake with a wire fence in the way. You don't; you extend fingers through the fence, rubbing them against the fingers of your opponents.

As any Texan can tell you, the term "U.S.-Mexican border" is a misnomer; its weight, in actuality, falls on Texas. When population and cities are considered, you have to conclude that it is a Texas-Mexican border, with a few miles of New Mexico, Arizona, and California added on as an afterthought. New Mexico, moreover, has no international ports of entry of any importance. About 9 million people live alongside the border, with perhaps 5.5 million of them on the Mexican side. One could add people in cities outside the perimeter of the geographic border that play an important role in border life, such as Los Angeles, San Antonio, and Tucson, all on the American side, and Monterrey, Hermosillo, and Chihuahua in Mexico.

Geographically, the region is hardly homogeneous. On the Mexican side, this vast territory is defined more by its administrative and legal characteristics than by its geographic, historical, social, and economic homogeneity. The lush landscapes of the Lower Rio Grande Valley, as well as parts of the Imperial Valley of California, stand in sharp contrast to the mile upon mile of desert expanse that separates them. The urban depots run from big cities, such as El Paso, to the rustic towns of Douglas (Arizona), Roma (Texas), and Palomas (Chihuahua), a town that has hardly changed since Pancho Villa rode through it on his way to attack Columbus (New Mexico), its neighbor.

○ ○ ○ 🖼 ○ ○ ○

Since their independence, most Latin American nations, including Mexico, have tended to measure themselves by the progress and order of the United States. Even today, Mexicans tend to evaluate their state of development by American standards, as Octavio Paz did in his famous *Labyrinth of Solitude*, retracing the steps taken by Rodó as well as the Cuban José Marti in *Nuestra América*. By this standard of measurement, the Mexican border fares poorly. But, as in life, things are more complex.

Along the boundary line, income levels drop as one travels south and rise as one goes north, as they do from west to east. The high family incomes on the Pacific Coast fall by as much as one-half on the Gulf of Mexico; counties on the Lower Rio Grande in Texas enjoy less than one-half the income of San Diego's. On the Mexican side, Tijuana boasts the highest per capita incomes, and Matamoros, the lowest; Ciudad Juárez straddles the middle. On the average, living standards are higher in the Mexican north than to the south; some two-thirds of Reynosa's population lives above the minimum income level. Yet, we must not forget that the cost of living is also higher, though access to cheaper goods across the border offsets that somewhat. In the United States, there is one automobile for every 1.9 persons; but there is only one for every 16.3 in Mexico. In Baja California Norte, where Tijuana and Mexicali lie, there is one for every 3.8 inhabitants, many with California license plates, the owners of whom, according to an irate letter writer to the newspaper *Zeta*, do not pay their share of taxes. Televisions sets are commonplace on both sides of the international boundary. In 1991, some 97 percent of U.S. border residents had a TV set, compared to 87 percent of their Mexican neighbors.

A binational paradox exists: Mexican average income rises as you near the border; on the U.S. side, it falls off. If affluent Tijuana—that is, affluent by Mexican standards—were a Mexican state, its per capita income would rank fourth in the nation, after the Federal District, Tabasco (petroleum) and Nuevo León (heavy industry). The six northern states of Mexico top the literacy rankings. But although per capita income in El Paso is low by U.S. standards, that of Ciudad Juárez is far lower, a symbol of the asymmetrical relationship that exists between the countries. With nearly twice the population of its neighbor, Ciudad Juárez has just one-eighth its budget. The gross product of San Diego, California, is twenty-five times greater than that of Tijuana, its neighbor. San Diego would have tasted rapid economic growth even if Baja California had not, but the same cannot be said of Tijuana if Southern California were underpopulated. Yet the development of such cities as El Paso and Ciudad Juárez, as well as the two Laredos, is the result of a symbiotic relationship. Between Tijuana and Mexicali there are three highways: Route 8 on the U.S. side is a divided, multilane freeway; on the Mexican side, the public highway is a winding and narrow road that drivers avoid taking; the much better private toll road is outlandishly expensive.

To reemphasize the point, Mexican border cities feel every fluctuation of the American economy, particularly those cities in Baja California, given the overwhelming presence of Los Angeles and San Diego. In the 1930s, they suffered most from the effects of the Great Depression, reeling from the massive decline in the number of American tourists and the subsequent rise in unemployment among restaurant cooks, bartenders, waiters, street vendors, and even prostitutes. Simultaneously, thousands of jobless Mexicans were driven out of the American Southwest and congregated along the border, adding to the woes of city fathers. However, the opportunity to earn dollars through tourism, entertainment, or auto repair, to name a few of the channels of opportunity, fuels the well-being of Mexicans. Exceptions exist, nonetheless, one being Matamoros, probably the most "Mexican" of the border cities, where tourism and the Prohibition era of 1919–1933 had less impact on development.

∘ ∘ ∘ 🏮 ∘ ∘ ∘

When we speak of the Mexican border, we are discussing cities. Not until one reaches the Lower Rio Grande Valley do farmers inhabit the expanses between cities; the one exception is Mexicali. West of Nuevo Laredo, virtually empty, arid lands greet the occasional visitor. This is a unique development; in few of the international boundaries of the world do cities loom as large. Today, 80 percent of Mexican border residents reside in localities of more than one hundred thousand people. These are no longer border towns that conjure up images of dusty streets, girlie joints, and cantinas. As Rick Cahill says in *Border Towns of the Southwest*, the cities gleam with neon lights, here and there a high-rise building dots the horizon, and automobiles rumble down at least a few tree-lined avenues.

Urbanization started early in the twentieth century, first in the northeast of the border region, due largely to the development of an export agriculture and the steel industry of Monterrey. The arrival of the railroad and migration northward from central Mexico further stimulated urban growth, as did the tourist and service industries, offshoots of the "golden years" of the Volstead Act (which inaugurated Prohibition in 1919) in the United States. As sin palaces blossomed, so did Tijuana and Ciudad Juárez. The Great Depression slowed urbanization, but World War II and the Korean conflict ignited it once more. Until the coming of the *maquiladoras,* the foreign-owned assembly plants, the service and tourist industries were the backbone of Mexican border urbanization. Spectacular urbanization walks hand in hand with the arrival of the *maquiladoras.*

Over time, the character of urbanization has changed. Some of the cities, formerly tourist havens, underwent transformations with the onset of the *maquiladoras.* As the fate of Avenida Revolución and the downtown of Ciudad Juárez testify, old core areas, where tradition holds forth, were relegated to the periphery by suburbs replete with their own shopping malls. Both Tijuana and Ciudad Juárez retain their tourist attractions—restaurants, nightclubs, and curio shops—but the heart of the local economy no longer beats there.

During the last three decades, the border emerged as one of the most urbanized regions of Mexico. In the last sixty years, the population multiplied over fourteen times, with growth centered in the largest cities, each with over one hundred thousand inhabitants. Ranked in order, the six largest are Ciudad Juárez, Tijuana, Mexicali, Matamoros, Reynosa, and Nuevo Laredo; only Nuevo Laredo shows signs of population stagnation. The other five cities are among the fastest growing in the Western Hemisphere. Ciudad Juárez, Mexicali, and Tijuana house one-half of the total border population. If current projections hold up, by the year 2000, Tijuana alone will have over 1.2 million inhabitants; its population growth rate is above the national average. Tijuana, unlike the other border cities, never went through an agricultural or mining phase; it was urban from the start. In 1996, northern Mexico, with the border municipalities leading the way, was the most urbanized region of the republic. Cities are the heartland of the border, and that is becoming increasingly true. In 1940, for example, 71 percent of border residents were rural; today, the percentages are almost reversed. In Baja California Norte, 90 percent of the inhabitants are urbanites. This process parallels world development; from 60 to 70 percent of the population of this earth now lives in cities.

Migrants play a huge role in the population of the border enclaves. From the start, urban growth responded to migration from sundry regions of the republic, including thousands of colonists of Mixtec Indians from far-off Oaxaca in Tijuana, Mexicali, and Nogales. Today's Mexican cities are truly melting pots of diverse cultures, dialects, and even, at times, of different languages. The migrants include the men and women who become the much-detested "illegal aliens" of the Southwest, many of whom return to make their homes in Mexican border cities. In Tijuana, for instance, over half of the population is of recent origin. Its inhabitants have a saying: "We are all immigrants. Our only difference is that some of us arrived earlier and some of us later." Mostly poor, the migrants settle largely on the outskirts of cities, in shacks, or *jacales,* as they are known. Urbanization encircles the cities with slums, beltways of poverty and misery, in the pattern of the Third World.

Middle-class people, a symbol of the economic changes occurring, increasingly inhabit border cities. Until recently, these cities were largely administrative centers, customs depots, and tourist meccas. More and more, with the arrival of the *maquiladoras,* they are becoming industrial bastions. Their tertiary activities, although still important, no longer set the tone. Official statistics largely equate "middle class" with "urban residency," and 37.9 percent of Mexicans fit this category. By this definition, the urbanized border has a high percentage of middle-class residents, surpassing the figure for the republic as a whole. Topping the list of middle-class cities, according to Bustamante, stands Tijuana, based, as he explains, on distribution of income, years of schooling, and levels of health. No other city in the republic, he maintains, is more middle-class; the pragmatic society of Tijuana worships capitalist values and is highly individualistic.

o   o   o   ✦   o   o   o

On the Mexican side, municipal subservience is much in order. At the top of the political hierarchy sits the federal government in Mexico City; next comes state authority; at the tail end of this system lies municipal politics. Except for Baja California Norte and Chihuahua, where the Partido Acción Nacional wrested political control from the PRI, local political officials, the *presidente municipal* included, require the blessing of the Priista hierarchy; their election, until recently, was a foregone conclusion. The patronage model of big-man politics, though increasingly under attack by opposition parties, reigns supreme. Under this system, the ambitious and opportunistic willingly exchange loyalty for access to public office, national coffers, or special deals in business and banking. The participation model of political negotiation, which Western democracies theoretically uphold, in which the interests of constituencies can be represented without fear of reprisal, is just now getting off the ground, as recent Panista (members of PAN) victories testify. Political manipulation and chicanery even include the PRI's financing campaigns of opposition party candidates—in order to give elections a veneer of democracy. "When I ran for the job of president municipal of Tecate" (a town not far from Tijuana), Crispín Valle Castañeda recalls, "though I was the candidate of the PAN, the campaign cost me not a penny—though I lost."

For all intents and purposes, local budgets are made and unmade in Mexico City. Some 80 percent of municipal revenues come from federal and state coffers. Federal authorities collect nearly 80 percent of local income but return just over 20 percent of it to the states and municipalities. Rural municipalities often do not even have funds to hire a town clerk. Of the nearly 3 million public employees in Mexico, only 150,000 serve *municipios* (municipalities). The power of *ayuntamientos* (city councils) to levy taxes is practically nonexistent. Federal intervention dictates even the nature and location of public services such as water systems and street lighting, and municipal services must also await state decisions. Despite the reforms of 1983, which theoretically granted more local autonomy, the centralization of power in the hands of the federal executive remains as steadfast as the Rock of Gibraltar.

This structural underdevelopment stems from the antiquated relationship of powerful federal authorities in the economic affairs of states and municipalities. Undemocratic and bureaucratic interference by federal officials reaches extremes in the border provinces. In the rest of the republic, only far-off Yucatan endures similar travails. Decentralization, the catchword of current political reform, seeks to expand municipal control of public monies for use on local projects. The platform of the PAN, which has captured voter support along the border, highlights local autonomy. Municipal independence also means freedom from the intervention of state governors, though not all these officials dictate in identical ways.

From Ciudad Juárez to Matamoros, one bone of contention that mirrors the differences between municipal and federal demands is the collection of tolls on the international bridges. The City of El Paso receives 20 percent of its budget from these tolls, which it uses to pay police and repair streets, among other services. At the opposite end of the bridges, Ciudad Juárez keeps almost none of this revenue; federal officials collect it. In the spring of 1995, with a municipal budget on the brink of bankruptcy, the Panista *presidente municipal* of Ciudad Juárez decided to challenge this inequity. To the surprise and anger of Mexico City, and to the applause of local residents, he installed municipal toll booths at one of the bridges, thus preventing federal officials from collecting that revenue. For this audacious usurpation of federal prerogatives, the *presidente* spent days in jail, but in elections later that year, the PAN retained control of Ciudad Juárez.

∘ ∘ ∘ ✿ ∘ ∘ ∘

Diverse factors explain the development of these border cities; the coming of the railroad is one of them. Between 1882 and 1892, the iron horse joined Ciudad Juárez, Nogales, Matamoros, Nuevo Laredo, and Piedras Negras to Mexico City and the United States. Another line linked Reynosa to Monterrey by way of Nuevo Laredo, and then to Mexico City. All the new lines connected these Mexican border enclaves with their counterparts across the border, and interestingly, by opening up jobs, they halted, at least temporarily, the flight of Mexican workers to the other side. As in the case of El Paso, these railroads also converted American cities into important commercial depots by joining them with Mexico City. Nevertheless, the railroad networks of both countries were quite different; El Paso had intercontinental links to both the West and East Coasts of the United States, but the railroad from Ciudad Juárez ran only to the south, which made that city economically subservient to El Paso. The trains that ran out of Ciudad Juárez encouraged the export of minerals and raw materials from Mexico but, conversely, opened the republic to a flood of imports from the United States. The railroad failed to join together the Mexican north.

The railroads ushered in an era of transformation in the life of border towns. There were jobs for their clerks, telegraph operators, and track workers and also, through the expansion of commercial activities, in warehouses, construction, and the service industries. Because of the railroads, all built by American capital, the population of the border enclaves multiplied. Ciudad Juárez and Nuevo Laredo blossomed into the major Mexican ports of entry. The railroad helped Reynosa weather the hard times brought about by the end of the *"zona libre"* (free zone), flashing a green light to import American goods.

Agriculture, too, had a hand in this drama. Despite the paucity of arable land (only 1 million hectares out of a total of 13.1), in the hinterlands of cities such as Mexicali, San Luis Río Colorado (Sonora), Matamoros, Reynosa, Ciudad Juárez, and Ciudad Miguel Alemán, a dusty but thriving metropolis across from Roma, Texas, agriculture became one of the pillars of the economy. Early in the century, cotton drove agricultural enterprise; in the Mexicali Valley, Americans invested millions of dollars on irrigation projects and planted cotton. With the advent of World War II, Mexicans in northern Tamaulipas and Mexicali, free of the American presence, continued to grow cotton. In the Valley of Juárez, the lack of an adequate water supply blunted the cotton boom. Nearly all of the cotton, a wartime necessity, was sold in the United States, with American companies controlling its ginning, sale, and financing. However, the bottom fell out of the cotton market when the Americans were no longer fighting in the war, a plague (labeled *pudrición texana* by Mexican planters) killed off crops, and scientists developed synthetic fibers.

Large quantities of Mexican produce still find their way to markets in the United States. Mexicali, once an oasis for cotton, now produces vegetables for California, principally green onions, broccoli, celery, and asparagus. Much of the farming is done by Americans, who rent the land from *ejidatarios* (farmers on communal plots) and employ cheap Mexican labor. According to scholars at the Autonomous University of Baja California, on some of these farms, children between the ages of six and sixteen make up one-fourth of the workforce, with three thousand of them working during the green onion harvest, a season that coincides with the school year. Few of them, of course, attend school. The companies pay $.11 for a dozen bunches of onions. These forgotten children, who symbolize the lower labor costs of NAFTA's export agriculture, help produce crops for dinner tables in Los Angeles, New York, Tokyo, and London. A handful of Mexicans, financed by American dollars, participate in this activity, which is labeled *agromaquila*, or assembly-line farming. A few individuals, mostly foreigners, come away with the profits, which they gain by relying on cheap labor, exploiting land that is not theirs and water that is subsidized by Mexican taxpayers. In 1990, the *agromaquilas* used up the equivalent amount of water consumed in two years by the cities of Mexicali and Tijuana.

From Matamoros to Ciudad Miguel Alemán, corn, alfalfa, sorghum, wheat, and cotton are farmed, and fruits and vegetables are shipped by truck to Hidalgo, Texas. From Sonora and Sinaloa, vegetables destined for households in the Southwest enter the United States. During the winter months, up to three thousand trucks pass daily through Nogales; the highest monthly volume of shipments occurs in March, the peak of the tomato harvest. The people of Ciudad Juárez buy virtually all the vegetables they consume from American farmers: potatoes, cabbage, lettuce, tomatoes, onions, cauliflower, carrots, and spinach. Merchants of the city, say critics, are the culprits. By buying and reselling leftover crops from nearby farms in Texas and New Mexico, they make impossible their cultivation in the Valley of Juárez.

The fruits and vegetables, and some cotton, derive from modern, largely privately owned farms. In Sonora, some big growers are Americans who finance their crops through U.S. banks and supermarket chains. Their seeds, fertilizers, and pesticides come from there. In the north, *ejidos* (village communal property) take a back seat to private property. It is not uncommon for *ejidatarios* in Tamaulipas, most of whom cultivate less than ten hectares, to rent out their lands and walk over the border to work on American farms. Only large private farms can cultivate sorghum, the chief crop of the region, at a profit. A similar pattern characterizes farming in Mexicali, where 80 percent of the *ejidos* are rented out. In these regions, agriculture, by providing jobs and attracting hundreds of thousands of migrants from the interior of Mexico, has encouraged the growth of cities. Yet today, agriculture engages only one-fourth of the population of the border states. At Palomas, a Chihuahua border hamlet, at Agua Prieta in Sonora, and particularly at Piedras Negras and Ciudad Acuña, both in Coahuila, ranching, too, is key to the economy. At the turn of the century, mining also helped lay the foundations of Nogales, Agua Prieta, Ciudad Juárez, and Piedras Negras.

∘ ∘ ∘ 🈺 ∘ ∘ ∘

On opposite sides of the border, cities face each other, their destinies inextricably linked together. As neighbors, most depend on each other rather than integrate into the social and economic fabric of their nations. One American, L. M. Holt, was the founder of two such cities. Known as "Limpy" because of a game leg, he baptized both Mexicali and Calexico, combining in the two the names of both Mexico and California.

The key pairs of twin cities are El Paso and Ciudad Juárez (the biggest binational market in the world), the two Laredos, and Brownsville and Matamoros. Some wrongly add Tijuana and San Diego, forgetting that San Diegans never think of themselves as living in a border town. As the only American city larger than its Mexican neighbor, San Diego belies the twin cities myth based on geographic proximity. From day one, San Diegans have prided themselves on being Anglos and Protestants, though they delight in bestowing Spanish names on their streets. To dwell for a moment on the irony of this, until a few years ago, the covenant that governed the plush community of Rancho Santa Fe in San Diego County barred all but Anglos from residing there, in a place where all the street names are in Spanish, including some that are grossly misspelled. The vast majority of San Diegans never venture south of the border and have no contact with Mexicans who live in Tijuana. San Diego's mayors refer glowingly to Mexican trade ties, but they speak no Spanish and know almost nothing about their southern neighbors. Tijuana ranks low in the esteem of San Diegans, and the fling with Spanish names is nothing but nostalgia for a romantic myth concocted by real estate speculators who wanted to sell lots to Midwesterners. The Anglo settlers quickly rid themselves of what remained of the "heritage of the Dons and Señoritas."

The military and the wars of the United States best explain San Diego's Anglo character. The naval base and the marine corps depot, and later Camp Pendleton, brought to San Diego not merely soldiers and sailors but their families, too; until after the Korean War, the great majority of these new residents were Anglos. The need to service the war machine, which included building thousands of warplanes during World War II, multiplied the number of Anglos, adding to their numbers technicians, engineers, and draftsmen, as well as semiskilled and blue-collar workers. Later, the high-tech and cold war industries, spurred on by the fighting in Vietnam, called for trained technicians, again almost all Anglos. An ideal climate, where the weather is neither cold nor hot, lures tourists from less benign regions of the United States, who, with the exception of affluent Mexicans, are almost always white and Protestant. Exorbitant prices for lots and homes have also helped keep San Diego white.

Actually, a small town separates Tijuana and San Diego. San Ysidro, as it is named, forms part of San Diego County; twenty-six thousand people, 87 percent of them of Mexican origin, live there. San Ysidro shares birth pangs with Tijuana, having emerged as a bedroom community for the midnight revelers of the Mexican beer joints and casinos in the 1920s, when Americans who worked south of the border demanded homes for themselves and their families on the U.S. side. Of those lucky enough to hold jobs, over half labor in the service industry or in retail trade, occupations that pay the poorest wages in San Diego County. In 1997, the annual median household income was slightly more than $21,000, in a high cost-of-living region. Since the 1950s, economic growth has been impressive on the Mexican side, due largely to proximity to the United States rather than to internal dynamics.

Tijuana, the youngest of the border cities, symbolizes this axiom: The machinery of American tourism originally drove its tertiary economy. Since the late 1960s, the *maquiladoras,* also sporting an American label, have increasingly become Tijuana's bread and butter. Its past, present, and most probably its future are linked closely to the ups and downs of the California economy, more so than to that of the Mexican republic. The tertiary economy suffered a setback with the advent of the Great Depression and the repeal of Prohibition in 1933. The number of border crossings plummeted, and a peso devaluation and the demise of gambling in 1936 led to rising unemployment. To correct this disastrous turn of events, officials in Mexico City declared Baja California Norte a "free zone," and two years later included the border towns of Sonora. Opening up the border to the importation of American goods restored life to the economy, and as a consequence, its population nearly doubled.

The story of these Mexican cities cannot be told without reference to the stationing of American soldiers along the border, beginning with the establishment of El Paso's Fort Bliss in 1848 and then the naval base at San Diego during World War I. Later, World War II brought millions of visiting soldiers, sailors, and marines from military bases, ushering in years of phenomenal prosperity that, in the matter of urban growth, has endured until the present. Mexicans from other regions of the republic came as braceros, workers in a lend-lease program of cheap labor for the war effort in the United States. With the war economy in high gear and money to spend, war workers from San Diego, a major aircraft production center, and El Paso, a military bastion, as well as other border cities looked to Mexico for scarce silk stockings, chewing gum, hairpins, and gasoline, while local merchants accepted U.S. ration coupons for the purchase of shoes and meat.

As the stories of Tijuana and Ciudad Juárez make clear, World War II and its aftermath spurred the economies of Mexican border communities. The tourist trade exploded in El Paso when the number of soldiers at Fort Bliss and Biggs Field multiplied manyfold. Similar experiences were shared by Tijuana, which was invaded by legions of sailors and marines and, to a lesser extent, by Nuevo Laredo, Reynosa, and Matamoros, also neighbors of U.S. army camps. The Ciudad Juárez of adobe buildings began to crumble, replaced by one of marble mansions, a Casino Juárez that catered to rich Mexicans, with plush movie houses such as Cine Plaza and Cine Victoria, and, for the first time, suburbs. The military bases and wartime industries of El Paso provided jobs for Juarenses. For Tijuana, the bonanza years meant massive invasions of poor people from the south, who moved into "spontaneously settled *colonias populares*," the hastily constructed settlements that confer on the city a chaotic character. The well-off occupied the downtown *colonias* of Chapultepec, Bolaños Cacho, and Hipódromo. After 1965, especially with the advent of PRONAF, a federal program to beautify border communities, the Zona del Río became the new business district, the renovation of Avenida Revolución followed next, and the suburb of Playas de Tijuana appeared. With this growth and the changes it wrought, old inhabitants of Tijuana found themselves a minority. As one of them confessed in *Puente México*: "I am saddened when I cannot find an old friend from those early days. The city I knew then no longer exists."

The war and what followed in its wake integrated the economies of the communities that straddle the border more closely. The classic examples are Ciudad Juárez and El Paso. Residents of the two cities speak of a binational metropolitan area that, by 1990, had nearly 2 million inhabitants. Every week, the three international bridges, the first dating from 1882, ferry 1 million El Paso-bound Mexicans, as well as nearly 300,000 vehicles. In 1994, over 750,000 trucks passed through Laredo. At times, traffic backs up for hours.

There are antecedents to this development. As early as 1926, Ciudad Juárez residents, with their purchases of fruits, vegetables, clothing, and other necessities, were spending $15 million in El Paso. From 1882 until 1935, when a Mexican concern replaced it, El Paso's electric company furnished the electricity used by the people of Ciudad Juárez, while another

American enterprise brought telephone service there. In 1882, a trolley began to run between the two cities, first pulled by mules and later by electricity. At the time of its demise in 1973, the trolley daily carried thirteen thousand passengers. Rivalry between business groups, each eager to discourage shopping in the other city, led to the close of the trolley line. During the days of the Mexican Revolution of 1910, Ciudad Juárez banks deposited their funds for safekeeping across the border, and the rich and prominent saw fit to move there.

A population explosion is still another phenomenon of this era. The growth can be attributed to tides of migrants from the south, especially after the appearance of the *maquiladora* industry in 1965, lower mortality rates, and fecundity, the survival of the newborn. According to the census of 1990, more than one-half of Tijuanenses were born in another state. One other factor bears mentioning—the appeal of living next door to a wealthy neighbor who may, under favorable circumstances, provide dollar-paying jobs for Mexicans who commute to work in the United States. Until 1975, the population grew by as much as 3.36 percent a year, then tapered off to about 2.10 percent. What this meant was that between 1930 and 1980, when the population of the entire republic grew annually by 4.2 percent, rising from 16.6 million to nearly 70 million overall, that of the border increased 10.5 percent, increasing from 276,000 to 3.7 million inhabitants. Today, the U.S.-Mexican border is the most heavily populated international region in the whole world.

Ciudad Juárez and Tijuana, with nearly half of all Mexican border residents, lead the urban population explosion. In 1940, Tijuana had just over 16,000 people, and today, nearly 1 million. Whether Ciudad Juárez is really bigger than Tijuana is debatable. Whatever the truth, the population of the Ciudad Juárez–El Paso metropolitan area has quadrupled since 1950. Ciudad Juárez, however, is twice as large as El Paso and is projected, like Tijuana, to have up to 1.2 million people by the year 2000. The two cities of Ciudad Juárez and El Paso represent one of the fastest-growing urban regions for both Mexico and the United States. By 1980, Tijuana had grown to over ten times its size in 1950; until the 1970s, annual growth rates had reached an incredible 12 percent, putting Tijuana alongside the fastest-growing cities of the Western Hemisphere. Of the fifteen largest cities in Mexico, three front on the border; only Mexico City, Guadalajara, and Monterrey have more inhabitants than Tijuana and Ciudad Juárez. Even Reynosa, which fronts on one of the poorest areas of the United States, had 750,000 inhabitants by 1995. None of the American border cities, despite their own impressive population explosions, has kept pace. The population of these cities is young; according to a recent census, more than half of the residents of Ciudad Juárez, a mirror of the demographic picture along the border, are eighteen years old or younger.

Demographers predict that 10 million people will inhabit the transnational border by the turn of the century. For Mexico and the United States, this presents policy implications of the first order. As a binational region, it is a source of revenue for both Mexicans and Americans—at the local, state, and federal level. Decisions on the environment, crime, drug enforcement, migrants, and trade, just to mention the heavyweights among issues, are international matters. Even national issues may be matters of foreign policy. As Lawrence A. Herzog writes, the border "is one of the few places in the world where urban and environmental planning is elevated to the level of foreign policy."

o o o 🏛 o o o

To bring this point to the fore once again, this distorted propinquity plays out in the urban enclaves that lie between the Pacific Ocean and the Gulf of Mexico. Its roots—as the pageant of the 1920s, for the most part an American melodrama featuring American actors performing on a Mexican stage, bears out—are not always deep. The historical legacy of these towns and cities ranges from the seventeenth century to the twentieth. The oldest locality, Ciudad Juárez, which was known originally as El Paso del Norte, dates from 1659, but San Ysidro, which faces Tijuana, did not exist until the 1920s. Both Laredos, as well as Reynosa and Matamoros, go back to the early years of the eighteenth century; Piedras Negras to 1849, and others to the turn of the nineteenth century. With the exception of Brownsville, their American equivalents began life at the same time.

Ciudad Juárez, *la mejor frontera de México* (the best border city), as its eulogists boast, was born as a Spanish mission, as was Ojinaga, on the edge of the Big Bend country of West Texas. The Misión de Nuestra Señora de Guadalupe, what is now Ciudad Juárez, served as a strategic gateway to the Spanish towns of New Mexico. The mission, which still stands and was the brainchild of a Franciscan monk named Fray García de San Francisco y Zúñiga, is a symbol of mission architecture, with thick adobe walls and hand-carved beams. Paso del Norte became Ciudad Juárez in 1888, named after the patriot president who took refuge there during the French occupation. As late as the 1920s, Ciudad Juárez was, to quote one account, "a poor and dirty little town, full of saloons and whores." El Paso, by the same token, was only slightly less bawdy. But Ciudad Juárez always possessed one advantage: It was the principal gateway, even more so after the coming of the railroad, for the exchange of goods between Mexico and the United States.

The old downtown core of Ciudad Juárez still shelters bars, hotels, discotheques, and curio shops, as well as the *plazuela*, better known as the *plaza de los mojados*, where the jobless congregate. On the east side, which has expanded rapidly, rise modern shopping malls, luxury hotels, and the homes of the rich. On the west side, out of sight of tourists, the contrast could not be greater: Here are the *jacales*.

The Spaniards came across the site of Ojinaga in 1581; they baptized it Presidio, now the name of its American sister. Ojinaga was not settled until 1759, when it became a stopping point on the trade route between San Antonio, Texas, and Chihuahua City. The building of the Southern Pacific Railroad to El Paso and Los Angeles cost Ojinaga its geographic importance. Today, historic buildings cluster around a quaint central plaza; the tidy homes of the well-to-do stand on a paved side street, far from the *colonias* of dusty streets and eroding adobe homes. Ojinaga, Tom Miller has written, is one of the last remnants of the Mexican West, where flour tortillas and cowboy hats are the vogue. Far removed from a big city, it is a "pueblito in Mexico's interior rather than a town facing its northern neighbor."

Far to the east, Palomas, the other border town in Chihuahua, once the headquarters for a vast American cattle ranch as well as the site of a gambling casino patronized by Americans during Prohibition days, reminds one of the way border towns looked decades ago. For three months each year, the streets of Palomas, a shabby place of no more than eight square blocks, are filled with cowboys herding cattle waiting to be shipped by truck to U.S. buyers. Columbus, New Mexico, a barbwire fence away, is ten times smaller than Palomas. To the east, in the state of Coahuila, lies Ciudad Acuña. Named after a poet who wrote garbled verse, Ciudad Acuña is a neighbor of Del Rio, Texas, and was not linked by highway to Mexico City until the 1950s. Piedras Negras, lying east of Ciudad Acuña, is six times larger than Eagle Pass and bears the name of coal deposits in its vicinity; in 1900, it was the third-largest Mexican border town.

Nuevo Laredo, which lies farther east, holds a special place in the hearts of Mexican nationalists. When it was founded by José de Escandón in 1755, the city was located on the north bank of the Rio Grande. After the War of 1847, when the international boundary was shifted to the Rio Grande, its Mexicans inhabitants moved their town to the opposite shore rather than live under Yankee rule. Its patriotic settlers baptized it Nuevo Laredo; the "old" Laredo, now part of Texas, stayed put. Since Nuevo Laredo's early growth revolved around its Texas cousin, ties between families in the cities still survive. Nuevo Laredo became a major international port of entry with the coming of the railroad in the 1880s. This was reinforced by the completion of the Pan-American Highway to Mexico City in the 1950s. By 1910, Nuevo Laredo was the second-largest Mexican border town. The historic business districts of both Laredos face each other; Mexicans shop on the American side by walking across the bridge. Since the 1940s, the city's growth has been to the south, alongside the railroad tracks to Mexico City and Monterrey, and to the west, where a third rail line joins Nuevo Laredo to Piedras Negras. In the late 1930s, it was a town of "dark and unsurfaced streets," to quote Graham Greene; today it has 350,000 inhabitants, who tolerate its hot summers and cold winters.

For years after the War of 1847, gangs of armed Americans invaded Tamaulipas, wanting to establish a republic of the Sierra Madre and, in the pattern of Texas, to annex it to the United States. Later, the American Civil War had a powerful impact on Tamaulipas, particularly Matamoros. Monterrey, the city in nearby Nuevo León, reaped a financial harvest. Trying to avoid the Union blockade, southern planters shipped their cotton through the ports of northeast Mexico, much of it out of Matamoros. The war brought prosperity to these Mexican towns; until then, their inhabitants, favored by climate, rainfall, and soil, raised cotton and cattle, adding to their incomes by smuggling goods into Mexico.

Matamoros, the biggest city in Tamaulipas, honors a hero of the Mexican struggle for independence. Its Spanish father, Captain Alfonso de León, was seeking a maritime port to give the region, eventually filled with small cattle ranches, access to the sea. The first colonists of Matamoros, the oldest town in the Lower Rio Grande, came from nearby Camargo. Old colonial buildings dot its downtown. In 1928, a highway joined Matamoros to Ciudad Victoria, the capital of Tamaulipas, and with the cotton boom of the 1950s, the city expanded rapidly after the establishment of cotton gins, cottonseed oil plants, and warehouses. After the boom collapsed, Matamoros turned to commerce and tourists. Its latest phase, featured by explosive population growth, corresponds to the arrival of the *maquiladora* industry.

Reynosa, unlike Matamoros, has only a glimmer of a historical past. One does not see architectural reminders; colonial cathedrals are absent from the city's central plaza. Only a tiny fraction of its residents have ties to families that lived there before the 1930s. Founded in 1749, Reynosa became a border city with the signing of the Treaty of Guadalupe Hidalgo in 1848. Unlike Matamoros, which added population rapidly, Reynosa remained a small town until recently; in 1930, it had fewer than five thousand inhabitants. In 1955, federal irrigation projects for large-scale cotton farming, and the coming of the PEMEX oil refinery, changed that. The region from Reynosa to Nuevo Laredo husbands rich deposits of natural gas. Initially, the gas went to Texas, but with the rise of industry in northern Mexico, PEMEX began to ship increasing amounts to the cities of Monterrey, Monclova, Torreón, Saltillo, and Chihuahua. PEMEX, which pays good wages and employs large numbers of men, is the cornerstone of the local economy. Until the arrival of the *maquiladora* industry in the late 1970s, and particularly with the appearance of Zenith, the economy of Reynosa, unlike that of the rest of Mexican border communities, had an internal dynamic of its own. Its geographic location did not dictate its economics.

An international bridge, inaugurated in 1926, joins Reynosa with tiny Hidalgo, Texas. But McAllen, the more important American city, lies just eight miles beyond. Each day, thousands of Mexicans wend their way to work over the bridge; hundreds of women, traveling on American company buses, shop in Hidalgo or McAllen; and heavy trucks loaded with merchandise rumble back and forth. On weekends, countless Mexican Americans cross the bridge, to shop, see dentists and physicians, or visit relatives. The distance between Reynosa and McAllen helps keep at bay the cultural influence so pervasive in Mexican border communities. Reynosa, they say, is another city adhering closely to Mexican culture, partly because of its physical isolation from a big American metropolis, partly because it sits not far from Monterrey, one of the largest and richest cities in the Mexican republic, and partly due to the presence of PEMEX. The availability of cheap used autos bought across the border helps explain its chaotic, sprawling nature, a blueprint not atypical of other Mexican border cities. With the aid of the auto, Reynosa's residents overran *ejido* lands, overcame the absence of bridges across its numerous canals, and circumvented the installations of PEMEX.

Nuevo Progreso, Tamaulipas, one of the youngest cities on the border, was born less than a half century ago, when a businessman in Progreso, Texas, wanted to import Mexican vegetables and built a bridge across the Rio Grande River. By then, Mexican farmers had planted corn, broccoli, and tomatoes on former brushland. Soon, Nuevo Progreso had streets of curio shops and restaurants serving American tourists. Some were "far younger" than the "Old Mexico" they had come to see.

Tijuana, in Baja California Norte, lies at the Pacific end of the border. Called the "most visited city in the world," its history is intimately bound up with that of San Diego, the California metropolis just eighteen miles to the north. Until 1957, no paved road connected Tijuana with the capital of the republic, despite unwelcomed and repeated attempts by Americans to acquire the peninsula from Mexico. For all the overlap of historic events, a huge gulf separates Tijuana, a Third World city, from San Diego, a wealthy haven. To quote the editorial lament of the *San Diego Union-Tribune*, "The sad truth is . . . that, throughout modern history, our two cities have maintained a distinct distance from each other—a divide that is far greater than that separating most other cities along . . . the border."

The economic boom of Southern California fueled the transformation of Tijuana from a *ranchería* to an urban settlement. A Mexican named Ricardo Orozco, formerly an employee of a Hartford, Connecticut, real estate agency that developed the port of Ensenada, laid out the city plan for Tijuana; he placed its downtown adjacent to the boundary line. The tourist industry controlled its location and the land-use plan. The bars, cabarets, and restaurants were on Avenida Revolución, and the residential *colonias* to the west clustered around the Parque Teniente Guerrero. As San Diego expanded as a naval base, so did Tijuana. Tourism fed on the reformist movement in California between 1900 and 1929. Gambling, the mainstay of the local economy, began in 1908 and horse racing in 1915. When U.S. authorities began closing international gates at 9 P.M., hotels sprang up in Tijuana. As one Mexican, among many who arrived in 1927, recalled, Tijuana inspired nostalgia *"por mi tierra . . .* the sight of the town plunged me into despair . . . everywhere houses of wood, unlike the adobe, brick and stone of my hometown."

Tijuana is changing. You still see Mixtec women selling trinkets on the streets; striped donkeys still stand on Avenida Revolución; and nearly everywhere, the fetid smell of poverty hangs heavy. But now there are also modern department stores, majestic hotels, elegant boutiques, condominiums for lawyers and physicians, banks, and freeways. La Avenida de los Heroes, a boulevard lined with trees and green lawns, is the heart of the new Zona del Río, where high-rises darken the skyline. It includes a $25-million shopping mall and a cultural center. To build it, "Bobby" de la Madrid, a callous governor with a heart of stone, drove out five thousand poor families living in slums, an eyesore on Tijuana in his opinion, and spent millions of federal dollars to channel the flood plain of the river. On the east side of the city lies La Mesa, where American tourists in their shorts and polo shirts seldom venture. It is a dusty suburb of shops and apartment complexes. On the Mesa de Otay are the buildings of the *maquiladoras;* the campus of the Autonomous University of Baja California lies nearby.

Middle-class Mexicans—*maquiladora* managers, government bureaucrats, businessmen, and professionals—can be seen everywhere in Tijuana. It is not uncommon to find their wives, yuppies in dress and values, in restaurants with cellular phones pressed to their ears. Anthropologists, economists, and demographers staff the Colegio de la Frontera Norte, a think tank on the highway to Ensenada. Tijuanenses enjoyed bonanza years until the late 1980s, when the bottom fell out of the neighboring California economy. Border crossings, always an index of local conditions, dropped dramatically, hurting commerce and service activities associated with tourists. Lower levels of public and private investment limited the construction industry, halting expansion and laying off masons, carpenters, and other tradesmen. Evidence suggests that per capita income might have decreased between 1970 and 1990, undermining living standards as economic expansion lagged behind the population growth rate. According to one study, the golden years may be memory: "Are we seeing," its authors ask, "the first signs of a bleak economic future for Tijuana?"

Mexicali, the only border city with a state capital, lies east of the coastal range, in one of the world's hottest and driest climates. Its citizens often drive to Tijuana to escape the heat; the better off buy homes along the coastal highway to Ensenada, largely an American paradise. Every year, the poor die from the heat in the summer and during the winter, from the biting cold. Tourists seldom visit Mexicali; it is a government town, replete with office buildings and bureaucrats. All the same, by one count Mexicali has at least eighty Chinese restaurants, famous for a cuisine known as Chinese-Mexican, largely because of its *chiltepín,* a hot chili pepper flavor popular among Mexican customers. Once a tiny village of Cocopah Indians, Mexicali today thrives despite its inhospitable climate.

Like Tijuana, Mexicali owes its original existence to American enterprise, specifically to an offshoot of the Colorado River Land Company, which, due to the largesse of Mexican authorities, enjoyed a monopoly on the land. Early Mexicali, a collection of wooden houses facing each other across dirt streets, was, for all intents and purposes, a cotton plantation. As late as 1930, its population was one-third Chinese (the reason for the scores of Chinese restaurants), a legacy of the days when American patrons imported thousands of Chinese to plant and pick cotton. Most had arrived in California during the gold rush of the 1850s, then had stayed on to help build the intercontinental railroad. When confronted with mounting racial bigotry— the Chinese Exclusion Act, for instance—and not wanting to return home, many moved to Mexicali. Principally from Canton Province, they lived in the *barrio Chinesca,* the Chinese enclave that stood on the international border. Another American company, the Jabonera del Pacífico, served as the only bank, sold the machinery and equipment, and, as owner of the sole cotton baler, monopolized its sale. The Compañia Mexicana de Terrenos y Aguas de la Baja California, also American, held the rights to the water of the Colorado River. Less than 2 percent of the planters controlled 95 percent of the land. Few Mexicans resided in Mexicali, though they toiled planting and harvesting cotton. Even in 1929, recalled a visitor, Mexicali was a small town filled with cabarets and whorehouses, patronized by Americans from the Imperial Valley.

Calexico, Mexicali's neighbor, is the tail on the dog. Dating from 1902, when it was a U.S. customhouse, it remains a small town. Mostly populated by people of Mexican descent, its stores, which cater to low-income Mexican shoppers, line the main street that runs parallel to the international border. Calexico lies in the hot Imperial Valley, a farmer's haven where jobs are scarce and poorly paid when available, with incomes among the lowest in California. To cite the *Calexico Chronicle,* for most families putting food on the table is the first priority. Among the inhabitants of Mexicali, many have relatives in Calexico; visits across the border are commonplace.

American tourists rarely visit Tecate, the third of the Baja California border communities, which lies thirty-three miles east of Tijuana and sits at 1,600 feet above the sea. For a long time it was principally known for its brewery, established in 1930, and its pottery, tile, and red brick industry.

Between Mexicali and Ciudad Juárez lie the Sonora border towns on the edge of Arizona: Nogales, San Luis Río Colorado, Naco, Sásabe, and Agua Prieta. Of the five, Nogales, which straddles a deep canyon, is the most important, and Sásabe, the least. Until the arrival of the *maquiladora,* Naco had not stirred in one hundred years. At the turn of the century, it was a depot for copper trains from the Cananea mines of William C. Greene; now, its corrals only seasonally hold cattle from Sonora ranches headed for Arizona feedlots. San Luis Río Colorado, a colorless town with a growing number of *maquiladoras,* acts as a service center for the cotton and sorghum hinterland. Agua Prieta, inhabited since 1897, faces Douglas, Arizona, where, before the closing of the smelter in Douglas, the copper mines of Cananea and Nacozari processed their ore, and cowboys herd thousands of Mexican cattle north to markets. An international accord links together the power, water, and sewer systems of Douglas and Agua Prieta, which is three times bigger; the two towns' fire departments respond to each other's calls. Even less significant than Naco is Sásabe, which stands on cactus-covered hills; lacking a PEMEX station, its residents buy their gasoline on the other side.

Until the fall of 1997, before Americans took to erecting walls, only a chain-link fence separated Nogales, Sonora, from Nogales, Arizona; without it, the two would have been one city. Mexico's Nogales, with over one hundred thousand inhabitants, is over six times larger than its neighbor. Without a decent bookstore or a library of note, or even first-class restaurants, Nogales is a homely commercial entrepôt clinging to two hillsides that abut a rail line and a highway.

3

Black Legend

The asymmetrical relationship between American and Mexican border regions is nonetheless relatively recent. Until the twentieth century, both sides of the border were, in the jargon of today's economists, underdeveloped out-of-the-way towns of little consequence to the financial capitals of Mexico and the United States. The border, in the eyes of most Mexicans and Americans, was still a frontier. For the United States, that began to change in the late nineteenth century, when the arrival of the Santa Fe and Southern Pacific Railroads opened the Southwest to mining and commercial agriculture and linked the cattle ranches of Texas to the stockyards of Kansas City and Chicago. Still, disparities between the American and Mexican borders were merely getting underway.

It was developments in the 1920s, for which Americans are largely answerable, that turned the character of Mexican border towns upside down and, in so doing, exacerbated the existing inequality between Mexico and its northern neighbor. What turned awry—and yes, perverted—the imbalance of yesteryear was the Volstead Act of 1919. Better known as Prohibition, this bit of puritanical mischief banned the manufacture and sale of alcoholic beverages in the United States. From that time on, the American fancy for booze and the Tartuffery required to give the lie to it, set the course of the border drama. For a decade or more, lines from *The Jester's Plea* aptly epitomize what transpired on the Mexican side of the border: "The World's as ugly, ay, as Sin,—And almost as delightful."

Mexicans are hardly blameless for what befell them. Whether eagerly or not, they embraced the American mafiosos of sin and booze and most of them eagerly rushed to bend a knee before the onrush of foreign visitors. By 1920, Mexicans had endured nearly ten years of internecine strife, as opportunistic politicos and tinhorn generals by the dozens fought over the spoils of public office. The Revolution, so baptized in national folklore, had come to a close. Peace descended on the republic; but the decade of turmoil and destruction of rail lines and rolling stock, mines, and haciendas had left Mexico in dire straits. There was urgent need for political tranquillity and reconstruction, lest the republic disintegrate into chaos. The army of the northern clique, the victors in the civil struggle, restored peace at the point of a rifle, but long-term stability required money and jobs—and Mexico was broke.

At this juncture in the country's history, developing the northern border provinces, a region only partly integrated into the republic, was not a priority. The scanty funds at hand were earmarked for other uses—the underpopulated north must fend for itself. Outsiders, namely Americans, proffered a helping hand, but accepting it required political sleight of hand because according to Article 27 of the Constitution of 1917, foreign investment, American by and large, was one reason that the Old Regime, toppled by the revolutionaries, had gone astray. That hurdle was overcome by simply ignoring Article 27 and welcoming foreign capital, as the Porfiristas had done.

For cash-starved Mexican politicians, the Volstead Act was an unexpected blessing. However, when they accepted its baggage, they sold their souls to the devil. One of those who did was Esteban Cantú, the military governor of Baja California until 1922. He owed money to everyone, for wages to his soldiers, to workers in Ensenada who were building a schoolhouse, and to others for building streets in Tijuana and Mexicali. But there was no money in the exchequer to pay anyone, and authorities in Mexico City turned a deaf ear to his fervent pleas for funds. Having no other source of revenue, his apologists maintain, he opened the door to vice. His successor, General Abelardo Rodríguez, amassed a fortune, his critics say, clasping the hands of American vice lords.

The story in Ciudad Juárez rings a similar bell. After the abolition of the *zona libre*, which turned Ciudad Juárez, more town than city at that time, into a free port in 1891, a severe depression got underway. The door out, according to politicos, was to make the city into a tourist mecca, which translated into saloons, bars, and gambling dens. A bullring had already been inaugurated in 1903, and two years later a race track. At the same time, El Paso's era of vice, which had arrived with the railroad, had come to an end, closed down by reform groups. Until then, games of chance, bars, and whorehouses were a feature of El Paso's social life. It was the original border "sin city," where a "ring," as it was baptized, of lawyers, businessmen, and politicos manipulated the Mexican vote and heralded the coming of vice and big-time gambling, believing that the city's sinful reputation helped finance projects and balance the budget. For a while, city fathers even allowed the local Chinese, who monopolized the laundry business, to operate opium dens. But in 1915, reformers elected their own mayor, and two years later, with the help of a straitlaced secretary of war in Washington whose hatred of bars and bordellos near Fort Bliss knew no bounds, they rang down the curtain on the old ways. This information comes from Owen P. White, a writer who mourned the passing of the ladies from the Tenderloin on South Utah Street, the whirl of roulette wheels, and the rattle of poker chips. Men now "shaved daily . . . changed their clothes by the clock, and began to play golf."

The transfer of saloons and brothels from one side of the border to the other brought a sigh of relief to the city fathers of Ciudad Juárez. As events transpired, on the eve of Prohibition, Ciudad Juárez rarely had enough funds to make ends meet. According to one account of the day, the people "live in poverty," wholly dependent on their neighbors. "We have no industry, no agriculture," aside from bullfights and cockfights. By the middle of the 1920s, however, the town was enjoying a bonanza, but lamentably, its sordid reputation had surpassed El Paso's earlier notoriety. One student of its society remarks, "Bars, cabarets, gambling houses, brothels, honky-tonks . . . dope parlors proliferated." The city's main street, a newspaper reported, had more saloons than any other in the world.

The smuggling of liquor into the United States was big business, an activity that drew bootleggers from as far away as Chicago. One of the early lucrative industries in Ciudad Juárez was the manufacture and sale of liquor, and some companies were transplants from the United States: The D&H and the D&W distilleries that produced Waterfill and Frazier Whiskey came from Kentucky. Antonio Bermúdez, later a Ciudad Juárez kingpin, made his first fortune as a wholesale liquor salesman. One of the original breweries was Cruz Blanca, for years a popular Chihuahua drink. Among the famous cabarets were La Linterna Verde and Nuevo Tívoli, both with dance floors and gambling rooms. The bordellos—another thriving business—were staffed by foreign women, chiefly Americans, Italians, Germans, and French. On American holidays, business on Calles 16 de Septiembre and Lerdo boomed, in spots called Big Kid's, Harry Mitchell's Mint Bar (acclaimed for its New Orleans Gin Fizz, slot machines, and polished brass spittoons), the O.K. Bar, and the Central Cafe. Americans from all walks of life patronized them, including celebrities such as Jack Dempsey, Amelia Earhart, and Mayor Jimmy Walker of New York. One famous dive was the Hole in the Wall on Córdoba Island, joined to the U.S. side by a wooden plank that spanned an irrigation ditch and served as an international bridge. Patrons simply lifted the wire fence that separated Mexico from the United States and walked across; no one bothered with the formalities of border inspections.

Booze and sin apparently paid off; the Ciudad Juárez of ten thousand inhabitants in 1910 had become a city three times as big by 1930. Mexican apologists, in the manner of the earlier El Paso Ring, say that there was no other source for the badly needed money from saloons and gambling halls flowing into the city coffers. The taxes and funds collected from the joy palaces represented most of the public revenue; this income paid for street lighting, water, and other public services. After passage of Prohibition, American liquor merchants, who were unable to peddle their merchandise at home, transferred their operations to Mexican towns, where their compatriots, though perhaps applauding the end of saloons at home, cherished the chance to drink across the border, far from the watchful eye of their neighbors. Prohibition marked the first time that large numbers of Americans visited Mexico.

The era of booze, which Americans largely sponsored, had antecedents, both in Ciudad Juárez, as already pointed out, and later in Baja California. In 1915, California outlawed horse racing and prostitution and, for good measure, banned dance halls and professional boxing two years later. With the closure of these activities, Mexican border towns picked up the slack. In Tijuana, when the San Diego–Panama Exposition opened in 1915, its promoters, among them Governor Cantú, organized the Feria Típica Mexicana, hoping to capitalize on San Diego's tourist bonanza. Their American cohorts, among them racketeers, sponsored boxing matches, held cockfights and bullfights, and set up games of chance. Two of them gave birth to a horse racing venture. John D. Spreckels, the sugar and railroad magnate, owned the land where the racetrack was built, and James W. Cofforth (Sunny Jim), a San Francisco boxing czar, handled racing. Gambling was the prerogative of Carl Withington, a nightclub owner from Bakersfield who also managed the Mexicali Brewery. Ed Baker was the czar of liquor imports.

Texas, too, had gone dry in 1918, so El Paso's bar owners simply moved to Ciudad Juárez, where they opened again for business. A sign in English over the Old Tivoli, the best bar in town, warmly beckoned to Americans. With the birth of Prohibition, most Mexican border towns—virtually overnight—became an escape valve for Americans thirsty for drink and hungry for good times. The barons of the liquor industry made Ciudad Juárez, dubbed the *gran cantina sin techo* (the great open-air saloon), and Tijuana their favorite haunts. Despite Tijuana's legendary reputation for sin, it was Ciudad Juárez, the big sister of border towns, that first acquired notoriety for its naughty entertainment. One American consul called it "the most immoral, degenerate and utterly wicked place I have ever seen or heard of in my travels." Hungry for additional revenues, the governor of Chihuahua made possible "quickie" divorces in Ciudad Juárez. The combination of the Volstead Act, American and Mexican hypocrisy, and Mexico's bankrupt finances transformed the border towns and, in the process, laid the foundations for the exaggerated asymmetry of future relations.

On the Pacific Coast, developments in California also helped. Blessed with an excellent harbor, San Diego was the ideal site for a naval base; with the start of World War I, sailors by the thousands came to San Diego, while Los Angeles, transformed into tinsel town by the movie moguls, went through years of explosive growth. New industries appeared in California; dams for storing water to benefit big commercial farmers were built, rich petroleum deposits were discovered, and highways were laid out for autos arriving from Detroit assembly lines. A railroad joined Los Angeles to San Diego, and American entrepreneurs erected a bridge over the Tijuana River so that tourists might come during the rainy season. Ford trimotor airplanes flew film stars from Hollywood to the Tijuana joy palaces. Oldsters recall that during his periodic visits, Tom Mix, the cowboy movie hero, filled his ten-gallon hat with coins and threw them to children in the streets.

As a result, a Mexican scholar laments, Mexican border towns changed completely, altering dramatically the way of life of their inhabitants. For all intents and purposes, they became the playground for millions of Americans hell-bent on enjoying themselves, who would, to cite one Mexican's opinion, "rather break our laws than their own." From that time on, the tertiary sector sat in the driver's seat of the local economy, and dependency on the other side of the border, like a narcotic addict's need for a fix, turned into a daily need.

From the 1920s comes what is known as the Black Legend of amoral border towns. As Raymond Chandler wrote in *The Last Goodbye:* "Tijuana is nothing; all they want over there is dollars. The boy who approaches your automobile to beg for money will, in the next breath, try to sell his sister." Chandler's biased version, a very American one, is not new; it symbolizes the Black Legend common to border towns, specifically Tijuana and Ciudad Juárez. Americans, and not just writers such as Chandler, had a hand in its manufacture. In national magazines and newspapers, American city fathers promoted visits to their cities, as in the case of El Paso, touting their proximity to the "good times" to be had across the border, where gambling and alcohol were readily available. Eager for profits, the barons of the joy palaces advertised their wares everywhere in the United States, the home of their customers. What they emphasized was the licentious nature of border towns—for which, of course, they were chiefly responsible. Postcards of the era pictured smiling Americans imbibing cocktails in exotic bars, frolicking in hotels, or spending a day at the races. Although often exaggerations of reality, these promotions helped inspire the notoriety of the Black Legend, which still lingers on. It is ironic that this hypocrisy stigmatized Mexicans, because most of them had little or no control over the illicit business.

For countless Americans, the Mexican border symbolized tantalizing evil, particularly after Hollywood began depicting Mexicans as both charming and deceitful in its films about the Wild West. A Charlie Chaplin film of the day captures the essence of this portrayal when Chaplin, who portrays an escaped convict, "runs along the border . . . one foot on either side, unable to choose between the United States," the symbol of "law and order, . . . and Mexico, representing lawlessness." It is ironic that in real life, Chaplin frequently cavorted in Tijuana. Sadly, Mexicans from other regions of the republic came to hold an identical view of border life.

With Prohibition, referred to as the "dry law," saloons and bars proliferated up and down the border. No town escaped their ubiquitous presence; each had its famous bar. In Nogales, it was La Caverna; in Agua Prieta, the Volstead Bar; in Nuevo Laredo, the New York Bar. Reynosa had the Crystal Palace, and Matamoros, the Moctezuma Bar. One of them, the Long Bar in Tijuana, advertised itself as the biggest in the world. Its walls were lined with concave mirrors that distorted one's image, and on Saturdays and Sundays, when tourists arrived in large numbers, a marimba band played for its mostly male patrons. Its proprietor also established the Mexicali Brewery. Two Americans owned the ABC Brewery, and another a whiskey distillery in Tecate. In ten years' time, the Bodega de San Valentín, a winery in Tijuana that dated from 1912, increased its production capacity from 10,000 to 650,000 liters. The Cetto Winery dates from this time as well. At the other end of the border, Reynosa, too, had its tourist zone, where bars, cabarets, and whorehouses were located; it was later baptized the *zona de tolerancia*.

One particular group of Americans, whose drinking and whoring won notoriety, shares responsibility for the Black Legend. Commonplace among the tourists of that day were the sailors, marines, and soldiers stationed in the military camps up and down the border. From San Diego, sailors and marines on weekend leaves, whose behavior astonished Mexicans, came to Tijuana. With their hair cut short, they were easy to identify in bars and whorehouses. Ciudad Juárez was the mecca of the soldiers from Fort Bliss in El Paso, as was tiny Naco for soldiers from Fort Huachuca in Arizona, who made the Rainbow Bar and Lux Cafe—where booze, gambling, and whores were the order of the day—their hangout. Later, the nearby air force base did the same for Nuevo Laredo, while soldiers from Brownsville kept alive the nightlife of Matamoros.

When, on occasion, Mexican officials attempted to put a stop to the worst abuses, they not infrequently found themselves out of a job. To give one example from 1921, Julio Dunn Legaspy, who had been named police chief of Tijuana and was asked to close down some of the bawdiest palaces, quickly learned that their foreign owners had more clout than he. He was soon jobless, with gambling and whoring back in business. As he told the story, the Americans controlled not only the vice but the Mexican authorities, who were in their pay and shielded them from the law. Tijuana thus went its merry way, and according to an article in the *New York Times*, it was a town that smelled of "saloons, dance halls . . . and gambling dens," where "the air reeks of . . . toilet perfume, stale tobacco . . . good spirits" and the sound of the roulette wheel." As to gambling, there was "every form invented by man. . . . Even the humble shell game, played openly on the sidewalks." Less opulent, Mexicali's cabarets and bars catered to farmers and ranchers of the Imperial Valley of California, the most notorious among them being the Southern Club, the Imperial Cabaret, the Black Cat, and the Tecolote Bar, a gambling casino and brothel where floor shows went on all night. In the Chinese district of Mexicali, tunnels led to opium dens and brothels, and for the convenience of bootleggers, one of them burrowed under the international line to Calexico. Nuevo Laredo, Piedras Negras, and Matamoros, like Tijuana and Ciudad Juárez, recorded impressive growth. Until then, the Matamoros-Brownsville region had been a farming backwater. After the puritanical reformers outlawed booze in the United States, one could, if lucky enough to live on the border, buy booze in Mexico, drink it there, or smuggle it back home. Prohibition, as Tom Miller succinctly puts it, "was the midwife of many Mexican towns." One of them was Río Rico, across from Thayer, Texas, on the Rio Grande, where enterprising citizens hastily constructed a wooden international bridge, which in tolls paid for itself within ten months. The bars, liquor stores, a fancy whorehouse, dog racing, and curio shops were the lifeblood of Río Rico, which survived until the end of Prohibition.

· · · ✤ · · ·

It takes two to tango, as Mexicans point out. Bars, saloons, and whorehouses proliferated along the border because gringos, told not to drink at home, visited Mexico to do it. And, "as is well known, when men drink and have money to spend, they want women who, fully aware of this, congregate where customers are found." Our Mexican observer went on to ask if anyone knew of "men who liked to gamble who did not drink?" Examples of these truisms were not difficult to find.

In Tijuana, the Sunset Inn and Casino, run by Americans with American employees for American customers, featured "eleven roulette tables, ten crap tables, four chuck-a-luck outfits, two poker tables, and two wheels of fortune. . . . Attached to this was the Monte Carlo Bar, and both were connected to the racetrack." Not too far away was Old Town, where the saloons paid young American hostesses to keep American "men buying drinks and to serve as dime-a-dance partners." Some of the girls sold their sexual favors. As the old adage goes: "First you do it for love, then for a few friends, and then you do it for money." The results of this American patronage are astonishing. In 1920, though Tijuana's inhabitants numbered no more than 1,000, on the Fourth of July of that year 65,000 Americans and 12,650 automobiles jammed the town. By 1926, American customers kept 75 bars in business, mostly on Avenida Revolución. For Hernán de la Roca, author of *Tijuana In*, a novel published in 1932, the city rose "before his eyes as the emporium of vice and moral corruption," the result, one should add, of American dollars, ingenuity, and fondness for drink.

During this age of booze, Mexican towns might as well have been towns in the United States. Only a few Mexicans profited from the bars, casinos, and brothels; most Mexicans competed for menial jobs. As one of them recalled of the early 1920s, "I was the only waiter to work at the race track; all of the others were Americans." Foreigners were in the saddle, even paying Mexican authorities to look the other way. Carl Withington, the owner of the Tivoli nightclub in Tijuana, for example, paid $60,000 monthly to Mexican officials for his gambling "rights" and, with the co-owner of the Tecolote Bar in Mexicali, 1,000 pesos a day to the chief of police, who, in return, left gamblers alone. In order to stay open, the Chinese gambling casinos in Mexicali paid a monthly quota of 28,000 pesos.

Along with Marvin Allen and Frank B. Beyer, Withington owned the Tecolote Bar and casino in Mexicali and the Tivoli in Tijuana. Withington, who had friends among influential Mexican officials, spoke Spanish and married a Mexican woman. Withington, Cofforth, and Baron Long were the czars of the bars and gambling casinos from one end of the border to the other. The lion's share of the capital that made the wheels turn for the Ciudad Juárez tourist emporium was American. Americans owned the Jockey Club, a racetrack that opened its doors in 1901; Colonel Matt J. Winn, of Kentucky Derby fame, was its general manager. The bullfights were an American enterprise, as were their customers. An American entrepreneur built the first international bridge with his own money; he got his profits from the tolls he collected. El Paso Electric Company, also American, later replaced that bridge with a steel and concrete one. As late as the 1960s, El Paso City Lines, a U.S. company, owned the bridge and ran the trolleys.

The opening of the Agua Caliente Hotel and Casino was the pinnacle event of that time. Owned by Long, Cofforth, Wirt G. Bowman, and Abelardo Rodríguez, it stood on the eastern edge of Tijuana, its buildings designed in the California-Spanish motif of white plaster walls and red tile then so popular in California. Its interior design was a medley of "art deco, Spanish colonial, Moorish, and French provincial." Palm trees from Hawaii lined its walkways and streets; my father, who knew plants and trees as well as anyone, judged the landscaping impressive. It had swimming pools, tennis courts, dog and horse racing, and a golf course, where each year Walter Hagen and Byron Nelson, the reigning kings, arrived to play for high stakes against each other. In the Salón Dorado del Casino, where Jean Harlow, Clara Bow, Wallace Berry, and Al Jolson frolicked, Margarita Cansino, who later changed her name to Rita Hayworth, danced flamenco and sang. Rumor has it that Buster Keaton, the Hollywood comedian, lost a fortune at the gaming tables. Expensive call girls made sure that single men were not lonely. The operation employed over two thousand workers. Gambling made the operation profitable; food and drinks were relatively inexpensive.

Demographic growth accompanied this frenzied activity. Between 1910 and 1930, Ciudad Juárez ranked among the five fastest-growing cities in the republic, with an impressive array of its citizens laboring to quench the thirst of American visitors. In the opinion of a Mexican politico, Ciudad Juárez, "without the booze industry and gambling, would be a heap of ruins." For this rescue from the jaws of neglect, Mexicans paid dearly. Tijuana, complained one of its inhabitants, "was the emporium where gold from gaming tables spilled onto floors but gringos took it home; for Tijuana there was only its shame." To quote Rubén Vizcaíno, a local intellectual bigwig, the "Americans corrupted us"; they "built a city to their liking," its story "a black episode in its history and culture." When Americans got into trouble in the border towns, Mexicans usually got the blame, as the famous Peteet case of 1924 demonstrates, when the police chief of Tijuana and a Mexican bar owner were blamed for the rape and suicide of drunken American girls and their parents. Of the four vice czars of Tijuana, only one was a Mexican; Rodríguez, the military governor during the 1920s, arrived, according to one version, with only a soldier's knapsack on his back. By joining hands with Long, Bowman, and Cofforth, he built a vice empire, which included the Casino de la Selva in Cuernavaca and the Foreign Club in Mexico City.

The American patrons and their customers brought with them old attitudes. One was race prejudice. None of the American owners of the liquor and gambling industry in Tijuana, for instance, hired Mexicans. In the casinos and better clubs and bars, Mexicans could not be found among the bartenders, waiters, and dealers. They were Americans who lived on the other side. The San Francisco Bar, where the wealthy went to drink, employed, along with Americans, Arabs and Chinese, but no Mexicans. Mexicans, when hired, earned less than Americans, although they did comparable work. Swarthy Mexicans rarely found a decent job. Only the California Bar and the Long Bar, both the property of Mexicans, employed them.

The first to take to the streets in protest were Mexicans who wanted to drive taxis, then monopolized by Americans. Under pressure from them, and from others who wanted jobs as waiters and bartenders, Governor

Rodríguez finally signed a law in 1924 that required proprietors in Baja California to hire Mexicans; but he enforced it only against the Chinese in Mexicali. Not until 1927 did it take effect against Americans, and then only after Mexicans had boycotted the Tivoli in Tijuana and, on one occasion, overturned its gaming tables to protest the recalcitrance of its owners to give them jobs. Labor unions of Mexican bartenders, waiters, taxi drivers, and musicians, who provided the music in the nightclubs, were then organized. The musicians, just the same, had to learn to play American tunes as a condition for being hired. Along the entire border, similar unions of waiters and bartenders appeared. Their militancy broke down the barriers erected by American employers.

A more overt form of racial bigotry also flourished. In some of the bars, not a few Mexicans, especially if dark-skinned, were asked to leave, and African Americans were not allowed in the saloons patronized by white Americans. Even Afro-American soldiers from El Paso could not drink in the elegant bars in Ciudad Juárez; one such bar was the Lobby Número Dos, which, for good measure, also excluded Mexicans. In Tijuana, African Americans had to drink in a bar reserved for them on Avenida Madero. Jack Johnson, the heavyweight champion, ran two nightclubs in Tijuana, one being the Newport Bar, which employed and served African Americans. This bigotry lingers on. At the Marabu, the "best" nightclub in the red-light zone of Nuevo Laredo, the whores, to quote one of them, will "not fuck a black man"; if they did "they could lose their Anglo clients."

None of the American promoters or their employees made their homes in Mexico. Those in Tijuana dwelled in San Diego, but El Paso was where the barons of bars and gambling halls lived. This was also true of middle-class Mexicans, including even customs officials. All of them spent what they earned on the American side. For them, as Roca wrote in his novel, heaven was San Diego, "a city clean of debris . . . where even the air one breathed had been disinfected." One of the slogans of La Liga Nacionalista Obrera, a pioneer labor group, was that those who "live from Tijuana live in Tijuana," a demand eventually incorporated into law. Off the tourist paths, Mexicans often inhabited shantytowns, taking what jobs were available. When Governor Carlos Trejo y Lerdo de Tejada arrived in Tijuana in 1931, he found, as he described it, "a forlorn city of dirty, wooden shacks. . . . the horse stables at the race track, by comparison, are "luxurious lodgings." He wanted adobe homes built, but when he attempted to carry out his plan, the political influence of the lumber companies in neighboring San Ysidro blocked it. That pattern was common to the entire border.

Most residents of these border towns did not think well of the nefarious activities; many were troubled, and some protested, including even a city councilman in Tijuana. A regulation in Ciudad Juárez, which sought to "moralize" the city and was no less nonsensical than Prohibition, forbade men to kiss women in public. Some years later, a civic parade to protest the bars and cabarets on Avenida Revolución in Tijuana drew participants from diverse sectors of society, including schoolchildren whose prostitute mothers watched proudly from their hotel windows. Authorities in Ciudad Juárez, perhaps pressured by city fathers in El Paso, who, worried about the gambling losses of Americans, wanted less of it, shut the international bridge down from time to time at an early hour.

∘ ∘ ∘ 🏛 ∘ ∘ ∘

Then suddenly, the house of cards collapsed. After the stock market crash of 1929, the opening shot of the Great Depression, and the repeal of Prohibition in 1933, the heyday of the 1920s ended. When Lázaro Cárdenas, the reform-minded president of Mexico, banned gambling two years later, only a memory lingered on, as bars and restaurants shut down. At the end of the 1920s, border crossings at the San Ysidro gate had totaled nearly 1.5 million, but not until after World War II did they reach that level again. Hard times and the availability of liquor in El Paso reduced traffic flows into Ciudad Juárez, leaving the tourist industry in ruins. With the closure of bars, restaurants, and nightclubs, people deserted the towns. In Tijuana, the foreign owners of the Tivoli and Midnight Follies nightclubs burned them down for the insurance money. Some twenty fires destroyed downtown Tijuana, mostly on Avenida Revolución. Their owners then left town. So ended the era of foreign domination along the border, and the notorious years of the Black Legend.

But not entirely. World War II, the biggest and bloodiest war in history, briefly revived the glory days of the 1920s. This time, customers were mostly military personnel stationed at nearby camps. This meant sailors from the San Diego naval base for Tijuana, and for Ciudad Juárez, those from Fort Bliss and Biggs Field in El Paso. Again a joy strip flourished from Tijuana to Matamoros, where young men cavorted far from the watchful eye of parents, neighbors, and military police. Korea and Vietnam kept a mild bonanza alive: Once again, a cabaret next to a bar, and a bar next door to a curio shop, all of them for American customers. The honky-tonks on Avenida Revolución in Tijuana—Aloha, Blue Fox, Ballena—remained, but now others, less pretentious, appeared on the north end of the city, for all intents and purposes a *zona de tolerancia*: Pelicano Bar, El Chupe Bar, El Infierno Bar, Salón de Baile El Bucanero, among others. "Ca'min, sir, ca'min, Sir. Beautiful senoritas," shouted the bar hucksters to soldiers and sailors. "Yes, sir. Rosa Carmina. Greatest ballerina from Mexico City," proclaimed a hustler at the Waikiki, a strip joint in Tijuana, Federico Campbell recalls in one of his memoirs. "Take a look inside, folks. No cover charge. The show is in, the show is in." As Rosina Conde writes: "The marines shouted more, more, eagerly reaching out with their hands to feel Lyn's rump, the queen of the rhumba, as she shook her hips." Also responsible for a new lease on life for Ciudad Juárez was the Texas ban on the sale of liquor by the drink, which drove soldiers to visit the saloons of Ciudad Juárez. Unfortunately for Mexican entertainment, the rise of gonorrhea and syphilis cases among the men stationed at Fort Bliss and Biggs Field put an end to their nightly escapades; military authorities, fearing a venereal disease epidemic, forbid them to cross into Mexico. So died the years of the border towns of the Black Legend, which, for Tijuana, José Galicot angrily recalls:

> *Tijuana, black legend . . .*
> *In the twenties,*
> *Booze mills for the gringos of the dry law.*
> *Tijuana, black legend . . .*
> *In the thirties,*
> *The casinos of Agua Caliente,*
> *Gambling and vice.*
> *Tijuana, black legend . . .*
> *In the forties,*
> *The war, bordellos,*
> *Where sailors cavorted.*
> *Tijuana, black legend . . .*
> *In the fifties,*
> *Marriages, divorces,*
> *Pornographic films,*
> *Abortions . . .*

With the end of America's wars of the twentieth century, the good times of yore are no longer the same; as one bar owner laments, "We lost our monopoly on immorality." But this is not entirely true. Avenida Revolución in Tijuana bustles with shoppers during the day, according to the *Los Angeles Times*, but "is positively electric with club hoppers at night" because the "clubs draw in thousands of twenty-somethings—and hundreds of kids who look far younger." The clubs, which "line both sides of the streets," make "it a sizzling boulevard for . . . dancers, drinkers and onlookers alike."

Texas, however, no longer forbids serving liquor over the bar; in 1971, it passed legislation giving counties a local option. El Paso quickly accepted the option. This law, as one observer recognized, killed off "one of the main attractions of Ciudad Juárez." A sexual revolution, if not exactly radical, also modified American attitudes toward sex; proof of this is the proliferation of topless bars, X-rated films, and sexual permissiveness. Another reason that men visited Mexican border towns no longer obtains. Ciudad Juárez, said one recent visitor, "used to be full of red-light districts, but if they exist now they are well out of sight." What shows continue are no longer on Avenida Juárez, the main street, but a block west, on Mariscal, where only the knowledgeable find them. Most of the nightlife thrives in discotheques. Strip shows and bawdy houses have been shunted off to *zonas de tolerancia* on the edge of town. There are also ladies' bars, where even Mexican women can drink. In Tijuana, the ponies no longer race at Agua Caliente; as Mike Marten of the California Horse Racing Board commented, "It was a sad turn of events . . . There was a time when Caliente was the premier track on the West Coast." But cockfights still go on at Ciudad Miguel Alemán, across the Rio Grande from Roma, Texas, at a *torneo de gallos* (cockfights) held each year; thousands of Americans drive over to bet and watch roosters fight to the death. No longer are quickie divorces granted in Ciudad Juárez; why go to Mexico when liberalized divorce laws, particularly in California and New York, make it unnecessary, and betting on horses can be done nearly everywhere by satellite, and Las Vegas and other gambling citadels beckon?

· · · 🏮 · · ·

There is a Texas saying: "I lost my virginity and had my first drink in a Mexican border town." That aphorism contains some truth, because long before the advent of prohibition, the world's oldest profession got a foothold in border towns. That was so both before and after World War II, when countless soldiers and sailors, as the adage goes, lost their virginity. That is still partly so today, even though Mexican law bans organized prostitution. One inflated estimate of the mid-1980s had fifteen thousand prostitutes in Tijuana; largely because of nearness to the United States, prostitution paid well. In this drama of sex for pay, Ciudad Juárez and Tijuana played leading roles, and Nogales does not lag far behind.

Now, however, that distinction belongs to Nuevo Laredo's *zona de tolerancia*, the largest and most famous red-light district along the border. Police who watch over the shenanigans in this *zona de tolerancia* keep a vigil a step or two from a medical clinic where the women are checked weekly. The Tamyko is the gaudiest of the nightclubs, with its building with red pagodas and patio with a fishpond and arched bridges. The best clubs woo Americans and, occasionally, wealthy young Mexicans. On weekends, crew-cab pickups carrying American college boys fill the streets of the red-light district. The prize for the worst of them belongs to Nuevo Progreso, where, to quote an American bigot, "even horny Mexicans won't go."

The profession, though no longer on center stage, continues to draw customers. According to health officials, in 1993, nearly 1,100 prostitutes labored permanently at "sexual activity" in the *zona norte de Tijuana*, where sixty-five bars and sixty-one hotels *de paso* (hotels for one-night stands) met customers' needs. Prostitutes came there from all over the republic. Some insist that jobs for women in the *maquiladoras* have reduced the number of prostitutes, but the evidence falls short of supporting this opinion. To the contrary, as the newspaper *El Mexicano* writes, prostitution is on the rise, the result of the poverty and desperation of thousands of young migrants who cannot find decent jobs in Tijuana, an argument that applies equally well to other cities. The poor pay of *maquiladora* employment may, in fact, encourage prostitution, an opinion voiced increasingly by women scholars. As a recent American visitor to Ciudad Juárez writes, "You never know if they are whores or simply seventeen-year-old *maquiladora* workers who moonlight on the side." A typical exchange: "How much," he asks? as she peers into the car window. The "equivalent of $14," she replies. For "how long?" he asks. "How long can you resist me?" she says with a laugh.

Poverty and oppression surely explain much prostitution; the blame lies with a society and a system that forces the poor to seek work in foreign lands or as prostitutes. A reminder of that is the girl on a bar stool beckoning to the men who pass by—"her face . . . empty . . . of spirit." To quote a young woman in Ciudad Juárez, "You have to do it because you need the money." Some of these young women, who sell themselves to poor and illiterate men from the provinces, must convince them to wear condoms.

In 1932, Tijuana had approximately five hundred registered prostitutes, mostly Europeans, Americans, and Asians, nearly all of whom lived north of the border. Even the pimps were foreigners. A Japanese man ran El Molino Rojo, the most lavish whorehouse on the border, with girls from all over the world looking to please American customers. Mexicans were conspicuous in their absence. A school now stands on the grounds of this "Red Mill." In Mexicali, Americans sought out El Gato Negro, La Copacabana, and El Molino Rojo. The world's oldest profession continues to pay dividends. In Ciudad Juárez in 1970, the total income from the prostitution business, tightly tied to the liquor industry, was over $2 million. Every day, *gabachos* (Americans) "would come up to you and ask, where can I find a good-looking chick," to quote one Juarense taxi driver, so "I would take them to Irma's, Caesar's Palace . . . or the Bunny Club."

Once upon a time, it was almost the prerogative of bars to be the locus of border prostitution; the brothels of earlier times had yielded their place to them. But streetwalkers are a common sight nowadays, as are more elegant call girls in the restaurants, nightclubs, and lobbies of hotels. Mexicans refer to the women who labor in bars as *ficheras*, who make certain that customers drink. On the side, they sell themselves, giving the bartender, who shields them from the police or Sanitation Department official, a percentage of what they earn. In the *zona norte* of Tijuana, most of the customers are Mexicans; in Ciudad Juárez, they are Americans.

There used to be a kind of hierarchy. Newly arrived families, whose menfolk came intent on finding work on the American side, settled in poor barrios, where the aspiring border jumpers got their first information about how to evade the *migra,* the border patrol. Some of the women found jobs as waitresses in the lunchrooms of the barrio. The attractive ones eventually moved on, in Tijuana to the bars on Avenida Revolución, where they became *ficheras*. As one of them told a reporter in the 1950s, "Don't think that I plan to be here all of my life . . . when I learn to dance I am getting a job at the Aloha." Now the willing and the young are usually recruited in their hometowns.

A footnote must be added to this sorry chapter of man's abuse of women. In Tijuana, the women of the night are starting to defend themselves. Over one hundred of them belong to an organization of their own that they call Vanguardia de Mujeres Libres Maria Magdalena, an alliance of "sexual workers" who seek to protect themselves from exploitation by men and unscrupulous municipal authorities, mainly the police "who extort money from us." During the Christmas holidays of 1993, they took gifts to the poor children of the nursery school of the *zona norte*. They hold workshops where the illiterate among them can learn to read, find out what their rights are, and alert themselves to the risks of their profession.

○　○　○　❖　○　○　○

A legacy of the 1920s is tourism, which is big business along the border, as it is in the contemporary world, where it claims approximately one-eighth of the world's gross national product. Along the border, tourism is particularly important for Ciudad Juárez and Tijuana. Tourist districts, as Americans know them, are unique to border towns; they exist nowhere else in Mexico. Only on the border does one find separate districts for commerce and tourists, with a mutual isolation of Mexicans and outsiders. "When I was young," recalls the writer Mayo Murrieta, "we walked everywhere in Tijuana but never on Calle Revolución . . . for fear of being treated differently." These districts offer abundant proof of the remarkable influence the border wields on the structure of Mexican cities. Once the key part of a city, today commercial zones dwarf the tourist district.

Of the billions of dollars that tourism confers on Mexico, two-thirds comes, either directly or indirectly, from border dollars. Over 90 percent of visitors to Mexican border cities come from neighboring counties and states. In 1993 alone, visitors from the United States—almost always the only visitors, in any case—spent an estimated $2.1 billion in the Tijuana-Ensenada corridor. So important is tourism for the entire republic that it has been a cabinet-level responsibility since 1961, when the Ministry of Tourism was established. Its first head was Miguel Alemán, a former president enamored of the American way of life, a friend of rich Americans, and a toady of American cold war diplomacy.

Hotels, motels, bars, nightclubs, restaurants, shops selling handicrafts (serapes from Puebla, wood carvings from Michoacán, *guayaberas* [shirts] from Yucatan, and leather saddles, shoes, and ladies' bags from Jalisco), perfume and jewelry stores, liquor stores, discotheques for the young, and racetracks (for horses or dogs) are the trademarks of border tourism. Pitchmen on the street, promising bargains galore, entice passersby to enter the shops. These sights and sounds, to quote a Mexican observer, "play on the preconceived image of what most North American tourists think Mexico ought to look like and what it ought to offer them for sale."

The purpose of this Mexican Disneyland is to please outsiders, especially the tall and blond. To cite David Nicholson-Lord, an English author, all of this adds up to what he refers to as "airport art" and the "trinketization of cultures." In diverse ways, tourism, he argues, "changes tradition," and "particularly in the Third World," where one must situate the Mexican border, "that change looks and feels like degradation." That bit of wisdom strikes you with startling clarity when you wait in your auto at international gates to enter the United States; on one side, there is row after row of wooden stalls ("the last chance to buy") displaying vulgar statues, grotesque clay pigs, and gaudy blankets and, on the other, vendors on foot hawking identical merchandise. Obviously, what Americans purchase determines what is made and sold. You wonder about the taste of the Americans who buy these eyesores, and if you are of Mexican descent, you feel shame for what has befallen the country of your parents.

Global second thoughts about these results led in 1980 to a conference in Manila called together by religious leaders in the peripheral countries worried about the impact of tourism on local cultures. It concluded, to the consternation of the West, that "tourism does more harm than good to people and to societies of the Third World." According to one of these nations' spokesmen, it exploits the majority, "pollutes the environment, destroys the ecosystem, bastardizes the culture, robs people of their traditional values and ways of life and subjugates women and children in the abject slavery of prostitution." Tourism, he went on to say, "epitomizes the present unjust world economic order where the few who control the wealth and power dictate the terms."

Although not always accurate, that portrait, despite the presence of assembly plants, does not stray far from the here and now on the border, a reality that is graphically depicted by Mexican novelists and short-story writers. In Tijuana, the sale of handicrafts claims over one-half of the tourist dollar, while restaurants and bars, next on the list, eat up nearly one-third. Over-the-counter sales of prescription drugs, too, attract countless customers, on the lookout for wrinkle-smoothing Retin-A or the hair restorer Minoxodal. A few of the restaurants are international landmarks, one being the kitchen of the Hotel Caesar in Tijuana, renowned for its salad, a recipe concocted in 1927. People who know good food eat at Martino's or Julio's Cafe Corona, two of the fine restaurants in Ciudad Juárez. Some years ago, Tecate, one of the smaller towns, attempted to lure tourists by "running bulls" through its streets, seeking to imitate the success of the event in Pamplona, Spain. But the ire the Tecatenses directed at drunken tourists who turned local life upside down put an end to the spectacle. Elsewhere, tourist impresarios, claiming to promote tradition and keep alive cherished ceremonies and popular customs, import "Aztec" Indians from Central Mexico to perform to the beat of leather drums and the wail of wooden flutes in pre-Columbian rituals on the streets of cities for the pleasure of gringo visitors. Yet the Aztecs, the legendary natives subjugated by the Spaniards, never set foot on the soil of today's border metropolises. The anthropologist Dean MacCannell refers to this false recreation of yesteryear as "staged authenticity." "Part of the problem," writes Nicholson-Lord, "is that tourism is colonialism in another guise," and because of that, it weakens the struggle to maintain an identity of one's own and the quest for "national self-determination."

For tourists, all Mexican border cities offer these attractions, though not to the same degree. Matamoros lacks the customary tourist district, and Nuevo Progreso comes alive merely on weekends. Mexicali, which prides itself in not being a tourist mecca, attracts visitors with a taste for fine Chinese cuisine. A busy port of entry, Nuevo Laredo, like Mexicali, does not live or die from tourism; neighboring Laredo is small and poor, and few of those who visit stay overnight. The money earned in these cities is far less than the amount Mexicans spend across the border. However, Nogales, which is also a major port of entry, has a large tourist zone and plentiful prostitutes, a response to the rapid growth of Tucson and Phoenix.

Reliance on tourism is a two-edged sword. Dollar earnings, either as profits or wages, are the obvious benefit. Eager to enhance this source of revenue, the Mexican government, with its National Border Program (PRONAF) of the mid-1960s, spent millions of pesos to erase some of the ugliness of border cities by turning narrow streets into tree-lined avenues, landscaping green parks, placing heroic monuments in areas traveled by tourists, and building history museums, theaters for ballet, and convention halls. The greater the reliance on tourists, however, the greater the dependency on outsiders and the greater the economic vulnerability of the society. It is a risky enterprise, when even changes in hairstyles of American women can hurt beauty parlors across the border. For all that, as the *San Diego Union-Tribune* reports, Mexico has only 10 percent of the foreign visitors of Spain, which is far smaller and less renowned for its tourist industry. Depressions north of the border hurt tourism. The collapse of the California economy in the early 1990s bankrupted scores of merchants on Avenida Revolución and shut down restaurants, while hotel occupancy rates dropped by half. As one taxi driver in Ciudad Juárez remarked about his trials and tribulations during an earlier downturn: "With tourism being in such bad shape . . . I am only surviving. I not only drive a taxi . . . I sell real estate and also fire extinguishers . . . sometimes I do well and sometimes I don't." On top of that, new tourist resorts in such places as Cancún draw the more affluent travelers; Hollywood luminaries no longer frequent Tijuana nightspots. To quote an article in *El Mexicano*, worse still, the young who visit have money only for the cheaper beers. Avenida Revolución, once a bastion of honky-tonks for servicemen, is now "a kind of teeny-bopper fantasyland." A goodly number of the dollars earned find their way back across the border because courting tourists does not encourage economic self-reliance at home. And the number of Mexican visitors to U.S. border cities almost always surpasses that of Americans traveling south.

Additional negative aspects include the increasing monopolization of the Mexican tourist industry by huge American conglomerates, including hotels, auto rental agencies, the credit card business, and restaurants. The world's hotel business, we must not forget, is a monopoly of U.S. multinationals such as Holiday Inn and Best Western, standbys in Mexico. Trickle-down economics, which drives the tourist industry, confers the most benefits on big business; only the leftovers remain in the host country, few of which "trickle down" to the poorest. As it is everywhere in the world, tourism along the border—even in urban hubs such as San Diego, "the finest city in America"—is a low-wage industry. Waiters, bartenders, cooks, and musicians, the staples of the tourist trade, never get rich off their wages. So what? say its apologists: Aren't low wages better than none at all? That, too, however, is a moot point; as Nicholson-Lord rightly points out, it depends on what alternatives exist, and sometimes there are none, because governments pursue a national tourism strategy that bars other approaches. As any visit to a border city confirms, the poorest subsidize the good times of the wealthiest; the result is a "twilight economy" where hordes of men, women, and children beg or tout. Although tourists are an important source of income for a Mexican city, most of them spend little time or money during visits and cannot be counted on to support blueprints purporting to fatten per capita income. At the same time, heavy influxes of tourists tax the capacity of municipal services such as the police and street and highway maintenance, a burden that hoteliers and others pass on to local taxpayers. Even buying binges by Americans can hurt; the sale of cheaper gasoline to visitors depletes local supplies or, as in the case of sugar, offers a shopping windfall to foreigners at the expense of the Mexican exchequer, which in the past subsidized sugar in order to keep the price low for poor Mexican consumers.

Given this reality, it is to be expected that Mexicans frequently express unflattering views of their visitors. To quote Vizcaíno, "They see themselves as supermen, leaders of the Free World, technological gods." When "they see Third World poverty—skinny dogs, the people begging, Indians . . . kneeling before them . . . they prove to themselves that they are God's children." When Americans spend a dollar, Murrieta goes on, "they feel they have the right even to desecrate our national flag."

To complicate life for Vizcaíno and his neighbors, in the 1960s the global economy, largely of American manufacture, pulled their homeland into its vortex.

4

The Global Economy

Today, life on the Mexican side of the borderlands only rarely conjures up that of the 1920s. For those of us who knew the old, the dissimilarity is striking. Since the 1960s, the arrival of assembly plants, an adjunct of the global economy, has radically altered the contours of Mexican border society. Old tourist hotspots recede into memory as urbanization, increasingly the offspring of offshore plants, takes hold, transforming hamlets into big cities; both Tijuana and Ciudad Juárez, plant kingpins, shelter hordes of inhabitants, hosting social ills typical of chaotic and unplanned growth. Migrants from all over the republic flock north, lured by dreams of jobs in industry. Yet globalization, what *maquiladoras* exemplify, merely shuffles the outlines of the asymmetrical relationship but hardly casts it to the winds. Mindful of their consequences, naysayers in Ciudad Juárez dubbed the society of *maquiladoras* Maquilamex, a metaphor that assents grudgingly to the weighty role that assembly plants play from Tijuana to Matamoros and captures the ambivalence of a people troubled by what they witness.

The term *maquila*, as one might suspect, has Spanish roots. In Spain in bygone years, millers who ground a client's corn called the portion they kept as payment a *maquila*; that is the genesis of the word *maquiladora*, the Mexican surrogate for assembly plant, often referred to, and rightly so, as *la maquila*. Today, its squat, drab buildings—faceless silhouettes shorn of the architect's creative genius—are a ubiquitous presence in Mexican cities of the border.

Workers in *maquiladoras* assemble articles of sundry nature from components of foreign manufacture, articles that range anywhere from television sets to doorknobs to windshield wipers; these articles are sold abroad, mainly in the United States, where the components originate.

Mexicans contribute their labor, as well as the water and the land on which the *maquilas* stand. These plants are offshoots of a global economy that has reshaped the role of the Third World, changing it from a supplier of raw materials into a purveyor of vast pools of cheap labor, which gives capitalists the means to lower the costs of their manufactures and to swell profits. That change relegates certain kinds of jobs to the dustbin in countries such as the United States and transfers them to places where women and children labor for a pittance. As Pat Buchanan puts it, capitalists "anxious to off-load their American workers on the junk heap of the global economy" make the Third World a mecca for transnationals.

The facts are simple enough: the Mexican border houses approximately 2,300 *maquiladoras*, their numbers multiplying almost daily. They are the cogs that drive the local economy and are the republic's chief source of industrial jobs. They employ over 630,000 Mexicans, predominantly young women, who account for one-third of the republic's labor force, a proportion that grows each year; they are 10 to 15 percent more productive, according to one study, than American workers. David Montgomery, a noted economic historian, writes that this grim reality explains why *maquiladoras* have generated during the last ten years a "47 percent increase in productivity coupled with a 29 percent decline in real wages." Taiwan, Hong Kong, and Puerto Rico were the original recipients of this largesse, but then it was Mexico's turn; by the 1980s, Mexico's *maquila* exports outstripped those of Hong Kong, not only because of its cheap labor but also because of its proximity to the United States, which reduces the cost of transporting goods to American consumers. At Tijuana, Joel Simon writes, *maquilas* converted "this border backwater into what some call Mexico's Hong Kong."

This is the global assembly line, where parts from around the world are assembled into a finished product in export-processing zones, such as the Mexican border, then shipped to the industrialized nations. The *maquilas,* part and parcel of transnational corporations, are highly mobile; always on the lookout for the most profitable location, they move easily from country to country. The threat of relocation and mass layoffs, like the legendary sword of Damocles, ever hangs over the host country. *Maquilas* are runaway shops; they are here today and gone tomorrow, as the workers of Cortland, New York, discovered in 1995, when the Smith Corona company closed down its plants and transferred operations to Tijuana, where Mexican workers now put together word processors, advanced typewriters, and office equipment. The overseas assembly plants are not factories in the usual sense but rather departments of huge corporations.

o   o   o   🔷   o   o   o

Maquilas in Mexico go back to 1965, when the Border Industrialization Program (BIP), the brainchild of Mexican entrepreneurs, was hatched. Events in the Far East, where American transnationals had established assembly plants in Hong Kong, Singapore, Taiwan, and the Philippines to capitalize on supplies of cheap labor, inspired them. The idea was to establish export platforms, at a time when Mexican leaders were struggling to find jobs for huge numbers of unemployed braceros and recent arrivals on the border. In some cities, one-half the workers were unemployed. Fear of political unrest was a key factor, as was arresting the flow of the jobless into the United States, where the increasing mechanization of agriculture made much Mexican labor superfluous. *Maquiladoras,* it was thought, would create jobs and earn dollars, an increasingly urgent need after the collapse of oil prices in the 1980s.

Begun as a temporary expedient, the *maquila* blueprint sought to capitalize on U.S. Tariff Items 806 and 807, which allow offshore subsidiaries of American transnational corporations to assemble products from American components for resale in the United States. Tariff duties are imposed only on the "value added," that is, the cost of foreign labor. The cheaper the labor, the lower the value added, and the bigger the profits. The plan was to entice American corporations to build plants along the border by allowing them duty-free import of all necessary machinery, equipment, and raw materials, including components to be assembled. To protect national industry, none of the finished goods could be sold in Mexico; however, NAFTA eventually opened that door, though how many more television sets and door hinges, to cite just two products, can Mexicans buy? Mexican legislation that sets limits on foreign ownership and management does not apply to *maquiladora* operations, an exemption that overrides a stipulation limiting foreign control to 49 percent. When legislation barred the transnationals from owning land along the border, which hampered their expansion, politicians rewrote it to permit foreign firms full use of Mexican land for up to thirty years. Although taxes on the *maquiladoras* are light, income from the industry each year brings in $7 billion in foreign currency, making it, after PEMEX, the biggest source of national revenue. In 1995, desperate for funds to weather the latest financial crisis, Mexican authorities belatedly levied an additional 1.8 percent tax on the value of *maquiladora* real estate, machinery, and other assets. In theory, management must enroll workers in the Seguro Social, the social security agency, and the national housing program. The loopholes, nonetheless, are formidable. The temporary nature of the program lasted only briefly; in 1972, legislation opened up the whole republic to them, with the exception of Mexico City, Guadalajara, and Monterrey, industrial citadels.

In this integration of the border into the economy of the United States, Mexican brokers were the movers and shakers. One of their publicity pamphlets from Ciudad Juárez promised prospective investors weekly wages only a few cents above $20 for a six-day week. In Baja California Norte by 1998, reports *La Jornada*, state authorities had joined these entrepreneurs, the influential Bustamantes for instance, in the campaign to lure foreign corporations south by dangling before them the promise of wages "lower than those of Taiwan, Hong Kong, and Singapore." Antonio Bermúdez, a former head of PEMEX and the owner of a construction company, employed an American to promote his Parque Industrial de Ciudad Juárez in the United States. His brochures, geared toward welcoming American corporations, advertised as one of the advantages the opportunity for plant managers and their families to reside in El Paso, where their American wives could make new friends, and their children could attend American schools. There were also, Bermúdez reminded his clients, American hospitals and clubs in El Paso, where everyone spoke English. This arrangement is now routine along the border. RCA was Bermudez's initial conquest.

On the heels of that success, other Mexicans followed suit. In Matamoros, along with Ciudad Juárez, Tijuana, and Nogales, now major *maquiladora* cities, they graded lands and put up buildings, baptized them industrial parks, and set about leasing them to Zenith, the Fisher Price toy division of Quaker Oats, and ITT. One of the first *maquilas,* the Electronic Control Corporation, assembled light dimmers. Later, Sergio Argüelles, a Mexican speculator, acquired more land and enticed, among other corporations, the Inland Division of General Motors. Less than two decades later, the three plants of General Motors were assembling auto parts and employing five thousand workers. The Consejo Nacional de la Industria de la Maquiladora de Exportación, which speaks for these entrepreneurs, campaigns actively to preserve the good image of the industry in the United States, tarnished, it alleges, by nefarious special interests.

These patrons of industrial parks, essentially go-betweens who serve *maquilas,* amassed fortunes by serving transnational management. They are the backbone of a class that identifies its livelihood with the *maquiladora* industry and that earns its money by exploiting, to cite a Mexican study, "the peculiar private-public sector symbiosis that exists in Mexico," at the expense of "the public interest." This relationship calls attention to the favorable terms with which public facilities are handed over to these entrepreneurs for the benefit of the *maquilas.* Many of the assembly plants employ Mexican managers who speak Spanish and know local politics yet earn less than their American equivalents; they, too, walk in step with the Mexican *maquila* bourgeoisie, a class not universally admired by Mexicans. To quote Mayo Murrieta and Alberto Hernández in *Puente México,* "Our bourgeoisie" dedicates itself "to industrializing our nocturnal life—drinking margaritas, tequila poppers, listening to mariachis, patronizing noisy discotheques . . . and alcoholic bars—keeping afloat the black legend of border good times."

Mexico's *maquilas* are closely related to the economic boom of the Sunbelt. They serve Sunbelt markets and, frequently, Sunbelt Americans, who help lure them south, the chief value being the supply and service business that accrues to them. In 1994, to demonstrate what this means for a Sunbelt state, the *maquiladoras* of Baja California imported $5.4 billion in goods and services, of which $810 million came from California. An International Trade Commission study for 1992 calculated that Tijuana *maquilas* poured up to $90 million into the San Diego economy. In another example, believing that they, too, would benefit economically, the city fathers of Brownsville and McAllen, Texas, actively recruited the establishment of *maquiladoras* across the border. The bank accounts of an international group composed of members of chambers of commerce in the United States and Mexican politicos, lawyers, bankers, exporters and importers, and land speculators hangs on the fortunes of the *maquilas*. So far, they have scant cause for worry. Drawn by the abundance of cheap labor, periodic peso pratfalls, and the favors conferred on them, the number of *maquilas* multiplies by leaps and bounds. Their euphoric Mexican proponents say that because of these plants, for the first time a strong middle class exists on the border.

In the United States, the *maquiladoras* were originally promoted as twin plants, a term designed to convey the idea of production in partnership. Capital-intensive facilities would locate north of the border, and labor-intensive activities would take place in Mexico. American border plants would provide the "inputs" to be assembled by the Mexicans; the finished product would then be shipped back to the United States. That did not occur. Most *maquiladoras* in Texas depend on parent plants in the Northeast, but the Silicon Valley and Orange County supply Baja California *maquilas*. Most maquiladoras have no twin plant. When such a twin exists, it is more than likely a warehouse with a handful of workers. Few industries in Sunbelt cities supply *maquiladoras*. One recent survey "found one Tijuana *maquila* buying tools made in the San Diego area, another . . . plant buying resin . . . and a Ciudad Juárez company buying tools and oil from El Paso." Nor, despite claims to the contrary, do *maquiladoras* create manufacturing jobs in the United States. There are exceptions, however; according to the *Los Angeles Times*, Sony, the Japanese corporation, assembles Trinitron color televisions and computer monitors from components produced by its Tijuana plant at a San Diego facility that employs 2,200 workers. Mexican *maquilas,* clearly, contribute to the economies of U.S. border cities.

Transnationals are also partly responsible for the emergence of vast pools of cheap labor in Third World nations. Huge agribusinesses now control immense expanses of land, as in Mexico, that are set aside for the production of cash crops for export or for processing into animal feed. The sale of expensive cuts of beef, pork, bacon, and sundry sausages to urban, middle-class customers promises fatter monetary rewards than cultivating corn and beans for buyers of lesser means. As this enterprise prospers, the number of campesinos who can survive by harvesting corn and beans on tiny plots shrinks, so they migrate to cities in search of jobs. Occasionally, young women in the family, many of whom move to border cities, find employment in the *maquilas*. Just the same, the transnationals did not ignite this horrendous rural flight; that dubious honor falls on Mexican politicos and planters who, in the 1940s, started to favor an agriculture for export over small farmers. Peso devaluations, which drive down the cost of labor, also account for the abundant pool of low-wage workers. At present, no country outranks Mexico in supplying cheap labor for U.S. transnationals; this should come as no surprise, because Mexican wages are among the lowest in the world.

Corporate America, first and foremost, is scarcely philanthropic, as one manager of a Nogales *maquiladora*, quoted in the *Tucson Weekly*, frankly admitted: "I don't think the companies came down here to benefit Mexico. They came down . . . to benefit themselves." Sandy Tolan, who interviewed this obdurate boss, concludes that the "'idea' is to keep costs down, stay in business, and maximize profits." When they locate their subsidiaries in Third World Countries, transnational corporations have specific considerations in mind. They avoid countries with traditions of labor activism, specifically strong unions, and stay out of countries racked by political instability. In both respects, Mexico offers ideal conditions; to quote Mario Vargas Llosa, the Peruvian novelist, it is "the perfect dictatorship," or at least it was until recently. *Maquilas* prefer to retrain workers rather than update old machinery. The cost of training workers is almost always minimal because, as one sociologist writes, the labor process involves repetitive, deskilled tasks that are easily transferable.

Foreign investment is the lifeblood of the *maquiladoras*, an industry beholden to foreign economic decisions and foreign legislation. The availability of cheap labor, in comparison with other world export zones, is still the principal reason for its existence along the border. At the same time, its almost sole reliance on the U.S. market makes it highly vulnerable to the ups and downs of that economy; it tends to ebb and flow with business cycles north of the border. A dip in the U.S. economy cuts into production and leads to a loss of *maquila* jobs. During the economic crisis of the mid-1970s, nearly half of the workers in the *maquilas* of Ciudad Juárez became unemployed; all told, as many as thirty-two thousand *maquila* jobs along the border vanished. American *maquila* operators, just the same, threatened to pick up and leave unless Mexico reduced their payments to social security and gave them more leeway in the firing of workers, asking that the probationary period, during which workers can be arbitrarily dismissed, be extended from thirty to ninety days. The Mexican government, which had just devalued the peso, granted all the operators' demands.

The absence of linkages to Mexican industry, either at the border or in the rest of the republic, ensures the survival of the *maquila* as a typical enclave operation, which, in turn, practically guarantees continued dependency on the Sunbelt of the United States. The border is an industrial enclave of *maquilas* that largely employ cheap labor and whose corporate offices are usually in the United States. Any Mexican attempt to alter this structure dramatically, for instance, by imposing a much heavier tax, will surely drive the *maquilas* to a safer haven.

Assembled goods, as explained previously, wend their way north. Clearly, these exports do not represent trade in the conventional sense. Even so, they do muddle the significance of trade statistics for both Mexico and the United States, a point emphasized by Victor L. Urquidi, a Mexican economist who talks of "hyperbolic figures given out by authorities and accepted by not a few economists." The Clinton administration—not surprisingly, since it sponsored NAFTA—yearly reports burgeoning exports to Mexico, claims that are disputed by dissenting watchdogs, the International Garment Workers' Union among them, whose own figures show that Mexicans purchase only one-fifth of these exports. The rest actually ends up in the hands of the subsidiaries of American corporations—the *maquilas.* Statistics are murky for the portion sent to free trade zones that also assemble and process goods. The two, nonetheless, account for over one-half the reported exports to Mexico; none of these goods, keep in mind, can presently be sold in Mexico. Mexican sources confirm that capital goods, most earmarked for *maquiladoras,* make up, more or less, over one-third of the exports. As former California governor Edmund G. Brown argues, "Most of our so-called exports to Mexico represent not final goods . . . but intermediate" ones produced for American or other markets after being assembled by cheap Mexican labor. Brown has the facts on his side. As the *New York Times* concludes, more than four-fifths of these exports "represent United States companies trading with themselves." These figures verify the role of Mexico as an export platform, but hardly its importance as a consumer market.

○　○　○　🏵　○　○　○

Recently, the *maquilas* acquired one more sponsor—a new kid on the block. The Asians are in town. Japanese investment dates from the 1980s. The first Japanese *maquiladora,* a subsidiary of the Mitsubishi Corporation, was established in Matamoros as a project sponsored by the Mexican government. Japanese investment in Mexico, when *maquiladoras* are included, more than doubled during the 1980s, rising to over $1.7 billion. Japanese *maquilas,* in typical fashion, assemble components for Japanese firms in the United States; they purchase little from Mexicans. In 1980, there were only eight Japanese *maquilas;* a decade and a half later, there were approximately seventy of them. By 1990, over one hundred Japanese transnationals were on the Fortune 500 list; of that group, thirty-three operated in Mexico. Like the American companies, they set up shop because of the cheap labor, lax regulation, and the need to reduce dependence on costly Japanese-made components; later, they chose Mexico because of NAFTA regulations, which require that key components such as picture tubes and tuners be produced in North America for the manufacturer of a color television to be exempt from paying duty in the North American trade zone. The Japanese goal, which Sony Engineering and Manufacturing pioneered, is to build a full-service center for television production in the Western Hemisphere. The border location gives Japanese products easy access to the United States market and helps circumvent possible American protectionist sentiment. Japanese executives, moreover, can live in the United States.

With Japanese investments, Tijuana has undergone a metamorphosis. The Japanese employ 15 percent of the entire Tijuana *maquila* labor force. Their plants manufacture everything from ballpoint pens (Scripto) to musical instruments (Casio). Today, the city is the world's foremost center of television production; together, the Asian corporations yearly assemble over 9 million television sets and employ almost twenty-five thousand workers, nearly matching the number manufacturing television sets in the United States, where over ninety companies once built them. The making of television sets and jobs has gone south. Components such as electronic tuners, which were formerly imported from Japan, are now produced in Tijuana. Sony, Sanyo, Hitachi, Matsushita, and Toshiba, among the largest Japanese manufacturers of television sets, own plants along the border. Daewoo assembles them in San Luis Río Colorado, as Goldstar does in Mexicali; Samsung, a Korean company, opened its $212 million plant in March 1996. By the late 1980s, over one-half of Japanese color television manufacturers had *maquiladoras* on the Mexican border. Thanks to them, Mexico became the leading supplier of television equipment for the United States, as well as a major exporter of color television sets.

· · · 🈷 · · ·

Have the *maquilas* lived up to their Mexican expectations? To begin with, for those who dreamed of replicating the Asian miracle, they are a huge disappointment. They did not sow the seeds for border industrialization, if by that we mean the development of a factory system from the ground up, not simply the introduction of assembly lines where Mexicans put together imported components. The truth is that *maquilas* buy no more than 2 percent of their raw materials, *insumos* as they are known south of the border, from Mexican suppliers; the rest is imported. Aside from paper towels, toilet paper, soap, brooms, and mops, Mexican manufacturing is a figment of the imagination in the world of border *maquilas.*

Furthermore, there is no evidence that they reduce levels of unemployment. To paraphrase Patricia Fernández Kelly, a Mexican scholar, "in-bond plants," as *maquilas* are also known, do not resolve employment problems for most of the working class. They account for 11 percent of jobs in Mexican industry and for 26 percent of the employed in the six border states. All the same, in this region *maquilas* stand out as employment powerhouses, accounting for over 40 percent of jobs in Tijuana, 75 percent in Matamoros, and, incredibly, 90 percent in Ciudad Acuña. Yet *maquila* workers, regardless of their importance, represent only a fraction of the economically active population in the republic. *Maquilas* provide jobs for just 2 percent of recent immigrants to border cities; although they surely help attract them, they do not hire them. Unemployment during the Border Industrialization Program actually grew, a testament to the size of the migrant influx and to the inability of *maquiladoras* to employ the new arrivals. The *maquiladoras* profit from this situation, as one manager explained: "Thanks to the high level of unemployment, which in Ciudad Juárez reaches 30 percent, we are able to be highly selective with the personnel we employ."

Maquilas, however, do provide jobs; they do not directly cause unemployment. They have failed to reduce unemployment rates because, generally, they do not hire members of the traditional workforce, that is, men. They look for women, members of a formerly inactive workforce: daughters, sisters, and wives who once stayed home. These women are the cheapest form of unskilled or semiskilled labor, the most vulnerable within society. Currently, women account for one-third of the republic's labor force, a proportion that grows each year. Whether women are hired because, as it is alleged, they are naturally more docile than men is not the point: The practices of the transnational corporations simply take advantage of Mexican women's customary subservience in a male-dominated society.

Men can surely do the identical work, but they would likely demand higher wages, better working conditions, and more flexible schedules. Mexican women perform shift work on a six-day basis, which U.S. workers have not been willing to do since World War II. All the same, women are not eager to put up with *maquila* jobs. They stay on the assembly line because, for the most part, no other jobs exist, particularly for those without skills or training and little schooling. In Tijuana, over four-fifths of *maquiladora* workers are unskilled, possessing on average no more than six years of schooling. They are young: In both Tijuana and Ciudad Juárez, they usually began to work at age seventeen or eighteen.

Workers in the *maquila* industry almost always lack job security; health and disability benefits hang by a thread, and hope of advancement is a myth. Job conditions, though perhaps not as bad as before, are often poor. Low wages alone, nonetheless, no longer explain the existence of *maquiladoras* along the border. When wages rose during the boom years, the *maquiladoras,* in order to reduce costs, updated their technology: Aldila, for example, a Tijuana plant that began in 1987 with nearly 300 workers manufacturing up to 1,000 shafts a day, now daily turns out 5,500 shafts, with the same number of workers and advanced machinery. Still, modernization, as a study by the Colegio de la Frontera Norte demonstrates, is partial and recent; nor do studies show that technology will ever completely eliminate the need for cheap labor.

Despite technological advancements, *maquilas* constantly advertise for workers; a cursory trip through a border city confirms that. Further, worker scarcity can promote changes in hiring practices. For example, in Ciudad Juárez, the lack of women has led employers to hire young men; the reason, according to Rachael Kamel, for "this seeming labor shortage" is that "with the value of their wages slashed by repeated devaluations of the peso," women, especially those with children to support, choose "to slip across the border to seek jobs as maids or factory workers." No matter how low the wages on the other side, they are usually better than those in the *maquilas*. Between 1980 and 1990, the employment of men rose from less than 20 percent to nearly 35 percent of the workforce, and in some sectors such as transportation, it rose to 50 percent.

By employing young women, the *maquilas* both expand the size of the workforce and simultaneously disenfranchise a majority of male laborers, the traditional rank and file. The *maquila* industry fractures the labor force by gender. Just the same, women scholars do not necessarily see the problem this way. For some, the *maquila* does not favor women over men in the labor market; quite the opposite, as one feminist says, *maquilas* do not lessen unemployment among either men or women. Whatever the truth, Mexico's economic architects have a tiger by the tail. A disruption of *maquiladora* operations will double the number of unemployed. One could argue that *maquiladoras,* by drawing migrants to the border and not hiring them, indirectly exacerbate labor problems of border cities. This is particularly true for rural migrants, most of whom are shunted aside by *maquiladoras* that prefer city dwellers, on the questionable assumption that they are "more stable, disciplined, and reliable." Approximately 1 million new workers annually enter the Mexican job market. *Maquila* jobs, notwithstanding that statistic, are predominantly for young females. One study in Ciudad Juárez shows that three out of four males who share a household with a female *maquila* worker, as husbands, fathers, or brothers, are either jobless or work as street vendors or occasional day laborers.

The *maquila* job picture is a mixed bag. Such workers are rarely skilled. Of the thousands employed, 83 percent toil at low-level jobs, slightly more than 10 percent perform "technical jobs," and only 6.5 percent hold managerial or administrative posts. Tijuana boasts the largest number of *maquilas*, but Ciudad Juárez has nearly three times as many *maquila* workers. The workers of Ciudad Juárez represent one-third of the city's labor force, or three out of four new jobs in the entire state. Chihuahua, once a state renowned for its cattle, mining, and lumber, is now, thanks to Ciudad Juárez, queen of the *maquilas*. The 565 plants in Tijuana employ 82,000 workers, and *maquilas* were responsible for nearly one-half the jobs created between 1980 and 1990. By 1990, the 94 *maquiladoras* of Matamoros employed 38,000 workers, mostly in automotive parts, electronics assembly, and contract sewing. Of the total number of jobs in Ciudad Acuña, 90 percent, as stated earlier, are in the *maquiladoras;* for all intents and purposes, the city was one big *maquiladora*. Still, the *maquiladoras* do not prosper everywhere. Those in Mexicali, to cite one case, employ fewer workers than before, and Nuevo Laredo has failed to attract more plants.

∘ ∘ ∘ 🔲 ∘ ∘ ∘

Labor costs, although currently perhaps less significant, are still the most expensive item in the budgets of *maquilas*. This is true all along the border. Yet wage rates remain low, kept there by plant decision, Mexican government policy, and "unforeseen" events such as peso devaluations, windfalls for management. Until the devaluation of 1982, wages were "high," better than those in Hong Kong, South Korea, and Taiwan. Some *maquila* operators, the evidence suggests, had thoughts about moving on, their executives talking of the "uncompetitiveness" of Mexican wages. The devaluation of 1982 ended the complaint, with wages falling from a historic high of $1.53 an hour to less than one-half that amount. At the Zenith television plant in Reynosa, after the peso's tumble of 1994, the weekly take-home pay dropped to under $20. The Asians toe the same line; Samsung, which employs young women who did not finish primary school, pays them 345 pesos for a forty-five-hour week, roughly $50.

Most *maquila* workers, theoretically, earn the federally mandated minimum wage, the equivalent of $2.50 a day; but to illustrate what this means, in the electronic *maquiladoras* of Tijuana, take-home pay is less than one-fifth of that in the United States. According to a recent article in *Businessweek*, wage differences between the two countries, depending on the type of *maquiladora*, loom large: In the mid-1990s, American workers in electronics earned $13.95 an hour, but Mexican pay was $1.54; in auto parts, Mexicans made $2.75, compared to $21.93 north of the border. In Ciudad Acuña and Piedras Negras, both in Coahuila, workers' wages amounted to 5 or 10 percent of those in the United States. But wages could be lower; for example, in Nogales, Sonora, workers make automatic door parts for Sears for $.55 an hour. Pay for garment workers remains at the bottom of the totem pole.

Maquila operators, just the same, claim that they pay above the national minimum; but even when that is occasionally true, they forget that almost everything costs more on the border. Before the devaluation of 1994, the average take-home pay of a *maquila* worker in Tijuana was less than the average per capita income in a city where prices of goods can be in dollars. Wages remain low even when performance is high, as in Matamoros, where twenty *maquiladoras* in 1994 received world recognition for quality. *Maquila* pay, by the same token, tends to control wage levels citywide.

How poor are *maquila* wages? The following verities cast light on this question. Current statistics reveal that street vendors in Ciudad Juárez make more money than *maquiladora* workers. Then there is the story of Perla, a woman from a village in Durango who recently settled in Ciudad Juárez and got a job in a *maquila* but, finding it impossible to survive on her paycheck, started selling Mexican produce wholesale in El Paso. Although her prices were rock bottom, on a good day she made four times her *maquila* wage. To survive on *maquila* pay, more than one member of the family must hold a *maquila* job. Mothers with dependents cannot live on the wages they take home; some, given this reality, turn to prostitution, an alarming development in border cities, or they become illegal aliens in the United States. This is not true for *maquila* executives, as the Zenith pay scale illustrates; the *Los Angeles Times* reported that the company's CEO made $1 million a year, though that is small potatoes compared to the salary of the CEO at Ford, whose salary was twenty thousand times the annual pay of a Ford worker in Mexico. Women are frequently paid less than men, even though they do identical work. The Japanese are no better. If the complaint of one Mexican political party is true, Asahi in Tijuana, for instance, pays employees a pittance for a ten-hour day.

Low wages explain why *maquiladoras* initially moved to Mexico. Why they remain low is another story. Obviously, better pay might tempt *maquilas* to go elsewhere, but that is not certain.

Competition for *maquilas* by city fathers promising to provide pools of cheap labor also partly helps explain the poor pay. *Maquila* operators can simply pick the highest bidder. What is clear, all the same, is that since the 1940s, conservative Mexican regimes that interpret federal statutes to suit their clientele ride roughshod over the bargaining rights of workers in order to keep them in line and keep wages low. At the behest of business, they rely on *charros*, puppet union chiefs, and manipulate labor organizations such as the Confederación de Trabajadores de México, the largest, and the Confederación Regional Obrera Mexicana (CROM), the oldest.

In theory, according to the Constitution of 1917, labor unions are free and independent. Workers enjoy the right to organize and join unions. In reality, less than one-fifth of the workforce is unionized. The unions are offshoots of the governmental apparatus and are manipulated by PRI bosses, as is the situation of labor on the border. In the *maquila* industry, they are virtually company unions, though affiliated with the national labor organizations, namely, the CTM or the CROM. Their character varies, however; some are more puppetlike than others. At one extreme are the Tijuana unions, whose leadership, one knowledgeable observer comments, is "totally corrupt." For all that, Reynosa, where PEMEX is the big industry, is a labor city.

That is not the way it began. Until the 1940s, when the early waiters' union fell apart, able and militant leaders headed the *sindicatos* (labor unions); after that, the traditional pattern of subservient union bosses took over. The corruption of leadership is less pronounced in Ciudad Juárez, and even less so in Matamoros, where a paternalistic chief built a personal empire. The level of corruption in unions, and elsewhere perhaps, can be measured by the degree of U.S. penetration in the service sector that depends on tourists. Since Tijuana was, until recently, the quintessential tourist town, corruption penetrated every activity, including the *sindicatos*.

The Matamoros labor picture, which is almost unique along the border, dates from the 1920s, when Emilio Portes Gil, the state cacique, announced he was expelling the CROM from Tamaulipas for attempting to destroy local groups. Whatever the truth of the matter, the departure of the CROM, then under the tutelage of the corrupt Luis Morones, opened the way for others. The *zona libre,* an incentive for the tourist industry in Tamaulipas, also played a role, as did the activity of labor in the port city of Tampico. It was in the tourist industry that the first unions appeared, organized by waiters, bartenders, and hotel workers. They were also the first to organize in Tijuana and Ciudad Juárez, again in the 1920s. Agapito González, the Matamoros labor kingpin, arose from this scene, getting to the top in the 1950s by siding with the state's leading politicos and taking advantage of the cotton boom of that time. When the *maquiladoras* appeared on the scene, Agapito, a CTM labor boss in the cotton industry, stepped in to organize their workers. A master politico, he convinced *maquila* workers and owners that both would be better off by dealing with him. His heyday lasted until 1992, when authorities in Mexico City jailed him for not paying his income taxes. This was merely a pretext; the Salinas regime, which sought to control labor with an iron fist, simply wanted Agapito out of the way, perhaps to rid the *maquila* industry of this pesky Mexican.

Union bosses, as one manager of a *maquiladora* in Ciudad Juárez acknowledges, "are very cooperative and understanding . . . they help us in the bargaining process between labor and management." The government expects *maquilas* merely to pay the minimum wage; the issue of whether to incorporate workers into the unions is left to the discretion of their operators. In Nogales, Sonora, which is staunchly antiunion, workers are "fired if caught talking to union people." In Ciudad Juárez, some of the *maquilas* demand that every three months workers sign a declaration of intent to resign; this allows employers to evade their legal obligation to help pay for social security benefits because workers employed for less than three months are not covered by the social security legislation.

Only a small fraction of workers in the *maquiladoras* belong to unions, probably no more than one out of ten. There are few if any independent unions in Ciudad Juárez, Tijuana, Mexicali, and Nogales, where most *maquiladoras* are located. The CTM, one should remember, is a mainstay of the PRI, which has dictated politics since 1929. Its *charro* bosses look favorably upon the *maquilas*, but the CROM, which controls 85 percent of labor contracts in the *maquilas* of Tijuana, is even more cooperative. In Tijuana, *sindicatos blancos*, or company unions, patronized by the CROM are commonplace; according to a labor spokesman quoted by the *Los Angeles Times*, "There is not a single *maquiladora* with an independent union." CROM leaders, the newspaper *Zeta* charges, provide protection for a price to foreign management against the demands of their workers. When workers attempt to organize, either the *maquila* shuts its doors, threatening to close down permanently, or police are used to break the strike. The labor agitators, as management labels them, are always fired. In Ciudad Juárez, according to the *Los Angeles Times*, operators of *maquiladoras* "freely admit that they sign contracts with government-affiliated unions before hiring a single worker."

The next story tells us in detail what this signifies for the individual worker. For three years, Armando Hernández, a welder at the Korean Han Young *maquila* in Tijuana, which assembles chassis for tractor trailers, had belonged to a union "he had never heard of, led by labor bosses he had never seen." His hourly wage of $.85 was negotiated behind closed doors in a contract he was refused permission to read. When he and his companions asked for a pay increase and a vote to organize a union of their own choosing, a right guaranteed by the Constitution of 1917, a man they had never set eyes on before appeared. He identified himself as their union spokesman, gave the lie to their complaints, and told them how "lucky they were" to earn twice the federal minimum wage. When they rejected his version of the good life and voted to organize themselves into a labor union, a board of arbitration, which the government controls, refused to recognize it. Meanwhile, the Han Young management fired Hernández and the other "agitators" and replaced them with welders from the outside. This appalling account is not unique: According to a survey carried out by an independent labor federation, only 5 percent of Mexico's organized workers had a voice in choosing their own union.

Yet in Tamaulipas, where Matamoros and Reynosa are located, a slightly different situation prevails. All but 10 percent of the labor force is unionized and, of course, nearly all under the CTM, but with a leadership at times more responsive to the demands of workers. One reason, aside from historical and political factors, is the existence of the PEMEX refinery in Reynosa, a union shop of independent bent. Another is Agapito González, the maverick CTM chief in Matamoros. These circumstances have paid dividends for labor. In 1983, management and González reached an agreement; in return for labor peace, management granted workers a forty-hour week and, eventually, slightly higher wages. Nonetheless, that has not stopped authorities in league with management from using state and municipal police to break strikes.

None of this implies that workers stoically accept their fate. Strikes do occur, especially in electronics. After the approval of NAFTA, when *maquiladora* operators no longer had to court Congress, the *Nation* reported that General Electric and Honeywell let go scores of workers attempting to organize unions in their subsidiaries. When workers in the RCA plant in Ciudad Juárez, the biggest on the border, went on strike in the winter of 1995, the company closed its doors; the strikers, who were asking for a 30 percent pay increase, had to settle for a mere 13 percent, far less than the cost of the recent devaluation. Yet the majority of the population of Ciudad Juárez strongly sympathized with them. Instances of labor unrest and protests, as newspaper accounts verify, occur up and down the border. To emphasize this point once again: Unfortunately, the failure of their efforts has resulted from an antilabor bourgeoisie, probusiness policies at all levels of government, hostile corporate leadership, the existence of large pools of unemployed labor, and the youth of workers.

All the same, the struggles of labor are not just manifested through strikes and official unionism. Beyond conflicts with corrupt *charro* bosses, management in the pay of foreign capitalists, and prejudicial boards of arbitration, the workers themselves carry on multiple forms of autonomous resistance, what scholars refer to as the "weapons of the weak." Their insurgency in the *maquila* runs the gamut from individual acts of sabotage on the shop floor to sporadic wildcat strikes that paralyze production for weeks on end. Workers have established independent unions, built interplant clandestine networks, set up legal-aid centers, and here and there, by collectively standing up for themselves, they have won concessions from management. They have also organized groups to speak for them, such as the Centro de Orientacion de la Mujer Obrera in Ciudad Juárez. These organizations handle issues of importance to women *maquila* workers, among them sexual exploitation in the workplace, the dangers of toxic hazards, wage equality with men, and strike support systems. As Devon G. Peña, author of *The Terror Machine*, argues, workers are not simply "quiescent dupes or powerless victims." Peña points out that workers employ the "weapons of the weak" because "the institutional deck is stacked against" them, since government and transnational labor politics are one and the same. They know that asking politicos in Mexico City to uphold their constitutional right to organize and join independent unions, to compel management to pay decent wages or improve conditions in the workplace is, more often than not, a waste of time.

○   ○   ○   ❀   ○   ○   ○

El Taller Universitario de Teatro, a theater group in Mexicali, puts on a play titled *Mexicali a Secas;* its dialogue examines the nature of *maquila* work.

> *I am a machine.*
> *No, I am not a machine.*
> *I work in front of a wall that looks at me, asking questions.*
> *I should never have accepted this job.*
> *Don't complain or ask for a raise. There are going to be layoffs, and*
>   *you may be the next.*
> *Unions are a forbidden topic. Don't ever think about forming one*
>   *because a* maquiladora *can disappear overnight.*

For a woman, a job in a *maquila* pays less than domestic work across the border, but it can provide medical care for these women and their families through the Seguro Social. This is one of the fringe benefits; wives work in *maquilas* just for the social security benefits. To quote one such woman in Ciudad Juárez: "My husband owns a restaurant and we have a fairly good income. But I have four children and one of them is chronically sick. Without insurance, medical fees would render us poor." White-collar jobs as sales clerks, receptionists, and secretaries grant more prestige but pay even less.

A *maquila* job entails hardship. The hours are long; for mothers, it means getting up at dawn to get children ready for school and be on the job by 7 A.M. A majority of these women, most of whom are under twenty-four years old, have never had a job before. They grew up in the city or town, tend to be single, and have had some schooling. Employers prefer them to married women with family obligations that might interfere with work. Few hire pregnant women, and some plants have compulsory pregnancy tests. A *maquiladora* in Ciudad Juárez, according to complaints by workers, requires new hires to "present bloody tampons for three consecutive months." Apparel *maquilas* employ older, less-educated women; some are migrants, heads of households, and in their thirties. For mothers, there are few if any day care centers, although child care can consume as much as one-third of a woman's salary. The women dwell in marginal homes in working-class *colonias*. When at work, they might remain seated for ten hours, repeating the same process day after day. At 5 P.M., after having inserted thousands of wires in a box or having sewed untold numbers of collars on men's shirts, they go home to take care of children, and perhaps a husband or boyfriend, and cook and clean house. Rosario, a woman of this sort in Ciudad Juárez, pays rent in dollars for two rooms with a roof that leaks, works a forty-eight-hour week at the RCA plant, and shares her home with her mother, a younger brother, and two aunts who have jobs in a garment *maquilas*. Some *maquiladoras* operate around the clock, seven days a week, including holidays. Aurelia, one of the women in Norma Iglesias's *La Flor Más Bella de la Maquiladora*, a big seller in border bookstores, labors ten hours a day, except on Fridays when she goes home two hours earlier. At the RCA plant in Ciudad Juárez, the women are instructed not to eat, talk, or read on the job and are prohibited from smoking or talking on the telephone. At some *maquiladoras*, the supervisor watches the time taken to go to the toilet.

Work conditions vary, from good to very bad. As defined by the U.S. General Accounting Office, most *maquilas* are sweatshops, workplaces that violate, at one time or another, laws covering hours of toil, minimum wages, child labor, and industrial homework. *Maquiladoras* also fall into the sweatshop category as defined by Pharis Harvey of the International Labor Rights Fund because they pay poorly, demand long hours of toil, and the conditions of the workplace endanger safety or health, although technically they may violate no laws. The worst are the garment *maquiladoras*, small plants that employ older, more experienced women. Often Mexican enterprises, most of them do jobs on contract for foreign firms, including Sears, the Warnaco Group, and Johnson and Johnson in Ciudad Juárez. Jobs can be unstable, conditions poor, the machinery, such as old Singer sewing machines, obsolete, and demands on productivity steep. At one plant in Ciudad Juárez, women are asked to sew a shirt pocket every nine to ten seconds, from 360 to 396 pockets an hour. Some of the garment *maquilas* pay by piecework; the less you sew, the less you earn. In 1994, the *Nation* magazine reported on one apparel plant where workers sewed jeans for Levi Strauss: "Rain poured through the roof and collected in puddles on the floor, causing workers to get electric shock from their sewing machines."

General Electric in Ciudad Juárez provides a better workplace. The company trains middle-level personnel and attempts to improve the skills of selected workers. Preferred jobs are in electronics. Additional incentives at some of these plants include savings and loan programs, periodic bonuses, and sports events. Management organizes beauty contests to pick the fairest of the *maquila* workers and sponsors picnics in the countryside. A dinner dance of the Liga de Futbol Intermaquiladoras celebrates the end of soccer competition between teams from *maquiladoras* in Tijuana. On Valentine's Day, managers can be seen distributing red carnations to their women workers. All of this, cynics say, is to keep down levels of discontent with wages and working conditions. Some of the *maquiladoras* have dining areas or cafeterias—modest benefits perhaps, but rarely found in the factories of underdeveloped countries. To eliminate the social gulf between labor and management, *maquiladoras* call their workers *operadoras* (operators) instead of *obreras* (workers). Some of these *maquiladoras,* unlike their apparel sisters, are in "air-conditioned buildings . . . but in terms of working conditions," Kamel argues, "they are sweatshops." To quote a women who had labored in assembly plants on both sides of the border, conditions are slightly better in the United States, but not much: "In Mexico only a ventilator kept the temperature down during hot summer days and only one's sweater and coat kept one from freezing in the winter."

Few studies exist on health and safety conditions. But government and puppet-labor collusion bodes ill for the maintenance of high standards. As related in the *New York Times,* just two other countries in the world have higher rates of industrial accidents, the costly consequences of loosely enforced regulations. Injuries to workers from machines shorn of adequate safeguards, toxic contamination from not wearing protective clothing, and other illness due to the absence of information on dangerous chemicals used in the shop are merely a few. A researcher at the Colegio de la Frontera Norte discovered illnesses at one plant from workers' inhaling lead fumes when soldering and injuring their eyes while bonding wires to circuit boards. The result of handling chemicals at a subsidiary of Allegheny International, one female worker testified, was "nausea, headaches, stomach problems, depression, and emotional change." The company doctor, the only one she was allowed to consult, called her problem "psychiatric."

The diagnosis, for reasons entirely different, may have been partly correct. The message in Charlie Chaplin's movie *Modern Times* applies perfectly here. Whatever else may be said, work at the *maquilas* is monotonous. For example, a young woman who worked in a doll factory recalled: "I sat on a bench in front of a fast-moving assembly line." The job was to take each doll as "it passed . . . dress it, and then return it to the conveyor belt. I don't remember how many dolls I dressed daily, but I know it was thousands, so many that in my sleep I used to dream that they were attacking me." No one should forget, as I mentioned earlier, that hardly any opportunities for advancement exist. As one plant manager in Nogales acknowledged, "If you know that you will die at the same level you're at now, how could you care about anything?"

One result is a high turnover labor rate, a headache shared by both American and Japanese *maquilas,* which by the 1980s was as high as 100 percent. Up to 12 percent of workers, according to a Mexican study, voluntarily abandon their jobs each month. This means that every month *maquilas* must hire one-tenth or more of their labor force and every ten months must face a complete turnover of personnel. The highest turnover rates are in Tijuana and Ciudad Juárez, especially in electronics, auto parts, and apparel. Men, particularly if better-educated, are more apt to leave their jobs than women. As early as 1982, there was talk of unacceptable turnover rates, a phenomenon labeled a "social problem" ten years later. And well it should be—because in Tijuana, job hopping is at an all-time high. It is so serious in Ciudad Juárez that *maquiladoras* are setting up shop in other cities of Chihuahua, as well as in Nuevo León and Tamaulipas.

Job hopping reflects more than just low wages, the absence of opportunities for advancement, and the monotony of work. What should be obvious is that women *maquila* workers "face the challenge of a job without a future, or a future without a job." The work, in reality, is a dead-end street. Workers have also abandoned their jobs because they fail to find adequate housing, good schools for their children, or nearby health facilities, or because they must use expensive or inadequate transportation, among other reasons. The public service infrastructure is unable to provide facilities for the ever-growing legion of *maquila* workers. Then, too, it is to the benefit of employers that workers move on; job hopping allows employers to evade labor legislation that covers seniority, indemnity, and vacation pay. *Maquila* operators even claim that worker productivity declines during the second year while absenteeism increases, largely, as independent studies show, because of low wages, the absence of advancement opportunities, and boredom. The abundance of cheap, young labor also explains management's reluctance to employ a permanent labor force of aging workers, who might logically demand higher pay and more flexible schedules. Still other studies demonstrate that young mothers with large families are even more likely to leave their jobs. Hard times, when jobs are scarce, keep workers at their jobs.

Even so, for many young women a *maquila* salary offers advantages. One is an opportunity for personal freedom—escape from the confines of the household of a domineering mother or a demanding father. For the first time, they have money to spend on themselves, for clothes, a washing machine, or a new stove. They may earn more than husbands, fathers, or brothers and can thus break the old dependency mold. Angela, a native of a rural village, comments: "[When] I went to work in the *maquiladora*, I felt tremendously happy, as though I had improved myself. At that moment God heard me and changed my life." A separate income, which translates into independence, helps to undermine traditional male authority; in Ciudad Juárez, certain bars and dance halls look for young female workers who, on payday, attract young men eager to court them. Whether *maquila* employment is responsible or not, in Ciudad Juárez, statistics show that the birthrate is down and the divorce rate up and there are more female-headed households. For traditionalists, this embodies a horrendous turn of events; women who work endanger family ties and neglect the raising of their children. But, as one Mexican author says, jobs in *maquilas* do not necessarily mean autonomy for women; unless women leave the parental household, they remain under the sway of both father and mother. Young women who surrender their weekly earnings to a mother who then gives them a small allowance are a common occurrence.

From the start, *maquila* operators spoke with forked tongues in order to justify their discriminatory treatment of women. In this mythology, women do better assembly work because of their small hands and fingers and their dexterity in certain kinds of skills and, of course, are better at sewing. Women endure monotonous jobs better than men. They are mainly interested in their homes and families; they take on jobs to add to the family income, but marriage and childbearing head their priorities. This rationalization, obviously, does not stand close scrutiny. The truth is that employers prefer young single women because they work for less since they have no family responsibilities. Yet when women work in countries such as Mexico, they do so frequently as the primary wage earners, not to simply supplement a husband's or father's pay. Many are single heads of households or the main source of a stable income. "If I do not work," asks one of them in Iglesias's study, "how will I find the money to feed my children?" These women, to cite an old saying, are "caught between a rock and a hard place": They have no real alternative. *Maquila* work represents survival.

Whether because of the myth or not, men hold the best jobs. They are the administrators, often the foremen on the assembly lines, who keep a record of absences and tardiness. In these positions, they earn more and can punish or reward women. Not a few take advantage of their authority to abuse them. As one supervisor for an American corporation boasted, "The system at the *maquiladoras* makes it easy for men with authority to enjoy relationships with women." He went on: "I had a girlfriend who worked on another shift under a friend of mine. I would ask him to let her go early." In return, "he . . . asked me for similar favors." At the Sylvania plant in Ciudad Juárez, the "personnel officer . . . liked the young girls who came through his office . . . the girls needed the work and he was the person who said yes or no." In her book, Iglesias tells the following story: "Everyone is always gossiping about who the line manager is dating, who is pregnant. If you complain, someone is sure to turn you in." At another plant, a worker named Lourdes quit her job because the "Japanese manager kept fondling her."

○ ○ ○ 🥡 ○ ○ ○

Are inhabitants on the border better off now than before the appearance of the *maquila*? The cites are bigger and, perhaps, wealthier, boast substantial middle classes, and more people have jobs. If that is so, why a dissenting view? One answer, according to the *Wall Street Journal*, hardly an antibusiness publication, is that *maquilas* are helping to turn the Mexican border into "a sinkhole of abysmal living conditions and environmental degradation." Advocates of this view say that the border was simply not ready to become an industrial bastion because of its lack of an adequate infrastructure. Unprepared for the arrival of hordes of immigrants, the cities were incapable of integrating the *maquila* phenomenon into their economies. Attracted to the border by the promise of high profits, *maquilas* seldom develop additional industry and pay almost nothing in taxes, since the city fathers, in order to lure them, grant them enormous tax breaks. Because they lack substantial sources of public revenue, the cities can do little to improve the quality of life of people drawn north by hopes of *maquila* jobs—people who, ultimately, bring others with them. Only a handful of these hopefuls fulfill their expectations. Most of the jobless add to the city's burdens or cross the border in search of work.

What should be obvious is the incapacity of border cities to absorb more *maquilas* and, simultaneously, to service increasing numbers of their workers. Something is terribly wrong when Ciudad Acuña, one of poorest cities, needs to build at least six thousand more homes for *maquila* workers. Worse still, even when municipalities enjoy added revenues, as in Ciudad Juárez, they go mostly to improve an infrastructure that benefits the *maquiladoras*. As early as the 1980s, bankers at Banamex cautioned that the cities of Tijuana and Ciudad Juárez, two of the most crowded in the republic, were saturated and could not adequately "support any more significant growth because of the lack of infrastructure." The *maquila* presence had overwhelmed roads, water, sewage, and power systems. This development, which stands logic on its head, characterizes every border enclave.

Maquilas keep on coming because, as the prevailing wisdom goes: "Jobs are what count along the border. Get jobs and the rest will take care of itself." This policy, to quote Mexican congresswoman Liliana Flores Benavides, has led to high rates of unemployment and underemployment, poverty, low standards of living, bad nutrition, inadequate housing, and poor schools, with a correspondingly high incidence of drug addiction, prostitution, alcoholism, and lawlessness. According to Samuel Schmidt, a scholar at the University of Texas, "the regional economy was integrated into the international markets with little economic diversification or improvement of the quality of life." It was a blueprint designed for regions of abundant natural resources, mainly water, but was adopted in a region poor in natural resources and arid. This development, he adds, depletes scarce resources, "a process that by now has resulted in a catastrophic environmental scenario" that has binational implications. Not everyone applauds when a mayor promises the sky to a foreign corporation, if the city's residents, to cite the *Los Angeles Times*, "are forced to ration drinking water in order to service a giant . . . maquiladora." Yet their owners, who never lack water, obtain it at lower rates than domestic consumers, and the quantity they are allowed to use is not limited.

5

The Disparate Society

Despite common antecedents among Mexican border communities, social disparities there, as in the rest of the republic, go from one extreme to the other. In the Forbes 500 list of multibillionaires, there are twenty-four Mexican families that together are worth over $44 billion, or the equivalent of Mexico's national budget for 1990. In a country where over 20 million people face hunger daily and, even by official statistics, another 40 million are poor, this lopsided distribution of wealth is a moral scandal—but neither is it terribly novel. From the Spanish conquest on, when the cross and the sword of the Europeans bent ancient Anáhuac to their will, the poor, usually bronze of skin and racially more Indian than Spanish, carry the burdens of Mexico, the victims of man's inhumanity to man.

o o o ❀ o o o

Affluence along the border tilts from west to east: Tijuana boasts the highest per capita income; take-home pay, as well as wealth, tends to drop as one approaches the Gulf of Mexico. But there are pockets everywhere of families rolling in luxury. in Carlos Fuentes's novel *La Frontera de Cristal*, the character Michelina, a young woman from Mexico City, recalls in astonishment that the chauffeur drove the family's big Mercedes up to huge wrought-iron gates "seen only in Hollywood films," through the entrance to one of sundry walled-in mansions ridiculed by local natives as Disneylandia—"half fortresses, half mausoleums"—this one with the neoclassical columns of Tara, the legendary manor of *Gone with the Wind*. The garages opened automatically, their "floors soiled only by the oil drippings of Porches, Mercedes, and BMWs." The estate belonged to a powerful and wealthy *fronterizo,* a businessman well known in the world of the border assembly plants of American conglomerates.

In Tijuana, the rich dwell on the hills to the south, in the *colonia* Lomas de Chapultepec that overlooks the modern Zona del Río or downtown in the Bolaños Cacho, one of the oldest neighborhoods. The less wealthy reside along the coast, in Playas de Tijuana and the municipality of Rosarito. Inhabitants of these *colonias* never lack for piped-in water, electricity, sewers, and paved streets. On the east side of Mexicali, palm trees line wide streets with imposing manors facing manicured public parks, but in Nogales the rich segregate themselves in the *colonias* Kennedy, Kalitea, and Chula Vista, all on the west side of town. In Ciudad Juárez, the Colonia Campestre, home to the affluent, shelters lawns and gardens in the American style that surround the chalets of bankers and businessmen. One of them, Rene Mascareñas, has a sixteen-thousand-square-foot home where he proudly displays the family coat of arms. Nothing on the U.S. side can compete with the fancy abodes in Nuevo Laredo, that of the Legorreta banking family among them, and some have more than a dozen bedrooms.

But the shacks of the poor never stay out of sight. The inequalities on the border are scandalous, as bad as anywhere in Mexico, where only a fraction of the population commands decent living standards and the urban poor are increasingly pauperized; as always, campesinos, the inhabitants of rural villages, stand at the bottom of the totem pole. That analysis applies equally well to border society. Since 1982, under the tutelage of neoliberals, the purchasing power of consumers has fallen by over 60 percent, unemployment stands at record levels, one-fourth of the workforce moonlights, and emigration north continues unabated. The poor of the border, as some maintain, may be less poor than the poor in other regions of Mexico, but they are poor nevertheless, especially if compared to the poor on the other side. In *Across the Wire*, Luis Alberto Urrea, who was born in Tijuana, vividly describes the borderlands as "a festering netherworld of orphanages and garbage dumps . . . where the poor . . . cling to the underside of the Third World." Yet tragically, as one woman tells him: "She had come to Tijuana from a still poorer province" and viewed "the borderlands as a kind of promised land."

One of the poorer *colonias* in Tijuana, where thousands of squatters have built their shacks, is the Colonia 10 de Mayo, one of scores on the sprawling hillsides of the city. Not quite half of the city's inhabitants dwell in these *colonias populares,* as such shantytowns are labeled. With shack upon shack hastily built of discarded materials, often from the other side, they are a stark reminder of Third World misery. These cordons of poverty surround the cities of the border. None of these poor residents have heat or insulation from the cold, running water, sewers, or

paved streets, and few such homes sit near schools—and yet they sym-
bolize the fulfillment of a dream. For the time being, the squatters are
lords over a plot of land—until the city or a "developer" evicts them.
Some of the families live in dwellings made from wood pallets, which
once served as platforms for tile or brick, with walls of black tar paper
and cardboard. Plastic sheeting serves as the roof. One such home was in
the *colonia* Matamoros, but it could easily have been in any city along the
border. When the weather turns cold, as it did in the winter of 1993, people die from exposure; one such was the three-year-old son of Gabriela
Mistral, a boy who slept on the floor with his mother. One evening, when
the temperature in Tijuana dipped to the low thirties, the child slipped
out from under the blankets: "When I awakened at dawn," cried
Gabriela, "my baby was dead . . . His little body was cold." During that
December in Tijuana, seventeen people, fourteen of them children, and
nearly all residents of squatter colonies, perished from the cold.

Ciudad Juárez, the other border megalopolis, is no different. It is a city
of contrasts, with extremes of wealth and destitution, where the filthy
rich and the very poor coexist side by side, where row after row of crumbling *jacales* rest not far from ostentatious mansions. It is at one and the
same time a rich and a poor metropolis, with its impressive tourist center
but also its dirt streets and slums. Over two-thirds of the city's inhabitants survive below the poverty level. Their hardships are mind-boggling,
as the trials and tribulations of Rufino Santos's family amply document.
As a youngster, he had come to Ciudad Juárez with his family, which left
behind a home on an *ejido* near Chihuahua City where they had lived for
five generations. When they arrived, they had no money or food, and
some had no shoes. There were only two sweaters to ward off the cold;
Santos's mother got sick from drinking polluted water, and his three-
year-old sister nearly died. Their first home was on the edges of the city
dump, in a shantytown that vanished in the mud when the first heavy
rains fell. His father, meanwhile, who had spent his life tilling the soil,
could find a job only at the city rubbish dump, making a living, to quote
Santos, "by turning garbage." Ironically, though homes may lack plumb-
ing and running water, TVs are commonplace, as they are in the slums of
other border cities. In this desert metropolis, people die of dehydration
and dysentery during the summer months for lack of water.

A middle sector straddles the two extremes of society. For the republic
as a whole, scholars estimate that it includes between 20 and 25 percent of
the population, although because of recent hard times, the figures are
probably high. Middle-class Mexicans earn between two and five minimum-wage salaries per month; in 1990, the minimum wage was equal to
a monthly income of $100; it is less now after the recent devaluation of the
peso. With even five minimum-wage salaries, and substantial underre-

porting of income, some middle-class families, most of whom average five members, live on no more than $400 to $500 per month. That income level places much of the so-called middle class among the poor; yet, as explained earlier, two-thirds of the population earns far less.

Within these parameters, the middle class is quite large, especially in Tijuana, which is designated by analysts as a middle-class city. Despite periodic lapses, income growth since World War II has been quite strong. From 1960 to 1980, per capita incomes in Baja California grew by 16.5 percent; by 1980, per capita gross domestic product there was the highest of all the border provinces, though all of them, with perhaps the exception of Coahuila, were above the national average. From the 1980s on, however, per capita income has fallen. Since World War II, many Mexicans have arrived in these border enclaves to partake of their relative affluence, but they pay a price because the cost of living is high in this dollarized economy. Take the case of assembly plant workers, the major industrial labor force on the border; according to a study of the Support Committee for Maquiladora Workers in San Diego, California, in early 1996, on the basis of the prevailing wage rate, they had to labor nearly 2.5 hours just to buy a dozen eggs; for 2 hours for a loaf of bread; for 8 hours for a kilo of beef; for 11.5 hours for thirty disposable diapers; and for a school uniform for a daughter, up to 86 hours. As the anthropologist John A. Price recognizes, "The pressure to hustle just to survive is strong." Even middle-class Mexicans must seek jobs across the border in order to maintain their living standard, particularly when a harsh climate demands heating in the winter and air-conditioning in the summer; inflationary pressures, on top of that, are seldom absent. Increases in the minimum salary, some economists maintain, are more often simply attempts to restore purchasing power to offset inflation.

In the opinion of scholars of border societies, Tijuana, which is blessed with assembly plants, tourism, and trade, is the epitome of the new city. As sociologist Leslie Howard notes, "What strikes the visitor most about Tijuana is the vigor and aggressiveness of its middle class." This is not confined solely to Tijuana; every border city has its middle class, especially Ciudad Juárez, which, like its cousin on the Pacific Coast, is blessed with assembly plants, tourists, and, because of its location as a railroad terminal, a thriving international trade. Ciudad Juárez also has an agricultural hinterland that once propelled banking and related business conducive to middle-class growth. Families of the middle class usually cluster in *colonias* adjacent to those of the wealthy; some were once the abode of the rich and powerful, particularly in the older cities. That is changing as the middle class, in the U.S. mode, moves to the suburbs, especially with federally sponsored construction of housing for government bureaucrats, university professors, and schoolteachers. Shopping malls, almost always with branches of stores from the other side, woo shoppers. This middle class owns automobiles, more so than sister sectors in the rest of Mexico, though rarely are they purchased new. To cite a study by Daniel D. Arreola and James R. Curtis, the shopping centers and avenues designed for automobiles "herald . . . the rise of a mobile and affluent . . . middle class."

∘ ∘ ∘ 🀫 ∘ ∘ ∘

Sociologists say that Mexico City embodies "pathological and calamitous" urban development. The terrible truth, for all that, is that other cities, both big and small, suffer from the malady once thought the exclusive prerogative of megacities. This is especially so along the border since the arrival of the *maquiladoras;* by attracting migrants, they exacerbate social problems, particularly housing shortfalls. To cite Ramón Galindo, mayor of Ciudad Júarez in 1997, "We face an enormous challenge: For the republic at large the annual population growth rate is 2.3 percent, but ours is over twice that." And, he adds, migrants from Durango, Coahuila, Zacatecas, and southern Chihuahua represent 70 percent of that growth. All Mexican cities, no matter where located, endure poverty, lack of housing and public services, and jerry-built infrastructures. These problems, which are characteristic of cities the world over, are most pronounced in the Third World, where the lack of economic resources exacerbates structural limitations and precipitates social crises. In Galindo's view, the demographic explosion of Ciudad Juárez means that per capita municipal spending always lags behind need.

This is true of every Mexican border city, where long-range planning cries for implementation in order to modernize and redesign urban cores, at the same time avoiding further environmental damage. Unfortunately, city planning lags—mainly due to lack of funds, expertise, and, equally important, the ignorance and unwillingness of politicians and businessmen to undertake it. Social Darwinism sinks deep roots in this neanderthal climate. The local elite, which generally advocates neoliberal doctrines, rarely demand policies of benefit to the downtrodden. The *ayuntamiento,* or city council, lacks both authority and funds for any undertaking of consequence. In Ciudad Juárez, which provides a microcosmic view of the political process, the council and the mayor are elected every three years in highly partisan fashion. Although border cities provide some of the services of their American counterparts, most such services are the prerogative of federal and state governments. Local budgets, which rely heavily on income from traffic fines, licenses, and permits, are severely limited by the ubiquitous federal presence, which collects more than three-fourths of local revenues. Only occasionally can municipalities count on funds to build a school, a public market, a jail, or a cemetery.

The results are horrendous. To illustrate what this implies, the *ayun-tamiento* of Nogales, Sonora, exists on a budget of 7 million pesos for a city of 125,000 people, but its sister American city commands a budget of $32 million for 22,000 inhabitants. Tijuana, a city of more than 400 *colonias*, has 170 firefighters and 17 fire trucks, one-third of them in disrepair. Without funds and a degree of political independence, Mexican munici-palities are largely ineffective as policymaking institutions; their primary function is to maintain political stability and civil order.

What little planning occurs confines itself to the encouragement of in-come-generating activities, tourism to start with, and overlooks the pub-lic need for housing, water, and schools, to list three essentials. In this ver-sion of the old trickle-down theory, what helps the well-to-do takes precedence over the necessities of the poor. Eventually, so goes this idea, what benefits the rich trickles down to the poor. The result is that busi-ness zones that turn a profit are modernized, but *colonias populares* are left to fend for themselves. In the Zona del Río in Tijuana, nearly thirty thou-sand people dwelling in *cartolandias*, shantytowns of cardboard shacks, were driven out by soldiers so that a concrete canal and malls could be built, a showcase for shops, hotels, restaurants, and discotheques where the affluent look for bargains, dine, and dance. Bulldozers leveled the shacks. The governor of Baja California, a corrupt politico with the back-ing of the federal government, sided with real estate speculators who hoped to feather their nest.

City fathers up and down the border embrace the Tijuana formula. They view planning and zoning with a kind of laissez-faire aversion. Money-hungry profiteers thus determine the urban blueprint. Private capital, helped by state financial and political support, "develop" some parts of the city, usually an undeveloped section or downtown area, as municipal and state authorities turn their back on the others, where un-planned growth occurs on flood-prone canyons and steep hillsides or, as in Matamoros, along canals, a situation that soon creates additional headaches. The experience of Ciudad Juárez illustrates this: The absence of planning and zoning led the city in the 1950s to expand to the south and northwest, where thousands of families settled on barren hillsides, later making it extremely difficult and costly to provide them with water, electricity, sewers, and streets.

The heavy rains that fell upon Tijuana in the winter of 1993 provide lessons for what unplanned growth implies, exposing for anyone who cared to see the correlation between poverty and suffering brought about by natural disasters; the poor, for obvious reasons, were the least pre-pared to withstand nature's onslaught. As one man complained, "I fled my house because it rained inside as much as it did on the outside." The rains caused heavy property damage as well as loss of life to a city whose growth had gone on in helter-skelter fashion, without adequate controls on housing development. Barely 10 percent of the city had drainage of any type. As one woman declared, "When it rains, all of the ills of Tijuana come to light." Flooding damaged countless homes, as mud slides toppled hastily constructed retaining walls on hillsides, particularly in El Rubí and Camino Verde, squatter's *colonias*. When one retaining wall collapsed at El Rubí, it fell on a house, killing two children. By the time the storm had vented its fury, thirty lives had been lost and thousands were homeless, the "predictable consequence," to quote a Mexican who was interviewed, "of years of governmental indifference toward the living conditions of hundreds of thousands of people." But the disasters of 1993 also testify to the greed of land speculators who sold lands where no houses should have been built without prior grading and drainage systems put in place.

∘ ∘ ∘ 🏵 ∘ ∘ ∘

Unplanned shantytown development accounts for three-fifths of the land area of Ciudad Juárez, a figure probably no different than that in other border cities. The influx of penniless migrants from Central Mexico, moreover, complicates the task of city planning; in their eagerness for a place to stay, they become *paracaidistas*, or squatters, who invade the unoccupied hillsides, canyons, and riverbeds of no value to real estate speculators. When they acquire a small nest egg, they are tricked into buying barren lots lacking water, sewers, and electricity. As they fill up, they become *colonias populares*. No wonder, then, that over the years social segregation worsens, helped along by unjust land policies that drive the poor to the least desirable fringes of the city.

Notwithstanding that dismal record, efforts have on occasion been made to dress up the cities. The first, dating from 1947, was the establishment of federal offices called Juntas Federales de Mejoras Materiales; their task was to improve social conditions of border cities, but as they were chronically short of money, they did little to meet their goal. From 1961 to 1965, another government project, the Programa Nacional Fronterizo, organized to combat the "physical and moral degradation of border cities" as well as to aid Mexican merchants to win back local markets from competitors on the other side, merely helped to beautify urban facades fronting on the United States, stimulate tourism, spur local commerce, and build modern hotels.

The consequences of this approach are horrendous. Each day, the gap between the needs of society and the pathetic response of public authorities grows bigger, exacerbating, as a Mexican economist remarks, "the decay of the urban infrastructure." This occurs throughout the republic, but especially in border cities where municipal and state governments cannot maintain social services at the pace of population growth and physical expansion. At the same time, access to running water, electricity, and sewers, a prerogative of the better-off, accentuates the polarization between rich and poor. This disparity, typical of Mexico, is particularly acute along the border; it affects even middle-class *colonias*. This means that in Tijuana—where 31 percent of the homes lack running water, 35 percent are without sewers, and over 16 percent have no electricity—these glaring deficiencies are shared mostly by the poorest. Yet as illogical as this may sound, the cost of living is higher for them because they end up buying their water from vendors and, because of the absence of sewers and electricity, they tend to get sick more often, which leads to bills for medicine and, when absolutely necessary, doctors. Living far from the center of the city, they must pay more for transportation, whether to go to work or to buy groceries.

The problems of Nogales epitomize this situation. During the 1980s, the city grew by leaps and bounds because of *maquiladoras*. Currently, the highest poverty indexes are found among migrants who dwell on the east side. None of the streets that join their *colonias* to the inner city are paved; they are poorly maintained if at all and, when it rains, virtually impassable. The local scene, remarks a Mexican scholar, resembles that of rural Mexico because of the "absolute absence of public services." Not one dwelling in this part of Nogales has electricity or sewers. The problems associated with excessive population growth and unplanned development are not confined to these eastern *colonias*. They plague most sections of the city, where the poor simply outrun the capacity of city fathers to provide necessary services, again a monopoly of the well-off. This lopsided pattern of inequality in public services repeats itself up and down the border, including the cities of Reynosa and Matamoros, where the poor are largely ignored. In Matamoros, four out of five residents dwell in forty-seven poverty-stricken *colonias* only partially serviced.

In these cities of the arid borderlands, a principal deficiency is water. The growth of the *maquiladora* industry exacerbates it. Not only do *maquiladoras* require vast amounts of water, but simultaneously, their growth attracts hordes of newcomers and that exacerbates shortages. On top of that, government policy favors unequal distribution of services and makes certain that the *maquiladoras,* business and commerce, and the well-off are never without it. That is the plight of Tijuana, where the shortage of water is an old problem. A good part of Tijuana's water system was installed between forty and fifty years ago, designed for a city of fifty thousand; leaks occur frequently because of rusty pipes. Where the poor live, inhabitants buy water from *pipas*, tank trucks that sell poor-quality water. Countless inhabitants who have running water in their homes cannot depend on it because of recurrent irregularities. Water flows only on some days of the week or during certain hours of the day. Water consumption in the poorer *colonias* falls below the minimum requirements of the World Health Organization. Only half of the homes have sewers; another 15 percent of them rely on septic tanks, and the rest empty their waste into the Tijuana River. The bilateral problems of Tijuana and San Diego revolve around the disposal of this sewage.

This litany gets worse as one travels east. Ciudad Juárez, for all intents and purposes a desert community, endures a perennial water shortage. It is the city's most urgent need. During the summer months, when water usage goes up, the *colonias* of the western hills go without water for weeks at a time. For that, Mother Nature is mostly responsible, but not entirely; the city government distributes water inequitably. The *maquiladoras,* which receive favored treatment from the authorities, consume water enough to supply eighteen thousand homes. Additionally, when farmers in New Mexico and Colorado siphoned more water from the Rio Grande, they contributed to the worsening situation of the *juarenses*. One-third of the homes in Ciudad Juárez, accounting for perhaps 250,000 people, lack sewers; their inhabitants use outdoor privies.

In Nogales, water scarcity creates a daily crisis, which is not surprising, since two-thirds of the desert state of Sonora lacks adequate supplies. Until the 1930s, this was hardly an insurmountable obstacle, since many Sonorenses lived in mountain towns where the climate, rainfall, and underground aquifers had welcomed settlements from colonial days. But then the population started to expand by leaps and bounds and turned urban; by the 1980s, over two-thirds of Sonora's inhabitants were living in regions that held just 29 percent of its water sources. As a result, Nogales, one of those exploding urban hubs, suffers chronic water deficiency, a condition shared by neighboring Agua Prieta. Only one-fifth of the *colonias* of Nogales enjoy the luxury of running water in their homes, and this holds especially for the *colonias* of the poor, where the cost of the water that must be purchased from tank trucks can be ten times what the middle and upper classes pay. Underground wells, many of which are privately owned, dry up or are contaminated. Of the seventy municipalities in the state, only nineteen have water treatment plants. Meanwhile, *maquila* discharges of toxic wastes, high in lead and arsenic, endanger public health; one recent study of female *maquiladora* workers in Nogales reveals that their babies tend to weigh less when born than those of mothers in the service industry. Projections indicate that Nogales's population will double by the year 2010, and the demand for water will rise sharply. As more *maquiladoras* enter Nogales, this will surely exacerbate shortages.

Elsewhere, water is both scarce and far from pure. People place their health at risk by drinking city water—when available. In Ciudad Acuña,

Piedras Negras, and Nuevo Laredo, for example, people customarily carry large containers to fill with drinking water when they travel to Del Rio, Eagle Pass, and Laredo; stores in these Texas cities provide faucets so that their Mexican customers can get the water they need. Ciudad Acuña has a water system for 25,000 people but a population of 150,000. Half of its homes have no sewers.

The appalling housing shortage takes second place only to water scarcity. Using Tijuana once more as the epitome of the urban model, economic growth has outstripped the availability of homes for the population at large. The first *colonias populares* appeared in the 1920s and have since become, due to massive waves of migrants, the typical housing pattern. Half of the city's residents call them home. People's massive invasions of land, visible proof of the inability or unwillingness of government to respond to the demands of the urban poor, are a practical response to homelessness. On the hillsides where these dwellings perch, retaining walls of discarded tires are the neighborhood trademark. Average occupancy by 1982 was seven people per one-room shack and three in dwellings with two rooms. Nearly one-third of the city's residents lived in homes with one or two rooms. These *colonias* occupy about one-half the residential area of the city. As already noted, these shacks are made of discarded wood, cardboard, tin, and tar paper and lack running water, electricity, and sewers. Oswaldo Pérez, a nineteen-year-old man from Puebla who earns just over $7 a day at the Hitachi plant lifting color TV tubes onto an assembly line the length of a football field, exemplifies what this means. He lives in the Colonia 10 de Mayo, a slum on Tijuana's east side that is bereft of paved streets, running water, and sewage facilities. He lives with five other men in a *jacal*, a dirty one-room shack, where gangs of "bums" and drug dealers, he says, prowl at night. "As soon as I'm home, we close our doors and don't leave"—and well he might, for he has already been mugged.

Ciudad Juárez, too, suffers from a severe housing shortage. Compared to Tijuana, its problem is less severe: Only 45 percent of families do not have their own home. Shantytowns such as Alta Vista, Francisco Villa, and Felipe Angeles account for three-fifths of the city's land area. Ironically, the names taken by these *colonias* are those of heroes of the Revolution of 1910, supposedly waged to right the wrongs of the past. The homeowners of Ciudad Juárez built more than two-thirds of the residences in the city themselves—out of waste materials. Most sit on public lands.

For *maquiladora* workers in Nogales, housing is also a critical need, but little is done to remedy it; authorities in Mexico City who control the purse strings plead that they have no funds, and they will not raise taxes paid by *maquiladoras* for fear that they will pick up and leave. Matamoros is hardly better off; thousands of people live in shacks, with sheets of corrugated tin for roofs. These dwellings frequently lack doors and windows. Holes in the walls, filled in with parts of discarded signs telling Mexicans to drink Coca-Cola or to drive a fancy car provide a surreal ambience. Clotheslines on which women hang the family wash link shacks together, and children play in the dirt around them.

Clearly, fine schools exist in these border cities, staffed with well-trained and dedicated teachers. But alongside them are countless others, and thousands of children do not attend schools because there is no place for them or attend schools badly in need of repair. At the primary school in El Pipila, a squatter town in Tijuana, five hundred children attend classes in a building without windows or heat; they sit on concrete blocks because there are no desks. Thousands of children in these communities cross the border daily to attend American public schools. Some, perhaps many, do so out of admiration for American education, but others undoubtedly do so because of the absence of good institutions at home.

The border regions have high incidences of diseases. Some are rather old fashioned, such as tuberculosis, whooping cough, measles, pinkeye, leprosy, and deaths from nutritional deficiencies. Forty-three percent of the tubercular, often victims of poverty, make their home on the northern fringes of the republic, an excoriating condemnation of living conditions there. Cholera transgresses on Ciudad Juárez and Nuevo Laredo, according to a health official in El Paso, because of "bacteria passed through sewage, which is the Rio Grande . . . Fish eat the sewage and people undercook and eat the fish." From Matamoros to Tijuana, cases of anencephaly (the congenital absence of all or a major part of the brain) are reported. Diarrhea is commonplace. The "difference between a developed country and a devel oping country"—to quote one more health expert—"is that in one, billboards hype remedies for constipation and in the other for diarrhea." Medical analysts speculate that one cause of so much disease might be chemical wastes dumped by *maquiladoras*. The rates of venereal infection in cities such as Tijuana surpass those of other Mexican metropolises, especially for syphilis. In the small enclaves of the border, as for all of rural Mexico, 60 percent of those suffering from AIDS had earlier worked across the border. For 1993, Baja California reported over four hundred cases of the disease; according to *El Mexicano,* that figure is too low, due to underreporting. One physician in Tijuana who is head of a health district declares that from ten to twelve persons die monthly of AIDS. Mexico as a whole, to cite statistics of the World Health Organization, ranks fifteenth among the countries afflicted with the virus. Despite the steel fences erected by the border patrol, these illnesses are easily transmitted to the other side.

○ ○ ○ 🏵 ○ ○ ○

The specter of unemployment, too, haunts the border. On the national scene, perhaps 40 percent of the labor force is either unemployed or underemployed; in addition, each year approximately 1 million Mexicans enter the job market, and in Tijuana alone sixteen thousand new jobs must be found annually. Samuel Schmidt believes that although border unemployment ranks below the national average, "the rate of the economically inactive population is . . . high." Only in Nogales, he goes on to say, "does the percentage of employed persons top 50 percent." Before the advent of the *maquiladora* industry, over 40 percent of Nogales's labor force was jobless. Then, too, the instability of the job market as well as the character of the jobs must be taken into consideration. Tijuana, for example, has had almost full employment until recently, but nearly 60 percent of jobs are in the tertiary sector, where unskilled workers frequently fill them; unemployment rates, therefore, are lower. Jobs of this sort, however, are low-wage and usually temporary or seasonal and without social security benefits, as in the construction trade.

Other factors also dictate the degree of unemployment. One such was the end of the *bracero* program in 1964, a sure sign that the era of labor intensive agriculture in the Southwest was drawing to an end. In the Lower Rio Grande Valley, the cultivation of cotton no longer ruled supreme, its sale on world markets mortally wounded by the development of cheaper synthetic fibers. Cotton gins, compresses, and warehouses, once hallmarks of cities such as Brownsville, sat idle as farmers shifted to more productive crops and embraced capital intensive technology, ending a time when *braceros* by the hundreds of thousands were called upon to plant and harvest crops. These developments left hordes of jobless men, many still hoping to find work on the other side, living in Mexican border cities from Matamoros to Tijuana. Unemployment, particularly in the tertiary sector, is hardly immune to the ups and downs of the U.S. economy; an illness to the north is a jobless disaster for Mexican waiters, bartenders, and hotel workers. Another factor that must be remembered is the demographic explosion, to a large extent because assembly plants attract migrants; and not all find jobs.

The informal labor sector has grown nationwide, as it has along the border. In every city, *vendedores ambulantes* (street vendors), their numbers multiplying daily, hawk wares on the streets, while others shine shoes, sell newspapers, or carry your luggage across the border. This proliferation, scholars say, is a response to the failure of the private sector and the state to provide jobs for large elements of society. This includes one out of three employable women. Child labor can be seen everywhere; children clean shoes, peddle newspapers, sell candy, wait on tourists, and, at corner stops, rush to clean the windshield of your car. Children of both sexes, no more than toddlers, drop out of school at an early age, and, when they reach adulthood, end up doing unskilled labor at low pay. Many eventually cross the border in search of jobs or become heads of families in the *colonias populares*.

American policy, as well as the exploding global economy, exacerbates these conditions. Today's unemployment morass partly stems from NAFTA, the free trade agreement that opened Mexico's markets to American goods and, as a result, bankrupted sundry Mexican industries for failure to compete with the transnationals that set up shop in their country. These small companies were the principal employers of Mexico's industrial workforce. NAFTA, similarly, encouraged the elite that runs the republic to privatize state-owned industries, the employers of yet other workers. Their new owners invariably, to use a current bit of jargon, downsized them, laying off countless workers. By altering Article 27 of the Constitution of 1917, Mexican politicos and their allies in business junked safeguards for the legendary *ejido,* village communal property. The reforms, as the establishment press glibly proclaimed, supposedly meant the modernization of agriculture, but actually, they favored big private farms that produced cash crops for sale in the United States, while at the same time opening domestic markets to imports of corn and beans, the crops that campesinos plant and harvest. From then on, they were free to sell off their parcels of land, which they could not profitably operate for lack of credit, water, and markets. Unable to compete with cheap imports from the United States, they have abandoned their plots and have either flocked to the cities or ventured north to seek their fortune. Untold numbers of them have ended up in border communities.

Recurrent efforts in the United States to stop the flow of illegal immigrants also plays a role. Every operation blockade, as Mexicans think of them, adds to society's woes south of the border. When hungry Mexicans come north—and many of them hope to find jobs on the other side but find doors blocked by the border patrol—they settle in communities from Tijuana to Matamoros, some undoubtedly awaiting the propitious moment when they can surreptitiously enter the United States. Others, nonetheless, choose to stay in these border cities. Once there, the hunt for jobs, housing, schools, and other scarce resources starts, which exacerbates the already overburdened plight of local communities. To illustrate: In Tijuana and Tecate, the demand for land on which to build homes grew by some 30 percent when American authorities enhanced vigilance along the border in 1994 on the eve of the Mexican economic debacle. When needs go unmet, the result is the illegitimate growth of *colonias populares*, which one sees on the fringes of all border cities, whose residents are either unemployed, only temporarily employed, part-timers, or street vendors.

∘　∘　∘　🏵　∘　∘　∘

A cursory reading of newspapers tells you that certain kinds of crimes currently flourish south of the border. This lamentable fact, however, is often reflected in behavior on the other side, to which reports of muggings, thefts, drive-by shootings, and murders for San Diego and El Paso testify. Whatever might be said about the causes of crime in the United States, it is clear that it thrives in Mexico because of the recent economic crisis, the harshest since the Great Depression. A sure manifestation of that, according to *El Diario de Monterrey*, is that crimes against property, whether armed robberies of individuals, banks, or businesses, stand at the top of the list. One of the principal problems of Baja California, adds *El Mexicano*, is a crime wave that is due to high rates of unemployment, among other factors. No business establishment is safe from thieves; their favorite targets, according to police reports, are liquor and video stores, gasoline stations, and pharmacies. Businessmen in Reynosa blame migrants who are unable to jump the international fence and therefore prey on the local population. But that alone does not tell the entire story. Popular behavior, as Machiavelli insisted, usually reflects that of its rulers, and Mexico's powerful oligarchical elite wallows in corruption, behavior exhibited by the PRI. A popular belief says: "If Carlos Salinas and his cronies can bring economic ruin to me and my family, and reap fortunes in the process, the least I can do is to look after my own survival regardless of the cost."

No wonder, therefore, that disrespect for the law often thrives. In Ciudad Juárez, one frequent visitor argues, "Violence is normal"; to cite a fruit vendor, "Even the devil is afraid of living here." It is claimed that *pandillas*, or gangs, kill 200 or more people each year. No fewer than 150 young women disappeared in 1995; the police say they are runaways, but they are often found dead, as was the case with a *maquiladora* worker found on the dusty outskirts of the city, her panties pulled down around her ankles. Robberies, followed by violence of one kind or another, homicides, and rapes top the list of crimes in Tijuana; at least two to three hundred robberies are reported each month, a situation not too different in Mexicali. As an editorial in *Zeta*, the Tijuana journal, says, "Despite measures taken to improve public safety, the sad truth is that residents feel insecure on the streets of our cities." Also, as I explain later, the drug traffic on the border obviously foments violence.

All of this was not so in the past, old-timers recall: "One could leave the house unlocked and know that no one would rob it." As Tito Alegría, an urban specialist, knows from personal experience, this is no longer possible; vandals have broken into his home in Tijuana on four occasions, although after the second theft, he put iron bars on the windows and kept a dog. That other types of crime were entirely absent from the Tijuana of yesteryear is doubtful, given its history of saloons, gambling casinos, and bordellos, antecedents shared by other border cities. In Ciudad Juárez, reports *El Diario de Juárez*, one homicide per day occurs because of the easy availability of guns and the failure to ban their sale, which explains why "gunfire wounds someone every fourteen hours." In the cities of Tamaulipas, crime rates are up, especially for robberies, shootings, and rapes.

Police corruption, an endemic ill, has been around for a very long time, not just on the border but from one end of the republic to the other. No Mexican disputes this gospel truth. Corruption rides high; no gendarme—whatever the rank and whether municipal, state, or federal—is completely immune. Mexicans will tell you they fear the police more than the criminals. No matter what else you do, friends told my daughter when she moved to Tijuana, "don't ask the police for help should your car stall at night." Justice, as Mexicans know all too well, is usually reserved for the rich or for those with *palancas*, meaning political or family influence. The *mordida*, or bribe, is a legendary evil. As an editorial in *Zeta* charges, the "municipal police are a disaster"; they are good only for harassing motorists for a minor traffic violation to exact a *mordida*. How many American tourists, often young men, have endured this experience?

Up and down the border, police have been caught driving cars stolen in the United States, a special type of binational crime. Gangs of car thieves, run by both Americans and Mexicans, operate from San Diego to Brownsville, stealing autos for sale in Mexico, sometimes for their fenders, carburetors, wheels, or driveshafts. This nefarious business poses a headache for drivers in such cities as San Diego, where people wonder whether the car they left parked on a street will be there when they return. That police profit from this racket, to quote the newspaper *Zeta*, "is anything but novel." In 1995, two Tijuana municipal police, according to the *Los Angeles Times,* were "directly implicated in car thefts around San Diego," a "graphic reminder . . . that Mexican police routinely drive vehicles stolen in California—and personally participate in auto theft rackets." In that same year, the Tamaulipas state police agreed to return 110 vehicles stolen in Texas. As to why gendarmes are less than honorable, countless explanations abound: There are the everyday examples of corruption in business and politics; police receive low pay, little or no training, and recruits are low quality; and sometimes, their appointments are won through family ties or friendships, as *palancas*. The job, after all, commands no respect from neighbors; to the contrary, being an officer of the law tarnishes one's standing in the community.

One of the emerging problems in these Mexican border cities, as in the United States, is juvenile delinquency, and not just among children of the poor, as might be expected. Juvenile misbehavior knows no class barrier. "It isn't the number of robberies or the blatant activity of prostitutes that astonishes us," proclaims *El Diario de la Frontera* in Nogales, "but that the perpetrators are young, almost children." Also, the "juniors," the sons of the well-to-do, frequently carry firearms and use them at will. The police, according to newspaper accounts, are unable to stop this behavior, supposedly because of the political clout of the delinquents' families. This leads one to wonder whether the much-praised Mexican family structure that allegedly hangs together through thick and thin is not becoming unglued? Are parents no longer making the rules for their sons and daughters? Is this, perhaps, the result of living in a society where the migrant experience weakens kinship ties and the role of grandparents, uncles, and aunts in the upbringing of nephews and grandchildren, believed to be the strength of the Mexican nuclear family?

Awareness of crime and other types of skullduggery, not surprisingly, rides high among residents of border cities, one reason, apart from the Mexican's cynical view of society, being efforts of the press. Until a few years ago, newspapers and journals were faithful stooges of the PRI, always ready to report what it wanted the public to know—not that people believed what they read. Fully aware that the press was prostituting itself, most Mexicans referred to what they saw in newspapers as official propaganda. That is no longer entirely so, because independent journals—increasingly a feature of the republic, especially along the border in Tijuana—have taken to reporting the facts. This reporting includes not just crime in general but also official chicanery and, to the journals' credit, the bloody deeds of the drug mafias. At times, the journals, as in the case of Tijuana's muckraker *Zeta*, identify the mafiosos and their gunmen by name. That hazardous activity puts them on a collision course with organized crime, whose murders are reminiscent of the mob warfare in 1920s Chicago during the Prohibition era of Al Capone and his gangsters. Journalists who break the rules occasionally pay a steep price, as in the murder of a noted reporter for *Zeta* and the recent attempt on the life of its publisher, Jesús Blancornelas, as well as in the slaying of the editor of *La Prensa*, a newspaper in San Luis Río Colorado, a Sonora border town. These bloody acts have been attributed to drug lords and the complicity of police authorities.

Much remains to be done before a truly free press exists in Mexico—or in the United States, where rich advertisers, conservative male journalists, and the Anglo establishment usually dictate what is printed. Yes, old journalistic values, more heralded in myth than in fact, are coming alive along the border, and not just simply because of similar trends in Mexico City, where some newspapers and journals, *Proceso* and *La Jornada* to name two, have shaken off the shameful subservience of yesteryear. That is not to say that press corruption has been banished from the republic. Nor, especially, has it ceased along the border, where authorities and the powerful continue to bribe reporters, with payments referred to as *el chay-*

ote, and local editors bow before local tycoons in government and business, who employ money and intimidation to get their way.

Currently, in border cities, as in much of the republic, high walls and iron gates, to cite Fuentes's *Frontera de Cristal* once more, encircle the manors of the very rich: "Today we need protection," says one of these fortunates, "armed guards and police dogs. . . . it is a sin to be wealthy." Thus, the well-off rarely venture out onto the streets without their bodyguards. The reason: Kidnappings for ransom have become a common occurrence. Only the Republic of Colombia, with its narcotics trade, outpaces Mexico in this almost daily and grossly underreported activity, which the scholar Eric Hobsbawm calls "social banditry." Official statistics verify the growth of the violence. During the last three years, according to crime experts, kidnappers seized 753 individuals in Mexico, at a total ransom cost of $45 million. In the first months of 1996 alone, Baja California Norte reported six kidnappings of this sort; it is anyone's guess how many others the victims' families kept secret. The collapse of the economy in December 1994, and surely the increasingly rampant drug scene, spurred on this wave of lawlessness. The *Diario de Juárez* claims that the nightmare started with the fall of the peso. In Ciudad Juárez, businessmen who hire bodyguards meet regularly to discuss how best to cope with the danger. The president of the farmers' association of Mexicali, a lobby for wealthy planters, warns that if this continues, investment and economic growth will suffer in Baja California. The abduction of the Japanese head of Sanyo Video Components in Tijuana in the summer of 1996 focused international attention on this nightmare. Until then, foreigners had been relatively safe.

6

Identity

Nowhere in the Hispanic universe is the subject of one's identity so central to life as in Mexico—and even more so, if that is conceivable, for those who dwell on its northern rim. Who are we? That, in a nutshell, is what countless Mexican thinkers have asked since the days when Hernán Cortés and his rapacious hordes subjugated the Aztecs and put the men to labor and bedded the women. Among sundry reasons, that is so because of *mestizaje*, the blending over centuries of two races and cultures, remnants from the Old World and the New; along the border, it is so because of proximity to the United States and, conversely, because many miles separate the region from Mexico City, mecca of the historic culture.

This question strikes at the core of basic issues. After all, border Mexicans—*fronterizos*—dwell in the shadow of the most powerful people in the world, and their way of life seduces even the cocky French. Yet they are hardly natives of the region. Few trace their roots to the border towns of the nineteenth century: Most arrived only recently, particularly residents of cities and towns west of Ciudad Juárez. Not until the 1950s did the trek north really get under way. Border residents are newcomers from diverse regions of the republic, and only their children and grandchildren can begin to lay claim to birthrights in the North. Culturally, they represent a kaleidoscope of colors.

For the haughty denizens of Mexico City, all Mexicans must swear allegiance to one culture, speak one language, and uphold common values. That centralist view dates, as María Socorro Tabuenca, a writer from Ciudad Juárez suggests, from the nineteenth-century fear of repeating Mexico's loss of half of its territory because its inhabitants, for want of a national culture, lacked the will to defend it. Thus, in the rush to create a sense of *mexicanidad* (Mexicanness), so as not to suffer a fiasco like that of

1847 again, all Mexicans, regardless of where they live, must adhere to one culture. Not to accept this truth turns *fronterizos* into *vende patrias* (sellouts) and Pochos (Americanized Mexicans), in short, the uprooted who betray their country in the rush to adopt what is not theirs.

This exclusive version of culture takes on numerous forms and relegates expressions, values, and customs that are at variance to the junk heap. It encompasses even popular music. In the words of Elena Poniatowska, a distinguished denizen of Mexico City, the bolero, as a musical symbol, epitomizes the spirit of the love life of all Mexicans: "If Stendhal evokes the sentiments of the French, the bolero summons ours." Mexico, announced one famous Mexican actress, is "one big bolero." For those of us who know Mexico and *fronterizos* and who danced to the bolero rhythms of the Clave Azul orchestra at the Castillo Club in the old days of Tijuana, that is a verity. Mexicans, no matter where they dwell, share much in common, and the bolero, at least for those of us who enjoyed the past, remains a nostalgic symbol of unity. All the same, differences do divide Mexicans, and *fronterizos* are no exception. As Tabuenca concludes, Mexicans embody multiple identities—individual, regional, and national ones. But that does not make them less Mexican.

The Shakespearean cliché "to be or not to be" encapsulates the essence of the rhetorical challenge that stands at the heart of what border Mexicans aspire to be. Like it or not, they live in the path of a "bulldozer culture," the crowning achievement of neighbors proud to be the biggest consumers on earth, of a society that overwhelms historic ways of life by destroying Mexicans' most cherished customs and questioning their values. Precisely because of that, for a majority of Mexicans the defense of the national culture starts at the border. Yet, at the same time, the border offers Mexicans the option of forging a regional way of life at odds with the age-old tutelage of Mexico City—and thus enriching national life.

∘ ∘ ∘ 🏵 ∘ ∘ ∘

Prosaic events, nonetheless, have dictated the course of border life. *Fronterizos* are, for better or worse, the offspring of a consumer culture à la the American way; a culture in which individual penchants and not societal needs mold responses; a way of life at odds, its critics believe, with that of their neighbors to the south. Caliban and not Ariel, to replay Shakespeare's *Tempest*, is its spokesman. At one time, tourism was its cornerstone, but now it is the *maquiladora*. "All you have in Ciudad Juárez," a person from Central Mexico tells a native of that city, "is El Paso." Chilangos, Mexicans from Mexico City, talk of the *tijuanazo*, the cultural shock that meets them upon arriving in Tijuana, a city so at variance with others in the republic. When "I lived in Morelia, a woman in Tijuana complains, "we were not a consumer society. Now I live in one." Carlos Monsiváis, the maverick intellectual, sees border life as "the subculture of prostitution which defines itself by accumulation," that is, "consumption." He bemoans the "tragic loss of Mexican identity" and writes of rootless bordello cities whose sole reason for being is to acquire vast quantities of American goods, whose inhabitants assume a *patria* (motherland) is constructed out of dollar profits. One experiences the sensation of being in cities whose sole goal is to be of service to tourists. Unfortunately, laments Monsiváis, the rest of the republic now tightly clutches identical values.

Fronterizos vehemently reject this interpretation. As one Juarense insists, the truth lies elsewhere: In actuality, Southerners, the recently arrived, are the most prone to fall in love with American consumerism. No other border in the world, according to this view, has a more unique culture. The way of life on the border compared to lifestyles in other parts of the republic is a world apart. True, proponents of this view admit that the most learned did not migrate north; rather, it was the restless and audacious, eager to strike out on their own. As one local writer explains, border society amalgamates cultural roots carried by migrants from all over the republic. The northern way of life evolved on the margins of the cultural imperialism of "Tenochtitlán," mother of Mexico City snobbism, imitating neither the Yankee model nor others. The configuration of northern society rests on the integration of and receptivity to Mexican regional variations, modified by daily contact with a neighboring country.

What is singular about border culture, writes Tabuenca, is its capacity, on the one hand, to resist being isolated from the traditional core while, on the other hand, concomitantly accepting a precarious but surely obligatory relationship with the neighbor next door.

To quote a resident of Ciudad Juárez: "I think that our *frontera* [border] is different because of the influence of the United States." People who live on the borderlands, according to this version, are more modern in their outlook, work harder, and take greater risks than other Mexicans. They are more ambitious and believe that hard work and frugality pay off, a notion that at times hides the ugly face of race prejudice.

The border, say numerous Chilangos, is a cultural wasteland, a belief also subscribed to by a host of pundits and even by natives. In the North, so goes this harsh opinion, "Fine arts, literature, and the social niceties are hardly priorities." The North is *gringolandia*, claim some Chilangos, who view with apprehension what they see as ties of Norteños (Northerners) to the United States, a country that inspires distrust in the souls of countless Mexicans. In *Puente México,* Mayo Murrieta and Alberto Hernández find it deplorable that when visitors from Mexico City arrive at the border, they consider themselves superior and discriminate against *fronterizos.* This attitude was manifested openly once class-conscious Central

Mexicans began arriving in large numbers. Until then, no sharp social distinctions had existed; no matter what their economic status, everyone had treated everyone else as an equal. Murrieta and Hernández say that with the appearance of the Chilangos, that changed, and the authors embellish this point by telling the following story. When a clerk from a dry cleaning business in Tijuana went to pick up the clothes of a physician who had just arrived from Mexico City, a Chilanga housekeeper met him at the door. Instead of asking him to step inside while she got the clothes, as Tijuanenses customarily do, she told him to wait outside, then not only closed the door, but locked it. A day or two afterward, when he returned with the clothes, she again kept him waiting on the doorstep while she got the money to pay him.

The view from Mexico City rests on historic antecedents. Since the days of the conquest, Spaniards and their descendants have disdained the "barbaric" North. An old refrain captures this sentiment nicely: "Outside of Mexico City, everything is Cuautitlán." That attitude survived into the twentieth century. In 1923, for example, the diplomat Federico Gamboa, in his *Diario*, described Sonora as "the state furthest from us [and] never . . . in tune with us" and noted that the "miles that separate Sonorenses from the rest of the country are nothing when compared with the moral distance between us." José Vasconcelos, another famous intellectual, recalled Sonora as the state where "the culture we know ends and that of beef begins." Or, to quote Monsiváis, "On the border there are no visible signs of high culture." From this viewpoint, the North, clearly, is a cultural wasteland: Aside from an oral tradition, no writers or artists of national stature exist in this region bereft of an educated ruling class, shorn of the popular arts, and isolated until the 1950s from centers of learning in Central Mexico. As one Chilango informed *Zeta*, "Tijuanenses are . . . *pochos*; they represent two nationalities; what customs or traditions, by the way, are you referring to when you speak of Tijuanenses?"

Given this attitude, it is no wonder that border Mexicans resent "Chilangos," a pejorative term accepted into the everyday vocabulary. "We are as Mexican as they are," is the answer from the North. "*Haga patria. Mate un chilango*" (kill a Chilango and forge a motherland) was one reply of the 1980s. Rubén Vizcaíno, dean of the Tijuana intelligentsia, comments that Chilangos, "when wealthy, are pompous, aggressive, brutal and racist, but also sycophants before foreigners." For Juarenses, the defense of their way of life signifies ridding their city of the notoriety it acquired in the 1920s; they do so partly by ascribing to themselves advantages denied others, among them easy access to the United States, to its culture, its goods, and its jobs.

Not all Mexicans on the border, however, share this anti-Chilango prejudice, which, in the opinion of José Manuel Valenzuela, one of the younger intellectuals, springs from local entrepreneurs who must compete with rivals from Mexico City, especially after the devaluation of 1982 opened business opportunities to Chilangos along the border. The fact is, whether *fronterizos* admit it or not, only the federal government in Mexico City supports the arts. Other sectors, private capital included, exhibit little interest in their promotion. According to Valenzuela, what Northerners who value art and literature want is "cultural decentralization," the end of Mexico City's tutelage. It is no longer a matter of "taking the lamp of learning" from Mexico City to the provinces. Decentralization means that Mexico City must respect regional endeavors and, in an equitable manner, help promote them throughout the republic.

It is clear that the cultural "uniqueness" of the borderlands cannot be understood without reference to the United States. The Mexican border, to quote one letter writer to *Zeta*, is "where two civilizations meet." Mexicans interact with another way of life and, sooner or later, invariably adopt aspects of its values and aspirations. That, nonetheless, can be a two-edged sword. Because they have accepted elements of another way of life, border cities are also seen as tawdry artificial outposts whose Mexican identity has been diluted by American television, McDonald's, and rock music. One could add the comics, which feature Donald Duck, Blondie, and Mickey Mouse, American icons. Writing in *Cuadernos del Norte*, Jorge Carrera Robles even speaks disparagingly of a "so-called culture of the *maquiladora*."

Old-timers decry this adaptability and recall a bucolic past. Traditions, recalled Crispín Valle Castañeda, who arrived in Tecate in the 1920s, "are no longer the same." In the past, life on the border was more rural, people happier, and no class pretensions disturbed their tranquillity. In Baja California, life underwent a change during World War II, when pleasure-seeking Americans, who arrived in large numbers for the wrong reasons, "corrupted our youth." They had no qualms about disturbing the public order, believing that in Mexico they were free to do whatever they wanted. Life was simpler then, but "today everything revolves around money, even baptizing a child costs a pretty penny." Yesterday, "friendships meant something." That is not so today because "friendships are bought and sold." In the old days, Don Crispín insisted, "One did not carry on with a young lady unless you had marriage in mind." Implied in this version of a bucolic past is the negative impact of American culture on its Mexican neighbor.

There is some truth in this criticism. *Fronterizos* often rely on the other side. They borrow and adopt what is foreign, whether in tune with Mexican culture or not. Even Vizcaíno, vociferously nationalistic, admits that the development of "high culture for Tijuana began in San Diego." It is "not always easy [for me] to travel to San Diego," acknowledges another

Tijuanense, though "I enjoy shopping at Tower Records," in a store that features one of the largest collections of classical music. This man also buys from U.S. catalogues, which is how he acquired his prized *American Dreamer*, a collection of songs by Stephen Foster interpreted by Thomas Hampton. The degree of reliance on the other culture also depends on what the American side offers. For many Tijuanenses, San Diego is a mecca because of its cinemas, art galleries, and museums. This cultural richness, just the same, does not extend the entire length of the border. On the art scene, for instance, little interaction occurs between Ciudad Juárez and El Paso, and when it does, it is usually among Mexicans and Chicanos. As Sito Negron, a reporter for the *El Paso Times*, recognizes, his city is not a cultural bastion.

Mexicans and Americans of Mexican origin do, occasionally, attempt to find common artistic and intellectual ground. One instance of this occurred between the two Laredos, one city being fully Mexican and the other virtually so. In 1989, residents of both cities organized a festival, entitled Laredo's Arte, in an attempt to utilize cultural ties that unite them. The goal was to celebrate jointly *el día de los muertos*, All Souls' Day, and reject, in the process, the ritual of Halloween, which is alien to people of Mexican origin on both sides of the border. Simultaneously, they wanted to find a substitute for putting up altars and bringing flowers to the dead in a cemetery, a custom of Central Mexico of little historical or cultural significance in either Laredo. To quote Hector Romero, one of the patrons, "We felt we had to do something of our own . . . The hope was to show the people of both Laredos that we have a common patrimony we must preserve."

All the same, in Tijuana, which is constantly under the gun of the American way of life, the issue of whether to celebrate Halloween takes on a militant, nationalist cast. For decades, the city had celebrated Halloween with goblins and witches, copying the behavior of youth in nearby San Diego. But now, Leobardo Sarabia, a writer and intellectual, explains, municipal leaders are trying to resurrect Mexico's Day of the Dead, so as "to preserve our own traditions." Some people, he goes on, who find the popularity of Halloween alarming, fear that this region will lose its sense of nationality and "be left with a very American culture." The campaign afoot encourages parents to take their children to the cemetery on November 2 for the customary outing, usually a picnic and, where a relative lies buried, to spruce up the grave, as I vividly recall my parents doing. For all of us, that November day was a special occasion to look forward to. In Tijuana schools, Day of the Dead festivals replace Halloween parties because as a border people we are losing our values. Alicia García, a school principal, remarks, "This is a call to rescue our traditions." The Day of the Dead, moreover, celebrates a very Mexican attitude toward death, the acceptance of the mortality of life, as José Guadalupe Posada, the famous artist, depicted in his engravings of *calaveras* (skeletons), cigarettes in their mouths, dancing the *paso doble,* riding galloping horses, or fighting bulls.

Indeed, the cities of the borderlands are cultural contradictions, some more than others. At one extreme is Tijuana, a city that every day reinvents itself and provides new spectacles. Once known as "sin town," it now boasts a cultural center and access to international networks of information. It is a city impossible to define easily, with both cosmopolitan and regional characteristics. Gay groups in Tijuana publish the magazine *Frontera Gay,* but the police routinely round up homosexuals, who revile the discrimination they suffer from city authorities, church, and citizenry. In what was unheard of a few years ago, gay activists convened a press conference and threatened to conduct a letter-writing campaign to denounce the "radio mafia" and to organize a public protest to demand their rights as citizens. The newspaper *Diario 29,* a government daily, reported on a series of talks by an eminent sexologist from Mexico City who discussed, in an adult class of over one hundred, masturbation and other topics "hidden under the table for centuries."

The old ways, just the same, survive. In Agua Prieta, where the heat of the desert sets the mode of life, old men, in the time-honored Mexican custom, sit on park benches; people refer to them as *banqueros,* a play on the words banker and bench. The old and the new ways clash: As an astonished American visitor commented, "Mariachis fill the air with soft melodies of traditional songs" while teenagers "try to drown them out with the latest rock and roll" from "huge ghetto blasters." Each year at Christmastime, *posadas* (festivals) are held up and down the border and *villancicos* are sung. *Tertulias,* a term Mexicans apply to gatherings of intellectuals and artists, go on as they did in the old days, with heated discussions over politics, art, literature, and public personalities, just as Guillermo Prieto, a literary mainstay of the nineteenth century, described them in his *Memorias.* Cockfights, as Mexican as any sport, draw large crowds of men, just as they did in the days of Antonio López de Santa Anna, the nefarious caudillo who presided over the loss of the Southwest in the War of 1847.

o   o   o   🏮   o   o   o

Furthermore, headway is being made to end what has been labeled the "cultural poverty" of the North. All the principal cities boast groups of plastic artists, novelists, and writers, and each has a surprisingly good theater. Nor are residents of the cities simply consuming what Mexico City or foreign capitals send but are writing for themselves and staging their own plays. "Tijuana," to quote a bookstore owner, "was all stores and bars." Now, with "more of a middle class, more people going to the university . . . people ask what about culture?" In Tijuana, which, along with Mexicali, leads the way in the arts endeavor, artists and writers discovered a haven in the Cultural Center, the big ball-shaped building in the heart of the Zona del Río, where they can see exhibits by José Clemente Orozco and Diego Rivera, attend lectures by Carlos Monsiváis and Carlos Fuentes, enjoy the Cuban Ballet from Havana, and listen to classical music played by an orchestra of Russian expatriates.

This growing sophistication came about not by way of Mexico City but, to the contrary, because of a developing educational edifice. For the first time, border cities can boast of artists and writers educated and trained within the region itself. Intellectual and artistic activity has ceased simply being an imitation of what goes on in Mexico City, becoming part and parcel, to cite an article in *Cuadernos del Norte*, of "our authentic reality and of our aspirations." It is the expression of a more mature society, where *fronterizos* attempt to bring to a close their traditional isolation in order to create an artistic and intellectual heritage worthy of taking a place alongside older ones. It steps away from the closed, centralized society of the past so that it might result in a more flexible national structure open to social, regional, and ethnic differences. The boom in the arts and literature, say its advocates, "celebrates a culture" that blends the "frontier spirit with the most vibrant parts of both sides of the border." That, nevertheless, does not imply economic equality for writers and artists on both sides of the border; as always, those in the United States are, as one Mexican exclaims, "spectacularly better paid."

It is no accident that the principal cultural bastions are Tijuana, Mexicali, and Ciudad Juárez. Each has a major university, respective branches of the Universidad Autónoma de Baja California (UABC) and the Universidad Autónoma de Ciudad Juárez (UACJ), although in the manner of American schools, they put their emphasis on technical and "practical" studies; in this aspect, tourism comes to mind. But they also provide programs in the humanities and the arts, and the UABC has schools of humanities on both of its campuses. The UABC in Mexicali also sponsors a school of fine arts, the dream of Rubén Vizcaíno and his colleagues. More than any other factor, universities are responsible for the boom in the arts and literature; for the first time, there are jobs for writers and artists and opportunities for intellectual activities without daily monetary worries. Doors are open to innovation. To elaborate on what this implies, faculty members of the UABC in Tijuana worked out an exchange program in 1994 with the University of Havana in Cuba, a first for the border. However, this in no way implies that professors, as in much of Mexico, are either well paid or adequately rewarded for their accomplishments.

The universities sponsor journals where writers and artists can publish or exhibit examples of their art. These journals, along with faculty jobs, best explain why cities such as Tijuana can be proud of their writers, poets, and novelists, who no longer have to look to Mexico City for publishers. Still, the life spans of university journals are mostly short; they are here today and gone tomorrow, the principal reason being budgetary limitations. Their sponsors keep running out of money. But the journals continue to appear, some achieving worthy reputations, such as *Amerinda* of the UABC, the voice of avant-garde poets. *Hojas*, another review in which writers and poets have been published, became one of the finest in the republic. In the 1980s, it sponsored *encuentros de literatura fronteriza*, meetings of writers from both sides of the border who got together to read and discuss their works. During the 1980s, the owners of a saloon, the Bar Río Rita in Tijuana, paid for the publication of *Esquina Baja*, one of the few journals devoted almost entirely to the essay and the short story. Its editors stressed the importance of "creating a reading public" for a journal of high quality in order to counter "the centralizing tendency that prevails in our country." There is a "prejudice against what we do in the provinces; if it doesn't make it in Mexico City it's not worthy." In rejecting what they dubbed the "missionary" activities of Mexico City, the editors provided their own version of what it means to be Mexican. Given their own experiences at the margin of United States culture, so went another of their arguments, they were not "as susceptible to its glamour as Mexicans of the more distant capital," as the Chilangos charged. *El Mexicano*, a newspaper read in Tijuana and Mexicali, prints a *Suplemento Cultural* every Sunday, with essays on subjects such as schools of art, and publishes poetry and short stories. A major purpose of *La Linea Quebrada*, another journal, was to define the nature of identity and culture on the border, for the sake of a generation that grew up watching *charro* (cowboy) movies and science fiction flicks and listening to *cumbias*. *Puente Libre*, a Ciudad Juárez review, carries articles on art, history, and identity, as well as publishing poetry.

The major border cities showcase important cultural landmarks. One of the most dazzling is the Centro Cultural in Tijuana, which opened in 1983 and was designed by Pedro Ramírez, the architect of the famous Museum of Anthropology in Mexico City. Called *La Bola* because of its round shape, the Tijuana edifice was built partly with the hope of promoting better understanding between Mexico and the United States; few Americans, unfortunately, attend its functions, which include international jazz festivals, ballet performances, displays of mural art, and, for aspiring actors and writers, a theater program. In Mexicali, the Teatro del Estado puts on plays from all over the world, the Galería de la Ciudad promotes art shows, and the Museo has on exhibit documents and photographs of modern Mexican history. Residents of Ciudad Juárez can listen to classical music played by the chamber group of the university or attend a performance by its Ballet Folclórico. The Museum of History is in the former Customs Office, which was built in 1889 in the French style during the Porfiriato. The Museo de Arte e Historia, housed in a modern building, offers visitors glimpses of Mexican art and history and features a collection of pre-Columbian artifacts. The former military hospital, which dates from the War of 1847, is today the Instituto Regional de Bellas Artes in Matamoros, which offers classes in painting and dance. Matamoros's artists exhibit their works in Monterrey and Mexico City. Since the 1970s, there is also a branch of the Universidad Autónoma de Tamaulipas in Matamoros.

○　○　○ 🏛 ○　○　○

Novelists, short-story writers and poets are relatively recent arrivals. Literature began to flower in the post–World War II era, when such towns as Tijuana became cities virtually overnight. There are, however, references to border towns in the novels of the revolution, which first appeared in the early 1920s with the publication of Mariano Azuela's *Los de Abajo;* both Martín Luis Guzmán's *El Aguila y la Serpiente*, a semiautobiographical tale, and José Vasconcelos's *Ulises Criollo*, an autobiography, briefly describe life on the border. Then, in 1932, Hernán de la Roca wrote *Tijuana In*, the first novel about the town. From then on until the 1970s, little of note appeared; most of the writing—short stories and poems—essentially appeared in newspapers.

The boom mirrored the changing times. Its standard-bearers were young, with few exceptions born in the 1950s, and were mainly poets and short-story writers. Critics maintain that poetry stands at the top of the list both in quality and quantity; *fronterizos* who write are, by and large, poets. For prose writing, the city of Tijuana led the way when Federico Campbell, Carlos Montemayor, Rafael Ramírez, Ignacio Solares, and Joaquín Armando Chacón started to publish their novels and short stories. Campbell, who calls himself a *cuentero*, a narrator of short stories, is the best known of the Tijuana group. Daniel Sada, from Mexicali, another luminary who achieved national recognition, is the author of *Lampa Vida* and is a master at capturing the essence of vernacular language. In his works, desert, sea, and death, which the author uses to probe the meaning of life, play central roles. Yet *Lampa Vida*, a stream-of-consciousness novel, is not about border life but about two lovers on the run from the girl's hometown; the lover, a buffoon despised by himself and everyone else, is a tawdry professional clown who goes from town to town unable to confront reality. Both clown and lover look upon their love as the means of their salvation. Gabriel Trujillo, also from Mexicali, is a noted essayist, poet, and chronicler. In one of his stories, *Hotel Frontera*, which takes place in the 1920s, Rudolph Valentino drives to Tijuana, takes a room in the hotel, orders a bottle of whiskey, and then asks for a "girl, virgin and no older than fifteen," preferably Mexican. He spends the night watching American men cavort, always with a "whore at their side."

Most of these writers focus on regional or local themes taken from their own experience as *fronterizos*: the cities and American tourists, the counterculture Cholo (counterculture border outcaste), whom Luis Humberto Crosthwaite writes about in *El Gran Pretender*, a collection of vignettes that attempt, in brief episodes, to describe the Cholo as he really is, not as outsiders picture him. Crosthwaite's characters talk in *caló*, the dialect of the barrio, and epitomize its life and times. Crosthwaite and his companions embody the rebirth of the Mexican school of provincial literature, made famous by writers such as José Rubén Romero, author of the much-read *Pito Pérez*, a *pícaro* (rogue) from Santa Clara del Cobre, a town in Michoacán. Emphasizing the region means writing multicultural stories; there is no national literature, only diverse Mexican literatures, as determined by place and time. The landscape is the desert, the mountains, or the sea, physical features of the North, and always bicultural border cities facing the United States. The literature reflects regional diversity; the border is not one homogeneous region.

The border detective novel, taking its cue from Dashiell Hammett and Raymond Chandler, incorporates geography with drug traffickers, clandestine landing fields, filthy jails, police brutality, and corruption. Its backdrop is the city and daily life, what fails to appear on the society pages of newspapers. Much of the literatures puts no stress on reason and ultimate justice, and good and evil play no role; brutal killings, as they do in real life, go unpunished. In "Lucky Strike," a short story by Gabriel Trujillo about a man petitioning for land owned by Americans in Mexicali, a lawyer in the pay of Americans hires an assassin to kill the plucky petitioner and then, in turn, is killed by the assassin. The story ends with the killer, unpunished, departing from Mexicali and the gringos, who continue to own the land, happy. Political power leads to police violence, and violence leads to crime. The border detective novel, unlike its American cousin, is not about the detective who, a bottle of bourbon in his hand, ties loose threads together to solve a crime.

○   ○   ○   🏵   ○   ○   ○

The arts appeared in Tijuana in the 1950s. Until then, art was decorative, usually appearing where tourists could be found, in hotels, bars, and casinos. Then, in the 1950s, painters and sculptors began to settle in Tijuana;

in 1955, the muralist painter Jesús Alvarez Amaya with Fernando Robledo Dávila opened a school of plastic arts, named after José Clemente Orozco, which produced a group of painters from Mexicali, the pioneers of the plastic arts in Baja California. The actual takeoff in the arts comes in the 1970s, with the work of the painters Rubén García Benavides and Enrique Estrada Barrera, who employed regional themes typical of Baja California. Their success is all the more remarkable since they had few buyers of their art and little encouragement from state and municipal authorities. There followed the abandonment of this school in favor of themes and styles common to the works of Mexico City and Europe, in short, contemporary vanguard painting. The art of Baja California painters was to be no different from that of their contemporaries in Mexico City or Guadalajara. With that about-face, a decline set in that is yet to be halted. In Ciudad Juárez, meanwhile, it is the support of the federal government and the local university that spurred the artistic awakening in the 1970s. But as Nestor García Canclini comments, the pressure is strong to embrace a noncritical "playful style of art . . . devoid of social concerns and aesthetic risks," in the manner of Western Europe and the United States.

One flourishing art form is photography, especially in Tijuana, home of numerous men and women of remarkable talent, one of them being Roberto Córdova Leyva, whose pictures vividly capture the dirt and grime of the cities, the plight of poverty-stricken children, the landscape of retaining walls of discarded tires. There is also a theater that shows vigorous signs of life, so much so that the Instituto Nacional de Bellas Artes in Mexico City sponsors in Tijuana a *diploma de teatro*, a degree in theater arts. Tijuana has a Chamber Ballet of the Border, the offspring of Ricardo Peralta, a native of Mexico City and a member of the National Ballet of Mexico City, He arrived for a month's teaching and stayed; ballet performances now draw audiences of six hundred or more.

∘   ∘   ∘ ▨ ∘   ∘   ∘

Something else, equally meaningful, occurs among women, in an epic still hard to assess but perhaps fated to rearrange the contours of conventional society. Women are on the move, demanding a new role in society and, at the same time, giving a fresh interpretation to the concept of national identity by questioning the importance of geography and, as even some men argue, asserting that social class, women included, is the key. In this interpretation, both the middle and urban classes of the principal Mexican cities are hardly the Lancelots of Mexican nationality, since they willingly embrace North American patterns of behavior and delight in using Anglo words and expressions. Above all, to posses an identity is to belong to a nation, a city, or a *colonia*, where everything shared by residents is interchangeable. In this interpretation, gender plays a role as well; the community is not formed just by the nation but also by women. In their poems and narratives, women challenge traditional values, which they associate with a male-dominated world. They cast doubt upon the family structure and the old relationship between women and men, a relationship linked to a system that seeks to keep women in their place.

The best known of these authors is Rosina Conde, whose cogently written short stories contemplate the Tijuana of the 1950s from a feminist perspective, in a time and place where drunken U.S. marines pay to watch go-go dancers in the bars of Avenida Revolución. Her latest collection of short stories, entitled *Arrieras Somos*, explores relationships between men and women. In "Estudias o Trabajas," a young woman is caught between being an old-fashioned girl who gets married and striking out on her own. When she chooses the latter course, she finds that the macho society of Mexico offers no way out. In Tijuana, where the story develops, the young woman recognizes that her choices of men to marry are slim: "There are no eligible men; they are either married or not worth a damn." In the best known of her short novels, part of a collection of her works titled *Agente Secreto*, Conde examines the conflict in Mexican families between the daughter who seeks to establish an identity of her own and the tyranny of the patriarchal father who, as she writes, tries to keep women submissive. The nub of this drama, as in many of her writings, revolves around middle-class family life and the lovers of the female protagonist who tells the story. This young woman, it becomes clear, is not the stereotypical female one finds in the usual Mexican novel. We know that from the literature she reads, the movies she sees, and the music she listens to. Instead of the Beatles, the favorites of her friends, she prefers rock groups such as the Rolling Stones or the blues and jazz of Ella Fitzgerald, Louis Armstrong, and Bessie Smith. She detests men who believe that women are good only for fornicating and caring for children, that women are unable to carry on an intelligent conversation. What angers her most is that her female acquaintances fit that mold. Conde is one of a number of able women writers from Tijuana.

In Ciudad Juárez, other women carve out names for themselves—young poets and writers such as Armine Arjona, Carmen Amato (also a fine photographer), Marcela Zaragoza, and Zula Méndez. One gifted writer is Rosario Sanmiguel, whose short stories are published in national journals. When compared to Conde's, her work is less belligerent and more reflective. Born in a small town in Coahuila, Sanmiguel taught Spanish in a junior college in El Paso, a job that opened her eyes to the realities of border life, which became the theme of her short stories. As she says, "We are trying to re-create what is special to us in Ciudad Juárez," but the subjects are universal—love, solitude, and death, "themes . . . treated through the eyes of characters from the border." In "Un Silencia Muy Largo," Frances, the chief protagonist, enters a bar in Ciudad Juárez, an act that raises eyebrows for women of her class do not frequent them. There she joins men, who supposedly go there to forget their cares and worries. She enters the bar determined to forget her lover, a married man she has been seeing for ten years. Her goal is to set aside the memory of his body, the symbol of her sexual desires and dependency, and then his memory. In this struggle to start life anew, Frances leaves home and finds a new job. In writing this, Sanmiguel gives the reader a woman of flesh and blood able to acknowledge her sexual appetites and resolute in her determination to get on with her life. "Las Hilanderas," another story, is about a mother and daughter who wade the Rio Grande to cross the border, believing that jobs that pay in dollars will better their lives. That never comes to pass. True, they find domestic work in an American household but also long hours, poor pay, and a matron who never lets them forget who is lord and master. Unable to tolerate this colonial relationship and nostalgic for her native soil, the mother returns home, leaving Fátima alone in El Paso, where, to find solace, she strikes up friendships with other undocumented women. Together, they spend Sundays in Ciudad Juárez, but on one occasion, when trying to return to El Paso, they are caught by the border patrol and sent back to Mexico. Fátima, instead of surreptitiously wading the river again with her friends, goes home to join her mother. She cannot, because, in her absence, her mother has died.

Patricia Ruiz, who was born in Sonora but grew up in Matamoros, is a weaver and, equally important, a sculptor. As an *artista matamorense* (Matamoros artist), she is a rebel against establishment art and fads. She wants, to use her own words, "to overcome the narrow confines of her traditional training as a weaver and do her own designs, "totally different from what I was taught" in Guanajuato. After a year of study in Poland incubating fresh ideas and concepts of her own, she returned home and exhibited solely in Mexico City. Eventually, she turned northward for inspiration, both for her weaving and sculptures, which she usually combines in one, making them totally *fronterizo*. "I live on both sides of the Rio Bravo," she emphasizes, where art must come to grips with the "violence and shock of life caught between two cultures." Her work, critics recognize, is her own, a *fronterizo* art shorn of ties to regional and national schools.

In the border cities, young women, and occasionally older ones, who performed under enormous handicaps in the backwaters of Central Mexico, are increasingly demanding an independent role for themselves. Drawn by aspirations for a job and for escape from male chauvinism—as Mexican as the tortilla—women flock north, so much so that they currently outnumber men; to demonstrate what this implies, in Nuevo Laredo there are seven women for every man. Ironically, another reason for the imbalance is that men, who are frequently denied opportunities at home, go off to work in the United States or Mexico City, leaving behind wives and girlfriends. These women must fend for themselves, never certain that their husbands or companions will return.

Women writers represent the tip of the iceberg. For countless women, the border symbolizes an opportunity for a different way of life. True, the baggage of yesteryear hangs heavy. Most abused women never file a formal complaint and most believe that men in the family should be schooled first, though divorced women assign a high priority to education. Most still think of marriage as their logical destiny, but here and there signs of other attitudes emerge, as Conde, an ardent feminist, illustrates in her short stories. Women are striking out on their own, postponing marriage, getting divorced, and living alone rather than subjecting themselves to the tyranny of macho behavior. At times, their views are strikingly unconventional, as opinions on abortion testify; to quote a young woman of an upper-middle-class family in Tijuana: "I would not have an abortion but others must decide for themselves whether they want one or not." This woman is not just Catholic but a faculty member of a Catholic college. Her opinions are not entirely atypical of educated women along the entire border—women who are attending graduate and professional schools in larger and larger numbers and becoming architects, physicians, lawyers, and university professors. They want to be able to stand on their own.

But then, resourcefulness has always been a hallmark of Mexican women, particularly those in the working class; they learned long ago how to take care of themselves, as the story of Chela vividly demonstrates. She lived in Ciudad Juárez but worked in a cannery in El Paso; every day, she illegally crossed the border, to a job that paid poorly. All day and every day, she sorted green and red peppers, tedious labor only made less so by conversations with Mexican companions. Her boss, who disliked Mexicans, was a slave driver, and the conditions of work were terrible. Her feet were always swollen, but she had to stand all day and virtually beg for permission to go to the toilet. Resentful of her job, she got even by stealing the "largest and most beautiful peppers."

One-third or more households are headed by women, and in not a few families that contain men, women are the principal breadwinners. Women work as professors in universities and as research scholars in the Colegio de la Frontera Norte, which has branches in every border city. They compose poetry, write short stories and novels, and publish articles and books on life on the border, often focusing on the role of women, as Olivia Teresa Ruiz does in her studies of *mujeres transfronterizas*, women who make both sides of the border their abode.

Young women professionals not only ask leave of no man, but they think for themselves, often espousing ideas at odds with those of their menfolk. Women, one study shows, are less inclined to worship at the capitalist altar and less reverential of the much-touted American way of life. Only a few see advantages to being in the United States, although some admit that there are benefits. But life there, they add, is work and more work; routine controls what one does, making it difficult to discipline children, accustomed to doing what they wish because they are left alone. Yes, American children enjoy certain advantages—learning English and obtaining well-paying jobs, to name two—but they grow up speaking and thinking in English, becoming more American than Mexican, more loyal to their place of birth than to the land of their parents.

Despite barriers of old, the feminist ideal wins disciples by the day, women who, insists Conde, "at fifteen years of age think as well as men of twenty." They no longer want to marry out of fear of being lonely or in response to nagging parents. Women of this persuasion scoff at charges that their attitude endangers the Mexican family: "We do not want to destroy it," they proclaim, "we want to change it." Their dream is a family in which women and men enjoy a harmonious relationship, in which both share household duties and the responsibility of raising children, with love and not fear dictating behavior.

Women are also fighting for their rights. In Chihuahua, they went to battle over bills submitted by the PAN to legislate the right to life into the state constitution and to deny women the right to decide for themselves whether they want an abortion or whether to use contraceptives. They asked the state legislature to abolish antiquated laws covering sexual abuse and domestic violence, asking for the removal of the age-old fantasy that women induce men into committing sexual acts and even violence against them, attitudes still embedded in the law.

These challenges are helped along by the emerging family structure, no longer based mostly on the extended family, as in much of Mexico, but on the nuclear one. When people emigrate they leave behind relatives, generally grandparents, uncles, and aunts, making necessary reliance on the immediate family. Fewer family members are around to tell women what they must do. Contrary to the assertion that there is an amoral family life on the border, the family prospers, though more and more as a vehicle for adaptation to changing circumstances; family bonds do not disintegrate because of migration, as is often charged—they simply take on new forms.

Women desire strong family ties, as the incredible adventures of *mujeres transfronterizas* document. They are the women who live in the United States but close to Mexico, who undergo the hazards of border crossings to visit family; more than men, they endeavor to maintain familial ties despite international obstacles. A majority are single parents;

no husband awaits them at home. Most eke out a meager livelihood, and so they travel to Mexico to buy cheaper groceries or medicine for their children, to get their hair cut, or to see a dentist or physician. So that their children will not forget who they are, they teach them Spanish at home. Mexican women who reside in U.S. border towns take their children to school in Mexico to escape, as they say, the lack of discipline and to avoid exposure to the drug culture. Many work full-time but still find ways to escort their offspring across the border daily and return for them in the evening, in an astonishing display of maternal love. Unescorted women workers, particularly in Ciudad Juárez, attend discotheques, dance halls, restaurants, and certain types of bars, behavior once thought characteristic of women who had strayed from the straight and narrow. At these places, observes Patricia Fernández Kelly, "Women laugh, joke, and talk loudly while they drink, frequently until the late hours of the day."

Northern women, a study finds, are more likely to use contraceptives than Mexican women in general. The young dress as young American women do, in miniskirts and designer jeans, and beauty parlors have been replaced by hairstylists and unisex hair salons. Women are taking a bigger role in politics, helping lead the PAN in Nogales or joining the PRI and the Partido de la Revolución Democrática (PRD). Because they are the ones who buy the groceries and know economic turmoil first hand, they are in the forefront of protests against peso devaluations.

○　○　○　🏵　○　○　○

One singular difference between the Mexican and the American inhabitants of the borderlands is that Mexicans are much more exposed to American ways than Americans are to Mexican culture. Mexicans, some claim, are less ethnocentric. One reason, perhaps, is the much heavier Mexican reliance on the American economy and, probably, the "colonial mentality" of the Third World that tends to see key advantages in the way of life of the industrialized nations. Border Mexicans are daily exposed in a variety of ways to U.S. influences, through commuters, undocumented migrants, workers in the *maquiladoras*, tourists, family ties among Chicanos and Mexicans, Mexican students attending schools across the border, and now, of course, the information highway. For some sectors of the population, the American way of life carries enormous prestige. Since the days of Hernán de la Roca, the first to write a novel about Tijuana, authors invariably compare differences between the two sides of the border. For de la Roca, of whom little is known, San Diego was "a temple of virtue and hard work" and Tijuana "a cruel and evil goddess." Mexicans come into daily contact with American customs through radio and television programs; in Ciudad Juárez, one study revealed that three out of

four residents watch American television, even when they do not understand English. Yet most Mexicans on the border prefer to watch national
television, in contrast to the youth of Mexico City, more likely to turn on
foreign channels. Univisión, Channel 26 in El Paso, nonetheless enjoys the
biggest audience in the region, which includes Ciudad Juárez, specifically
for its news broadcasts. But, as Luis Humberto Crosthwaite, a novelist
with a national following, remarks, *fronterizos* who watch television as an
alternative to boredom have the following choices:

- Push the On or Off button
- Select Channel 8 (CBS)
- Sit on a sofa or bed and watch commercials while you wait for the
  program to start; you do this if you are bored and you are alone
- Three commercials: the best stain remover, the best bargains in
  stereos, the best pizza once in the oven cooks in three minutes
- Another commercial: the best remedy for stomach disorders is
  Alka Seltzer, the best hamburger is McDonald's.

Crosthwaite's commentary documents that not everyone is duped by
American propaganda. People, for all that, are seldom fully aware of cultural influences that endanger national identity, values, traditions, and
historical patterns of behavior inherited from the past. Border Mexicans,
whether they know it or not, through exposure to American television
and radio live under the influence of American aspirations and patterns
of consumption. That explains why the border is thought of as a strategic
zone for the Mexican republic; that is where differences start. Maintaining
a Mexican way of life becomes a priority, which makes necessary activities designed to keep it so, including the propagation of a national art. As
Leobardo Saravia, a literary critic from Mexicali, points out, few factors
shape life along the Mexican border more than proximity to the United
States, not simply in economic terms but also culturally. As with any
dominant group, American culture sells itself as the culture par excel-
lence, the only one that opens the door to "true economic development."

This idiosyncratic relationship goes back to the early part of this century. Up to then, the movement of people and goods across the international boundary was relatively insignificant; both sides of the border were
scantily inhabited, cultural exchanges were minimal and, when they did
occur, gradual. Since Mexico is the economically weaker neighbor, that
fact predisposes its society to accept a subordinate role when dealing
with the Americans next door. It also means that Mexican culture is more
apt to imitate and adopt values from across the border. This unequal relationship, as John A. Price, the author of a book on Tijuana, explains, "is
the basis for much of the stress and poor adjustment . . . in the symbio-

sis." As Olivia Teresa Ruiz, a Mexican anthropologist, demonstrates, the proximity of two socioeconomic systems generates "transborder habits" that are lived on a day-to-day basis.

But that is only partially the case. Yes, countless Mexicans envy the material wealth of Americans and wish to acquire their technical expertise. "Sometimes I envy the Americans for the beautiful things they have," a young woman told Price. But they are Mexicans, and wish to remain so, and events in their country are their primary concern. Their interest in the United States is limited to personal concerns. That is not to say that there are not border Mexicans, as well as others in the republic, who would gladly embrace American citizenship, as Gerardo Cornejo, a novelist from Sonora, laments. Some Mexicans hold dual citizenship, although, until recently, it was illegal. It is not difficult to find Mexicans who are decidedly "pro-Yankee," as Cornejo puts it, particularly among the Catholic clergy, conservatives, and the local bourgeoisie, a class that every day has closer economic ties with the other side. Yet Cornejo believes that this attitude is less pronounced along the border. The pro-Yankee attitude that Cornejo talks about might also be due to shared values, in this case neoliberal ones, lately perhaps because so many businessmen, engineers, and technicians are graduates of schools in the U.S. mold.

That neoliberal ideals, whatever the reasons, are popular among local businessmen, lawyers, and engineers is indisputable. The concept of privatization has a wide following, even among some in CANACINTRA, the industry lobby, who advocate selling off PEMEX to Americans, as I learned in conversations with them. When industrialists speak of class distinctions, there is little reference to a Marxist concept of class. Instead, a popular explanation for the poor in society is to talk of fate and individual luck, rhetoric that also stems from traditional Catholic doctrine. The responsibility for poverty lies with the individual. In Ciudad Juárez, as well as in other cities along the border, it is not uncommon to hear natives describe themselves as "hard workers," so as to separate themselves from Central Mexicans who are not. It is as if in the buying of durable goods on the other side, to cite Pablo Vila, a sociologist, the Protestant ethic of work also comes along. Those who live in deplorable conditions in Ciudad Juárez, it is charged, must be migrants from the interior of the republic, for how else can you explain their poverty, since hardworking Juarenses overcome these barriers? Wages in the *maquiladoras*, according to this discourse, are not low, they are simply foolishly squandered by lazy and stupid workers, people from the interior with cultural deficiencies. Some Juarenses emphasize that their commitment to hard work flows by way of their contacts with the United States. These people even adopt the racist rhetoric of the United States, using highly pejorative language when discussions of Mexican Americans arise.

People along the border—despite the opinions of Chilangos, who poke fun at what they describe as the "singsong" northern accent—speak good Spanish, better than in some other states of the republic. One explanation for the richness of expression and vocabulary in this regional speech is that people from all over Mexico, each with their own vocabulary, their own *dichos* (sayings) and *refranes* (proverbs), colonized the border. True, "Anglicisms" abound, though no more so, Monsiváis admits, than in Mexico City. The use of English words or of words concocted from both languages, referred to as Spanglish, is primarily the result of the economic and technical dependence of Mexicans, as well as the impact of American radio and television. English is a necessary tool for certain kinds of employment, certainly in tourism, the traditional standby, where waiters, bartenders, and hotel clerks must be bilingual, as well as in industry, where the new technology demands it. Secretaries in the *maquiladoras* are often fluent in the two languages, which they might join together in common, everyday expressions. At the end of a day at work, they might take leave of each other by saying "Bye-bye, *mi hija.*" Ironically, total competence in English is limited to small numbers of individuals who are truly bilingual, as a study of Ciudad Juárez shows, although a majority of Juarenses study English in school and hear it spoken on radio and television and in their contact with Americans.

Imitation of American behavior, which is increasing in much of Mexico, is not unusual and takes diverse forms. On the eve of World War II, the invasion of Tijuana and Ciudad Juárez by Pachucos, Mexican Americans from Los Angeles and El Paso, encouraged young Mexicans to wear long coats, peg-leg pants, and chains that dangled nearly to the floor. Later, the Pachucos became the border *cholos,* poor outcastes in a society that turned its back on them, who spoke in *caló* and danced, according to *Esquina Baja,* to the worst rock music in Mexico. All of the border cities have teenagers who, in the American manner, wear "mod" clothes—the girls in tiny miniskirts and the boys sporting baggy pants with the visors of baseball caps turned around—and listen to the latest rock. Mexicans of all classes, though often bronze of skin, worship whiteness; yet, in the American manner, the young offspring of the well-to-do, who would never dream of marrying a "darker" person, spend vacations on the beaches of Acapulco getting a "tan." Discotheques, which epitomize American culture, are the rage in Ciudad Juárez, while music and dance styles follow in step.

Juxtaposed with this worship of things foreign lies an anti-Americanism just below the surface. On this subject, a study of *maquila* workers is revealing. A majority of the women polled believed that factories in the United States provide better working conditions, better schools, and more room for individual initiative. Yet only one-fourth of them would want to have been born there. On "three occasions," said a music teacher, "I was offered legal residency in the United States, but I said to myself, if not in my homeland, I am a nobody elsewhere." In one of his writings, Crosthwaite tells of a conversation between a Mexican father and his young son in the United States that touches directly on this matter of national loyalty. The dark-skinned boy of thirteen had no problem; he had made up his mind: he wanted hot dogs, a vanilla shake, and french fries. It was the father who objected: "So many years of hard work so that this damn son of mine can think this way." The father wanted his son to ask for refried beans, *champurrado* (a heavy chocolate drink), and *chilaquiles*, tortillas cooked in a sauce. "Remember," he shouted, "we are Mexicans." The boy, "with his lips full of catsup, looked at him with brown eyes each day bluer, and left for his bedroom to see more television." Years later, Crosthwaite writes, "I asked the father: Oye, Jefe, if you are so Mexican, why did you stay in the United States, why didn't you save your dollars and return home?" After that, the father never again broached the subject, "and the eyes of his son turned dark blue with little white stars." Mexicans in Ciudad Juárez, according to another study, prefer their way of life: Yes, Americans work harder, but only because they have greater consumer aspirations. "In the wake of the collapse of the Soviet Union," to cite an editorial in *Cuadernos del Norte*, "old shibboleths surface again in the opulent society of the United States . . . racism, the myth of the chosen people, the desire to spread liberty American-style to the entire world."

Given this ambivalence, admiration for the United States, as well as envy, sits side by side with fear and distrust. It should be no surprise that Proposition 187, the California initiative to eliminate free emergency care in hospitals for undocumented immigrants and bar their children from public schools, exploded like a bombshell along the Mexican border. No city escaped public protests, as teachers, students, parents, and civic leaders in Reynosa, Nuevo Laredo, Ciudad Juárez, Nogales, Mexicali, and Tijuana roundly condemned what they labeled the "xenophobia" of Americans, at times hanging in effigy Pete Wilson, the governor of California who sponsored the measure. Protesters stood alongside the lines of cars leaving Mexico for the United States, exhorting their drivers to turn back and boycott American stores.

· · · 🏛 · · ·

But back to the matter of identity, to the question asked at the beginning of this discussion: How Mexican are border Mexicans, men and women who live in the shadow of the omnipotent gringo? Does love for the motherland, a cornerstone of Mexican nationality since the days of Father Miguel Hidalgo, still hold sway, as it did when José Antonio López

Alavés, a native of Huajuapan de León, a town in the state of Oaxaca, composed *Canción Mixteca*, a nostalgic remembrance of the *patria chica* (native region) joyfully sung today wherever Mexicans congregate. In 1912, when he gave life to this most Mexican of romantic ballads, López Alavés was a young man of twenty-three, had been a student in Mexico City for the previous six years, and was homesick for his native land. The words of his song, tender and sad, recall that *patria chica*:

> *How far I am from the land where I was born.*
> *Intense nostalgia captures my thoughts,*
> *And to see myself alone and forlorn as a leaf in the wind,*
> *I want to cry and die of a broken heart.*
> *Oh, land of the sun, I crave to see you.*

Unlike many today, José Antonio, the composer, knew who he was and where he had come from. But is that also true for the many who live on the northern fringes of the republic? One of these mornings, laments Rubén Vizcaíno, the people of Tijuana will awaken and ask themselves, "Who am I . . . North American, or Mexican?" When he arrived in Tijuana in 1949, he remembers with sadness, the people even "made love in English," part and parcel of how "Tijuana lost its identity." Critics frequently refer to these Mexican borderlands, as indicated earlier, as in danger of losing their nationality, though locals speak of the border as a bulwark of the national identity. The *fronterizos*, so goes this version, "are in a constant struggle, a battle . . . with the most powerful civilization on earth, daily defending not only national sovereignty but also that of Spanish America." Or, to quote Marta Paláu, a Mexican scholar of border affairs, "The impact of the United States on our lives is tremendous. . . . Our response as artists and intellectuals must be emphatic: not allow them to set the rules, and not accept the patterns they seek to impose."

These views, despite the bombastic rhetoric, do not withstand close scrutiny. Yes, gringo influences such as shopping malls, fast-food restaurants, miniskirts, and discotheques are a usual sight, but no more so than elsewhere in the republic. What is certain is that questions of identity, of the place of the border in Mexican society, are today much more complex than before the arrival of hundreds of thousands of Mexicans from the interior.

How does one begin to analyze this matter of border identity? Which of the two forces, the centrifugal or the centripetal, is the dominant one? Any answer, it appears to me, must first delve into the historical background, in order to identify which influences gave form to its contradictory unfolding. That means taking into account the traditional isolation from the heartland and the deficient means of communication and travel of the day. We cannot ignore the impact of the American conquest of 1847, nor the overwhelming presence of the United States, nor, as Mario Margulis and Rodolfo Tuirán remind us, today's impact of transnational capital in the guise of *maquiladoras*. NAFTA intensifies this concern over the loyalty of border residents, on the age-old assumption that the more contacts with the United States, the greater the loss of Mexican identity. Given the asymmetrical relationship, as well as the preponderance of American films, news broadcasts, television, popular music, and even fashion, the trade opening will inexorably lead to an erosion of the Mexican way of life. The final outcome, however, is still uncertain, because "one lives next door," to cite *Esquina Baja*, to a "culture so exclusive that it tolerates no rivals."

Young Mexican scholars, however, are not convinced. For them, the argument that Mexican culture is diluted at the border is a "tired, Byzantine discourse." "I know who I am," says Marco Antonio Samaniego, whose first novel won the Agustín Yañez prize for literature: "We are not *agringados* (Americanized)," but, he adds, "we are not, because of the border, just like other Mexicans." Are "we to believe," continues Sergio Gómez Montero, that "we are less Mexican because we don't dance the *jarabe* (hat dance) . . . don't pay homage to the cult of the Aztecs and don't worship the Virgin of Guadalupe?"

As José Carlos Lozano, whose views coincide with Tabuenca's, argues, geographical proximity is not the determining factor. On the basis of a study of popular opinion in Tijuana, Ciudad Juárez, and Nuevo Laredo, conducted by the Colegio de la Frontera, he concludes that social class and sex are better indicators of attitudes. Proximity to the United States aside, Mexican youth of the upper class, including those on the border, are less likely to uphold values associated with Mexican culture than those of the middle and working classes. Lozano stresses that benefits of class tend to determine the degree of loyalty to Mexican traditions on the one hand, or American ones, on the other. The well-off at the top of society's ladder are more apt to embrace values characteristic of a capitalist system, but underdogs hold on to traditional elements of popular culture—witness the homage bestowed by the poor of Ciudad Juárez on the Day of the Dead. The festivities may not be identical to those in Oaxaca, where they are earthshaking, but they are a celebration nonetheless. It serves to remind one that workers have a say in their culture, insist on ancestral contacts, reverence for their families, family gatherings, oral traditions, and respect for the past. Workers, after all, were the first to embrace the sport of baseball. Class alone clearly does not explain everything; gender, age, and years of education must also be taken into account. Women, to emphasize this once more, identify more closely with Mexican values than men, even when of identical social status. The middle class is the most ambiguous, at times mirroring the views of the lower class, at times those of the upper. Interestingly, Lozano concludes that Juarenses, whatever their class, are the most prone to ape U.S. culture and values.

Some analysts go even further, among them Jorge Bustamante. He tells everyone willing to listen that residents of border cities hold on more strongly to Mexican values. Geographic proximity, he says, reinforces the national identity: It "provides us with the means by which to measure ourselves. We are what the others are not." The American neighbor, in this equation, is "what I am not." We "tend to be more Mexican," to quote a businessman in Nogales, "precisely because we live next door to the United States." Miguel Escobar, a novelist from Sonora, echoes this view: "The constant confrontation with what is not Mexican accentuates the Mexican self-image." Border Mexicans, adds Bustamante, are not *agringandose* (becoming gringos) as much as they are joining a universal middle class. They behave more and more in the manner of middle classes throughout the world, not simply as an American version, as also occurs with the middle classes of Mexico City, Gudalajara, and Monterrey.

Obviously, other bonds unite Mexicans, no matter where they dwell. A common language is one of the pillars of a nation, and border Mexicans speak Spanish, whatever Chilangos may say. Yes, as Don Crispín acknowledged, scores of *fronterizos* speak English "because it is so necessary." Religion is another pillar, and nearly all Mexicans are Catholic, whether they attend church or not. A common historical heritage is one more cornerstone, which Mexicans, regardless of where they are, share. That past dates from preconquest civilizations, witness the giant statue of Cuauhtémoc that stands in the Zona del Río in Tijuana or those of Benito Juárez and Miguel Hidalgo, heroes of yesterday, elsewhere. Family ties also bind, and they are as strong along the border as in Mexico City.

∘ ∘ ∘ 🏵 ∘ ∘ ∘

Religious unity is another national pillar but, for all that, it is shaky on the border. The Catholic Church, to which Mexicans pledge allegiance, is as ancient as the border itself. Nuestra Señora de Guadalupe, the oldest temple, has stood in Ciudad Juárez since 1680. Yet Northerners, unlike Mexicans to the south, are not known for their intolerance on religious issues. In 1970, for instance, clergymen from Latin America and Mexico of the School of Liberation Theology, hardly a doctrine in accord with the Catholic leadership, met in Ciudad Juárez, to the applause of residents. Countless *fronterizos* are only nominally Catholic; men, as in other regions of Mexico, seldom attend mass, designated a woman's function. Children go because their mother wills it; but as they grow up, the boys stop attending church. Unions between men and women outside of the church are common and, among the working class, those who engage in them suffer little stigma.

Protestant groups, just the same, are making inroads, even when priests and nationalists label adherence to the sects an "assault on the Mexican identity." *Esquina Baja* calls "religious fragmentation" a "common spectacle in the cities of the border." Protestant preachers make inroads, yet their conquests are largely confined to the peripheral *colonias* of the urban poor. Nearly all belong to the most conservative sects, which are largely Fundamentalist and Pentecostalist. Some of these sects are throwbacks from the mid-nineteenth century. What is new is their success in converting *fronterizos* to their way of thinking. At present, there are approximately two hundred different sects in the five largest border cities. They represent more than two-thirds of those that operate in Mexico.

They first arrived in Monterrey and Matamoros about 1860, then the two most important towns. Melinda Rankin, of the American Biblical Society, was the pioneer, along with James Hickey, who did yeoman work on behalf of the Baptists. Along with Thomas H. Westrup, Hickey founded the first Baptist church in Mexico, and by the turn of the century, Monterrey had the largest Baptist congregation in the republic. By 1853, there were Protestant missionaries in Chihuahua, who mainly devoted their efforts to urban settlements, mining, and railroad centers. In towns such as Monterrey, Chihuahua City, Piedras Negras, Matamoros, and Ciudad Juárez, they established schools; by 1910, Tamaulipas had more Protestant than Catholic schools. Six years later, in the person of Andrés Osuna, Tamaulipas had the first Protestant governor in Mexico. By that time, schoolteachers, shop owners, railroad workers, and government clerks had embraced sundry sects. In the repatriation of Mexicans in the 1930s, hundreds of converts to Protestantism helped spread the gospel.

Until the 1960s, Protestants made only limited inroads but then gained ground due to the rapid urbanization and growing disparity between rich and poor, making their biggest gains in *colonias* of migrants. Few of these churches established up and down the border, most of them by Mexican converts, have ties to their counterparts in the United States. Where misery is the lot of the people, the Pentecostalists, with their doctrine of community and mutual aid, rapidly win converts—at the expense of the Catholic Church, which, like the PRI, provides scant solace for the desperately poor. Far behind the Pentecostalists are the Baptists, who enjoy moderate success, and then follow Presbyterians and Methodists. A recent addition is the Jehovah's Witnesses, with a total of over 1.3 million adherents, conferring on Mexico the distinction of having more of them than any other country in Latin America. Jehovah's Witnesses are also the only group that enjoys success among middle-class Mexicans.

Part Two

Binational Dimensions

7

Unwelcome Strangers

Migrants from other parts of the republic, as has been noted before, settled Mexican towns along the border and then built the cities, becoming a goodly part of the countryside and creating urban cores across the region. That was the experience of my parents, who, driven out by tumultuous times in Mexico, traveled north and settled on the California side of the Mexican border. My father, when my mother died, returned home to Mexico, but the blood of my mother darkens the soil of California where she lies buried. In this part of the world, to quote Eleanor Roosevelt, we are all "fellow immigrants"—aside from the Indians, quickly displaced by Spaniards, Mexicans, and Americans alike. To talk of borderlands, no matter which side, without including Mexican migrants is nonsense; they are integral to the history and development of the region.

Today, on both sides of the international boundary, Mexican migrants dwell among us, too, because of developments that transformed the contours of the American Southwest, changing it from a place of idle lands and lonely cowboys, as yet untouched by the progress of the twentieth century, to one of commercial farms, factories, and big cities. The lure of dollar-paying jobs drew people to the Southwest and, similarly, to the Mexican border, where dependent growth took root, first because of American dry laws that transferred liquor and gambling south, followed by raucous years of drunken soldiers, sailors, and tourists bent on seeing "Old Mexico" and, finally, the arrival of assembly plants. Mexican urbanization, essentially a migrant phenomenon, occurred in response to changes north of the border during World War II, which transformed cities such as San Diego and El Paso, pulled into the vortex of the national economy, into dynamic metropolises. The coming of age of the American Southwest summoned an influx of job-hungry migrants to states such as

California and Texas and simultaneously drew them to Baja California Norte, Chihuahua, and Tamaulipas.

Yet currently, these migrants rarely set eyes on a welcome mat; a majority of Anglo-Americans clearly do not want any more of them, and certainly not their women and children. Most demand that Washington beef up border control, and nearly three out of four want illegals rounded up and deported. Although at times displaying greater ambivalence, Mexican Americans, as a rule, share similar opinions. A recent study of attitudes in Brownsville, a city largely of Mexican origin, illustrates this. Of those polled, four out of five were Mexican by ancestral lineage and one-half were unable to reply in English; some 80 percent of them wanted migrants kept out. Attitudes vary, nonetheless: The more affluent voice greater understanding for the plight of migrants, as do the better-educated. Those in harmony with Mexican language and family traditions are far more sympathetic than Pochos, who worship the Anglo way of life; to be identified with Mexicans is anathema to them. The more time spent in the United States, the greater the hostility; third-generation Mexican Americans are less understanding than their grandparents. All the same, exceptions to these attitudes abound.

The behavior of El Pasoans, residents of a city also heavily Mexican, mirrors this generally unsympathetic attitude. When border patrol agents closed the gates to El Paso, a majority of its residents celebrated. Some people tied green ribbons, the color of the patrol, on their car antennas, while others took coffee and doughnuts to agents on duty on the levees of the Rio Grande. There were letters to newspapers from subscribers delighted that their tax dollars would no longer be spent on "illegal alien freeloaders at the food stamp offices and county hospital." "I don't want them over here," said Isabel Rodriguez, a young vendor. "I know they're human like me, but I don't go trying to wash people's windows when they don't want me to." Yet there was also a bit of ambivalence, particularly among the better-off. To quote one emcee at a Mexican-American Bar Association gala: "His wife was so cranky about doing her own housework," because her maid from Ciudad Juárez could not get across, "that she'd lost her libido." Operation Blockade, he joked distastefully, "impeded more than one kind of entry."

American dislike of Mexican immigrants, nevertheless, takes on the hue of a love-hate relationship, depending on what you do for a living and the economics of the times. Employers of cheap labor, who in past years were almost always growers, welcomed Mexicans with open arms. Eras of large-scale Mexican immigration and periods of deportation oscillate. In the days of World War I, when American boys went off to save Europe, stalwarts of the Cotton Growers Association in the Southwest avidly recruited Mexicans; when the war boom collapsed, their representatives, blaming Mexicans for domestic unemployment, deported them. Recovery enticed more Mexicans north, and later more deportations followed during the Great Depression. World War II, this time with American boys fighting to save the world, opened the door for more Mexicans, but another massive deportation, dubbed Operation Wetback, occurred with the end of prosperity in 1954. The cycles ebb and flow. Some scholars refer to this schizophrenic behavior as the "revolving door" and call the border patrol the gatekeeper.

Conversely, south of the border, some Mexicans fear that migrants exacerbate social problems—by building ramshackle housing, polluting water, spreading disease, and stressing an already decrepit public transportation system. Further, they tend to think their presence has caused a rise in the crime rate, a belief made worse by the recent arrival of newcomers from such places as Chiapas, Oaxaca, and Guerrero, where swarthy types prevail, never the darlings of old-line Northerners who prize lightness of skin and European attributes.

One of the headaches for some border residents is the incoming Indian tide from Oaxaca, made up largely of Mixtecos, with over five thousand of them dwelling in Tijuana. One-third or more are bilingual, speaking both Mixteco and Spanish; and some were born in these border provinces but, amazingly, remain Indian, keeping alive in these alien lands ancient traditions and customs, including the use of Indian tongues, while maintaining ties to the homeland. This is all the more impressive since their culture is predominantly oral; they employ their folktales, jokes, advice, and *refranes* to re-create what they left behind and thus uphold their own identity. The Mixtecos are poor people who make their homes in hovels on the hillsides of border cities. Discrimination from other Mexicans is their lot. They do the dirty work at the lowest pay. The sale of tourist crafts, which they make themselves, is one of their mainstays. As street vendors, they are part of the "charm" American tourists seek, yet they are the first to be driven off their place of vending by the police, who not infrequently prey on them. In Nogales, Indian vendors are shunted off to the least desirable tourist locations, but municipal authorities in Saltillo, the capital of Coahuila, have shipped them back home.

These racists believe that *indios* are a national embarrassment because they contribute little to society and lower Mexico's standing in the ("white") nation next door. Leonardo Barroso, the wealthy wheeler-dealer from a border city in Carlos Fuentes's *La Frontera de Cristal,* openly displays his bigotry when he comments that he finds it "annoying to purchase first-class tickets and still have to sit and watch *prietos* (swarthy men) in dirty work clothes and straw hats" file past while he awaits the departure of an airplane. These swarthy types, all the same, flee grinding poverty, poor jobs, and unemployment wrought by recurrent economic debacles, not infrequently the consequences of ill-advised policies urged by those like Barroso.

Scholars concede that in the United States, the immigration question antedates Mexicans. Popular concern in the United States surfaced when the character of the newly arriving changed. Until then, Northwestern Europeans, Germans, Scandinavians, and the English held the upper hand. They were usually light-skinned Protestants and could easily adapt to the prevailing cultural norms established during the colonial era. Anxiety over the nature and number of the newcomers emerged as Italians, Slavs, and Jews from Southern Europe became the immigrants. They were different, according to the prejudices of the day, often Catholic, speaking strange languages, culturally apart from Nordic peoples, the original colonizers. So long as the economy prospered and there were jobs for everyone, popular misgivings remained beneath the surface. The depression of 1893, and those that from time to time followed, ended the honeymoon. When hard times surfaced again in the early 1920s, Congress, in response to xenophobic outcries, legislated quotas for the unwelcome.

∘ ∘ ∘ 🏵 ∘ ∘ ∘

That historical introduction provides a backdrop for the issue of Mexican immigration to the Southwest, so much in the headlines in the 1990s. In this region of the world, Mexicans, of course, have been around for centuries. At first, there was merely a handful of them, but as the railroad opened up Texas, Arizona, and California to mining and agriculture, Mexicans passed over the border in larger and larger numbers, lured by the promise of better-paying jobs. The ten years of civil strife prompted by the Revolution of 1910, as well as by World War I, when American men went off to Europe, drew more Mexicans north. Some of the immigrants even ventured as far as Chicago.

The curtain on that era was lowered with the Great Depression, which left Anglo-Americans competing for jobs once relegated to Mexicans. Rural communities throughout the Southwest had a surplus of labor, particularly after Okies from Oklahoma, Arkansas, and Texas appeared in California by the hundreds of thousands, driven out of their communities by poverty, unemployment, and dust storms, as John Steinbeck vividly documented in *The Grapes of Wrath*. Soon a cry could be heard that Mexicans were a burden and should be sent home; there were no jobs for them. In the early 1930s, perhaps half a million were deported and sent back to Mexico. The children of many of those departed were U.S.-born and legally American citizens. That was a matter of no consequence to federal and state authorities, who rounded up Mexicans by the trainload. This draconian policy, slightly modified, was repeated again in 1964, this time

with the repatriation of braceros, Mexicans imported during War World II
to relieve labor shortages, who had lingered on during an era of economic
expansion.

The collapse of the bracero program dealt a harsh blow to Mexican border communities. Expecting to return to jobs in the United States, former
braceros clogged the streets of border cities, especially in Tijuana and Ciudad Juárez, and their numbers were increased by rural migrants from the
interior of Mexico who had been pushed off their lands by the Green Revolution, which favored big agriculture. Border cities became way stations
on routes to the United States, but as so often happens, transience led to
permanence, an occurrence that swelled border populations and multiplied unemployment horrors.

Until 1986, Washington's policy on illegal or, to use a Mexican term,
"undocumented" immigrants, consisted largely of intercepting them at
the border or occasionally at their jobs and dispatching them home. The
Immigration Reform and Control Act of 1986 (IRCA) sought to keep them
out by granting amnesty to those who had resided in the United States for
a specified period. It declared the hiring of illegal migrants to be a civil
and sometimes criminal violation of the law. The legislation temporarily
slowed the influx, until Mexicans realized that the act was more bluff
than substance because employers were not punished. Job-hungry migrants, as well as employers of cheap labor, were delighted. As Leslie
Sklair notes, the absence of sanctions for employers who hire these Mexicans shows the interests of the U.S. government: The border, as official behavior demonstrates, is a source of cheap labor for American employers,
"both explicitly as in the bracero program . . . and implicitly in that employers" take "no risks in hiring undocumented labor." Evidence reveals
that the U.S. government has usually given employers access to Mexican
labor. Clearly, the act of 1986 did not resolve the problem of illegal immigration; the number of apprehensions climbed upward, the result of a
beefed-up border patrol, but so did successful incursions by migrants.

º º º 🏛 º º º

Behind this scenario lies a racial prejudice as American as apple pie. To
cite an American scholar, "Ideas of race superiority are a clear and per-
ceptible thread that runs through the warp and woof of the American fabric," a belief that is "ingrained . . . with a tenacity almost unmatched by
that of any other doctrine."

Like the Southern Europeans of the late nineteenth century, Mexicans
were different, poles apart from Anglo-Americans. They were dark-
skinned, Catholic, and spoke Spanish, and they represented distinct cultural norms. They did not fit in, so went the popular prejudice. Before the

Great Depression turned public opinion openly hostile, horse-riding rangers had lynched Mexicans in Texas, and conditions for these Mexicans included segregated communities, "Mexican schools," speak-only English rules in schools, balcony seating in movie houses, and bans on their use of public swimming pools.

Racial prejudice, though more subtle, still lingers on. It may be strongest against migrants from Southern Mexico, from states such as Oaxaca and Guerrero, whose citizens, their facial features undeniably Indian, suffer the greatest likelihood of being victimized by Americans. As with African Americans, a racist criteria is applied since it involves Mexicans with Indian traits. Yet this is only partly true, as Mexicans shorn of "Indian features" are also prey to discrimination. Occasionally, just being Mexican and poor ignites the hostility of whites. The truth is that when one is poor and Mexican in the Southwest, one never knows what might occur. As civil rights advocates justly claim, if the preponderance of immigrants, legal or not, was Northern European, the outcry would be muffled. Today's targets are Mexicans, Central Americans, Haitians, and poor Asians, and the lies told about them resemble what was earlier said about Jews, Italians, Greeks, and, of course, African Americans. It is not uncommon to hear Anglo-Americans refer to Mexican immigrants as criminals, welfare cheaters, and, as the *Diary of an Undocumented Immigrant* recalls, also as "*chivos,* or goats, because of the odor we exude"—the accusers forgetting that, if true, the "odor" can be explained by the absence of bathing facilities and clean clothing.

Today, when a global economy upsets traditional labor patterns, these attitudes again jump to the fore. Public opinion polls, especially in California and the Southwest, show growing public antagonism toward Mexican immigration. As a *Los Angeles Times* poll verifies, a majority of Californians "are fed up with illegal immigration, with 86 percent calling it a major or moderate problem." Three out of four Californians want to use the national guard to patrol the Mexican border. Governor Pete Wilson of California, whose presidential aspirations led him to make illegal immigration a key plank of his campaign, has even called for a constitutional amendment to strip citizenship rights from American-born children of illegal immigrants. Obviously, that hardly fits in with the view of Mexicans, who see outmigration as basically an economic phenomenon of benefit to the United States, since Mexicans fill jobs shunned by American workers.

If there is a cost to be paid, what is it? That is the question asked by most Americans. Do illegal immigrants contribute more than they take out? The debate on that is yet to end, though most analysts agree that Americans profit from their stay. As Michael Fix and Jeffrey S. Passel show, "when all levels of government are considered, immigrants generate significantly more in taxes paid than they cost in services" rendered.

But, as they acknowledge, the surplus is unevenly distributed, with the federal government getting the lion's share.

Unfortunately, the literature on the contributions of immigrants is both sketchy and contentious; the pool of data is small, so informal guesswork, assumptions, and value judgments usually control results. In the arena of policy studies, claims to objectivity must be taken with a grain of salt; more often than not, researchers' beliefs about the nature of the world mold conclusions. In the view of one of them, "Most . . . tend to make assumptions that maximize costs and minimize revenues," and "most are done by and for governments with an agenda." Thus, there are sundry interpretations. The multiplicity of studies on immigration, as one expert advises, "strongly counsels caution and prudence." That, in my opinion, makes good sense.

Moreover, since statistics, which all of these scholars utilize, are easily manipulated, they seldom tell the whole story. In the immigration debate, they are used to support widely divergent views: One set of figures can claim that illegal and legal immigration drains $42 billion yearly from the national economy, whereas another, from an entirely different perspective, can cite a net contribution of $25 billion. In California, the Urban Institute estimates that in 1994 illegal immigrants paid $732 million in taxes, about 17 percent of the taxes collected. Yet Texas is the only state that calculates the net cost of illegal immigration. According to a report for that same year by the Texas Office of Immigration and Refugee Affairs, 550,000 illegal immigrants contributed $290 million in annual revenues, but their cost to the state was $456 million. Of that sum, education ate up 68 percent and health care 19 percent. Statistics from the governor's office in California for 1993 claim that state and local governments spent $2.4 billion a year on illegals, calculated to be a population of 2.83 million, with nearly half that money going to education. A study by the Urban Institute insists that schooling illegal children costs only $1.28 billion, nearly half of that claimed by California's figures. Another study, this one generated by the Clinton administration for 1992, reveals that California, Florida, Texas, New York, Illinois, Arizona, and New Jersey, the states most heavily affected, "spend more money on federally mandated programs than they collected in taxes from the overwhelmingly young and poor population of illegal immigrants." A recent study conducted in 1997 by the National Research Council reaffirms some of these assumptions. Mandated and financed by the federal government, it concludes that immigrants, both legal and illegal, give an annual net boost to the national economy of $10 billion, while providing much-needed low-wage labor and helping to keep some consumer prices low.

An *argumentum ad hominem* is that public costs are high because illegal immigrants feast on welfare. That is highly doubtful, though, as in the case of California, taxpayers share a bigger burden. With few exceptions, immigrants are of working age, young men and women less likely than natives of the same age to receive welfare benefits. At the state level, the picture is mixed, because not all state governments assume identical responsibilities. Most migrants, in fact, are barred from receiving public assistance, except for emergency care under Medicaid and the federal nutrition programs for women, infants, and children. Only a small minority benefits from aid, largely through relatives who are American citizens. Texas denies welfare help to illegal immigrants. Nonetheless, the fastest-rising state expense for Aid to Families with Dependent Children, until recently the main welfare program for California, is for American-born children of illegal immigrants. Spending for them has nearly quintupled during the last five years. The Los Angeles County Department of Health Services figures that almost two out of three mothers who give birth in the county's four public hospitals are undocumented. These women account for 28,000 births, and because of their American-born children, they will be able to claim welfare benefits on their behalf.

One thing is clear: States, counties, and local communities bear the burden of immigration. To cite an editorial in the *New York Times*, "States . . . inundated by illegal immigrants are unfairly bearing the costs." The National Research Council bears this out. The head of a household in California, one of six states with huge immigrant populations, yearly pays $1,178 in added taxes, money used to pay for schooling and health care for immigrants. Cities such as Los Angeles are burdened by costs associated with new immigrants. The plea of the governors of Florida and California for extra money to provide for education and emergency health care for these people, the editorial of the *Times* proclaims, "is just." The newspaper cites a study by the Center for Immigration Studies showing that education and medical care represent about two-thirds of the $7 billion spent each year on illegal immigrants. Nationwide, the same study concluded, it costs $4.5 billion each year to educate both illegal immigrants and children born to them in the United States. At this level, state governments provide most of the public services the undocumented receive, but the federal government collects nearly all of the taxes they pay. In California, for instance, perhaps 16 percent of the students enrolled in public schools are foreign-born, although they are not necessarily illegals. That cost is borne by the state's taxpayers, not the federal government.

Given the nature of this debate, it is not surprising that over three-fourths of Californians who read or hear these claims by politicians and others believe illegal immigrants take more out of the economy than they contribute. For example, an unhappy Anglo-American resented cutbacks in his Medi-Cal benefits that he felt occurred because "these people come over from Mexico and they get on welfare. The more I talk about it the angrier I get." The polls reflect, says the *Los Angeles Times*, "the historical tendency to open the door when the economy is growing, and to shut it when times are hard."

Visibility, I believe, is crucial here. Due to changes in the global economy, Americans are more aware of Mexican immigrants than before. In the past, they put down and maintained the tracks of the railroads, entire families staying in "section houses"; they planted and harvested the crops on farms; and in states such as Arizona, they dug the ore from copper mines in Bisbee and Globe. These activities occurred far from cities where most Anglo-Americans made their homes. The global network changes that. Now, Mexicans work increasingly in the cities, where they are more visible, especially in California, home to a majority. The total numbers are not the issue; certainly, there are more undocumented today, but not in relation to the entire U.S. population, which has multiplied since the 1940s. Currently, there are about 22 million foreign-born residents in the United States, or about 8.5 percent of the population. That figure may sound high, but not if one remembers that from 1870 to 1920 the percentage was nearly twice that number. During that historical peak, about one in seven Americans was born in a foreign country. Today, of the 1.1 million foreigners who settle annually in the United States, only 200,000 to 300,000 are illegals. Of these, only one out of five is a Mexican. Despite the distortions, the truth is that a majority of illegals enter the United States quite legally but overstay their visas; they form the majority of illegal immigrants. Only one-third of the "undocumented" population is Mexican. Of this number, two-thirds, perhaps as many as 1.7 million, reside in California, largely in Los Angeles, and about 15 percent live in Texas. San Diego County, which is closer to the border, has fewer than 200,000 illegal immigrants.

International migratory flows have been around for a long time—just witness the centuries-old settlement by Europeans of the United States, Argentina, and Uruguay. By 1930, some 38 million Europeans had come to the United States, most of them determined to work for a short time, save money, and return home. More than one-third of them did. And for some nationalities the figure is even higher; 80 percent of Balkan immigrants did not stay. The two-way flow did not end until World War I. Without the forced migration of Africans, Brazil and the Caribbean would be entirely different. Demographers estimate that, at a minimum, the number of international migratory workers exceeded 20 million, not counting their families. This was a worldwide phenomenon, which included Europe, Africa, the Middle East, the Americas, and Asia.

To emphasize this once again: Mexicans are simply more visible; they stand on street corners of cities in the Southwest anxiously waiting for a job offer; they are janitors, dishwashers, cooks, maids, waiters, and gardeners. Everyone sees them. There is always a time lag working here—between the time of the public perception and the actual number of Mexican immigrants. So long as Mexicans stayed on farms or mines, they tended to remain "invisible" for a longer time; but as they join the service industries, the public becomes more aware of them. They are part of the urban milieu. When hard times strike and jobs are scarce, Anglo-Americans, and Mexican Americans, too, focus their ire on the visible alien.

In the past, the Ku Klux Klan, the Native Sons, the Daughters of the American Revolution, and organizations of similar bent, as part of their "whites-only" propaganda, fanned the anti-immigrant fires. Today, that crusade has been taken up by others, Malthusian ideologues among them, who vent their ire on Mexicans. One is the Federation for American Immigration Reform (FAIR), the offspring of Zero Population Growth advocates who, according to the *Nation*, received at least $800,000 from the Pioneer Fund, a right-wing philanthropic group that sponsors studies on race and intelligence. FAIR, which labels immigrants the real menace to American life, urges sealing the borders. One Republican assemblyman in California, who shares FAIR's stance, calls for the "mining of the border" to keep out Mexican illegals. With a membership of fifty thousand, the well-funded FAIR wields political clout in Washington, Sacramento, and in the courts of public opinion. In 1986, it opposed the Immigration Reform and Control Act, which opened doors for residency to about 3 million undocumented aliens, half of them in California.

It is not simply the recession of the 1990s that explains this anti-immigrant sentiment; many Americans, as the support for FAIR symbolizes, do not want "their culture and race" diluted any more. During 1993, in the legislature of California, over twenty anti-immigrant bills were introduced, mostly by conservatives who once hailed cheap Mexican labor as healthy for the economy. On occasion, the anti-Mexican sentiment is striking, as when William J. Knight, a Republican assemblyman from a Los Angeles suburb, circulated this piece of doggerel from one of his admirers.

> *Everything is mucho good.*
> *Soon we own the neighborhood.*
> *We have a hobby: It's called*
> *Breeding.*
> *Welfare pay for baby feeding.*

Or, as Elton Gallegly, another California Republican, warned, "Our nation is being quietly and systematically overrun by wave upon wave of illegal immigrants."

The evidence indicates a rising prejudice against Mexicans. Illegal immigration can be harmful to the immigrants themselves; as we shall see later on, migrants are victimized on both sides of the border. Employers pay them as little as possible, housing is expensive and poor, and community services such as medical care through doctors and hospitals not always available. Acts of violence increase, particularly in California and Texas. The abuse includes beatings, insults, humiliations, and arbitrary confiscation of personal documents by police and the border patrol. People throw garbage at the newcomers and bulldoze immigrant camps, and criminals prey on them. In November 1992, bullets from a high-powered rifle killed two young Mexicans walking on a road in north San Diego County. The killers, two high-school students, belonged to white-supremacist groups. At the trial, one of them declared that he "hated Mexicans." Residents of San Diego are especially active in demanding that the federal government take measures to stop Mexicans from illegally crossing the border. In the spring of 1992, more than a thousand of them stood at the San Ysidro border and turned their car lights on Mexico in order to show public support for the struggle to seal the border. Rodger Hedgecock, a former mayor of San Diego jailed for political fraud, was one of their leaders. One Young Mexican from the Colegio de la Frontera Norte recently told me about how frightened he was when driving from San Antonio to El Paso. One evening when he was low on gasoline, he left the freeway to enter a small town, only to see four white men beating two Mexican workers. Fearing he might be next, he wanted to drive on, but finding the one gas station in town closed, he stayed in a motel. He slept poorly, he told me.

Pete Wilson banked on that sentiment when he made immigrant bashing and, covertly, race the focus of his successful reelection campaign and his amateurish bid for the presidency in 1995. Illegal immigration, as he recognized, had emerged as red-hot politics. In a time when global economics are turning the job hopes of millions of Americans topsy-turvy, Wilson and his fellow demagogues are telling voters that illegal immigration is the culprit. Why, asked Wilson in a full-page political advertisement in the *New York Times*, "does the United States government continue to reward illegal immigration at such cost to the American people?" That he had Mexicans in mind was made clear by the demand that President Clinton "use the ratification of NAFTA as a tool to secure the cooperation of the Mexican government in stopping massive illegal immigration." Wilson, as Robert Rubin of the Lawyers' Committee for Civil Rights, a San Francisco group, recognized, was raising the red flag "in a racially divisive manner."

Demographers predict that California will have a Latino majority by the year 2040. Whether that occurs or not, it is still certain that by the turn of the century, Hispanics—the official term for all Latin Americans—will represent about 13 percent of the total national population and will be the largest minority in states such as California, which already is nearly 30 percent Hispanic. This frightens many white Americans, who see their universe changing and their monopoly on culture endangered. To "Save Our State," the slogan of Californians in 1994, the voters passed California's Proposition 187, which denies schooling to the children of illegal immigrants and medical help to their parents. As Jim Gogek of the *San Diego Union-Tribune* wrote, Proposition 187 "is the last gasp of a segment of white Americans who are trying to . . . return national demographics to the 1950s."

That is frightening because, in some ways, they are succeeding. "All I wanted was a job," one Mexican woman complained, "but they made [me] feel like a criminal. Crossing the border was simply not worth the price; it is better to stay here [Ciudad Juárez] and struggle." One place where the hostile enjoy success is in the public schools. According to the Harvard Project on School Desegregation (1993), despite three decades of efforts to integrate public schools, the population of Hispanic students in largely minority schools is on the rise. Like blacks, poverty concentrates them in large cities, mostly in the Southwest. Enrollments in these schools are over 50 percent Hispanic; 66 percent of Hispanic students, or 3.7 million out of a total of 5 million, attend them. These are the highest percentages in a quarter of a century. The states with the most segregated schools are Texas (41.7 percent) and California (35.4 percent), followed by New Mexico and Arizona. The percentage of Hispanic students in predominantly segregated schools has gone from the 55 percent of 1968 to 73 percent in 1991.

Mexicans, for all that, are not just victims. They fight back, as the history of agricultural workers in California fields amply demonstrates. Caesar Chavez became a national hero by leading strike after strike on behalf of field hands in California and their right to organize and join a labor union. Earlier, Mexican workers battled valiantly against Phelps Dodge in the copper mines of Arizona. Mexicans in Tijuana, who wanted to protest what they refer to as Mexican bashing, specifically Proposition 187, organized a boycott that caused, the *New York Times* reported, a loss of several million dollars to San Diego business. Proposition 187 awakened young Mexican Americans in high school and college to take to the streets, reviving the dormant Chicano movement. In October 1994, the *Los Angeles Times* reported that up to 100,000 demonstrators marched from the East Side of Los Angeles to downtown in a boisterous condemnation "of Proposition 187 . . . and its best-known advocate, Governor Pete Wilson." And the results of the elections in California in 1996 show that Mexican Americans are voting in larger and larger numbers.

o   o   o   🏛   o   o   o

Concerning why Mexicans come to the United States, there is both a push and a pull factor, as sociologists argue. In the United States, jobs await Mexicans; and Mexico, clearly, is hardly a wealthy country. Despite the often-stated claims of American pundits, Mexico is not a horn of plenty waiting to be efficiently exploited by the expertise of knowledgeable men and women (read: Americans). Much of its land is poor and lacks water for agriculture, particularly in the northern provinces, most of them being arid or virtual deserts. By design and accident, Mexican architects of national policy allowed population growth to get out of hand; unless a scientific miracle occurs, Mexico, given today's blueprint, cannot adequately support its 90 million people. Since the 1940s, to exacerbate matters, economic thinking favors the better-off, particularly urbanites, at the expense of workers and dirt farmers. For this shift away from the ideals of the Revolution of 1910, Washington's politics also bear some of the responsibility; increasingly conservative American administrations, at the beck and call of transnational corporations, openly side with Mexicans who rush to dismantle the safety net left behind by reformers of an earlier era. The cold war antics of the Truman administration, for example, opened the door for the assault of the corrupt Miguel Alemán regime on independent labor; the tenure of Fidel Velázquez, at ninety-four years of age still boss of the CTM, the biggest of the puppet unions, dated from this time. The sabotage of Article 27, the agrarian plank in the Constitution of 1917, by the Salinas clique is just the latest blow. The resulting neglect of Mexico's poor, for which both the Mexican *burguesía* (bourgeoisie) and American policy architects are responsible, partly explains why migrants from that country invade the United States. Unless Mexico puts its economic house in order, which will require a major change in Washington's designs, the Mexican immigrant tide is bound to continue.

Bad times in Mexico, when jobs that pay decently dry up, simply push more Mexicans northward. In *Diary of an Undocumented Immigrant,* a poor Zapotec from Oaxaca laments: "My luggage is a small vinyl suitcase that holds one change of clothes. It's a bag for a person who has left home for a couple of days, but I don't know when I'll return to my village." For young Mexicans, there are either no jobs or poorly paid jobs. As Carlos Talavera, bishop of Coatzoalcos, says, "The undocumented go to the United States for economic reasons." Or to quote Art Torres, a former California senator, "If there are jobs here, people will come. No matter if you have . . . the National Guard or the Seventh Fleet in the Sea of Cortes."

That said, it must not be forgotten that the jobless, the worst off, seldom venture north, and for a simple reason: It takes money to make the trip, to survive in cities such as Tijuana or Ciudad Juárez while waiting to get across, to pay a *coyote* (a guide), and to buy food in California or Texas until work is found. Approximately three out of four undocumented immigrants held jobs in Mexico before setting off on their adventure. A wage differential primarily lures Mexicans north; so long as they earn one-eighth of the American wage, they will come. It is a matter of marginality. As the sociologist Joan W. Moore says, "Given rising poverty and the horrendous inequality of income in Mexico, the real question is not why so many Mexicans come to the United States, but why so few?" Or, to quote one Mexican worker, "I would like to go back to Mexico, but I like to eat too." The terrible poverty of rural Mexico, partly induced by government policies, Alicia Castellanos reminds us, explains why some Mexicans migrate. They come not because they think that life is that much better but because there is no hope of improving their lot at home. As one woman said: "If you are alone and have children to support, there is no future for you. That is why I am trying to go to the United States." Life is better in Southern California, a man from Guerrero commented, "than it was three years ago when [I] gave up selling T-shirts to tourists in Acapulco at $7 a day to compete for jobs paying $5 an hour in Santa Ana."

Similarly, the evidence indicates that instability at home, such as peso devaluations, may encourage some Mexicans to leave, but not everyone. How, after all, does the fall of the peso affect a poor Mixteco campesino from Oaxaca? Whatever the monetary gyrations, he is simply poor; when he comes to the United States, he may do so for reasons that have little if anything to do with the current value of the peso. All the same, after the devaluation of 1994, arrests at El Paso by the border patrol, in January 1995, rose by 25 percent over the same month of the previous year; a Ciudad Juárez expert quoted in *El Paso Times* testified that this was one sign that the slumping peso was boosting illegal crossings. Detentions of illegal migrants, by the same token, are up along the entire border, at some points of entry more than at others, one such being Arizona crossings, partly the result of crackdowns by the border patrol at San Ysidro. Still, care must be taken not to confuse the number of crossings with the ups and downs of tides of migrations; they can be vastly different, as Mexican scholars rightly point out. However, devaluations or not, as a border ballad laments, Mexicans trek north:

> *I am going to the United States to seek my livelihood.*
> *Goodbye my beloved patria, I carry you in my heart.*
> *Do not think ill of me because I abandon you; poverty*
> *and misery are to blame.*

Then again, Mexicans travel to the United States because they find work there. If they did not, they would stay home—that is obvious. This is the pull factor. Patterns of migrations from Chihuahua, for instance, coincide with demands for labor in Texas. Economic reasons, as Bishop Talavera argues, are what motivates Mexicans to look for work in a foreign country that, if public opinion polls are correct, does not want them. There is always some kind of need for cheap Mexican labor in certain regions of the United States. And "cheap" is the key word, as Jorge Bustamante remembers from personal experience: "They took us to a ranch" and "the driver of the truck got out. . . . His first words were 'there's lots of you.' Then he said: 'let's see . . . raise your hands if you want to work for a dollar an hour.' Nearly everyone . . . raised his hand. 'No . . . there are still too many of you.'" Bustamante reports that the driver repeated this procedure until he found seven men willing to work for $.50 an hour. He told the others to "get on your way fast so I don't have to call the police and have you cited for trespassing."

As noted, the need for Mexican labor fluctuates during economic downturns. Yet with the exception of the Great Depression years, when one-fourth of the labor force had no jobs, demand never disappears entirely. To the contrary, hard times drive employers to hire cheap Mexican labor in order to lower operating expenses. That way they survive the crisis or, as their critics argue, keep profits up on the backs of cheap Mexican labor. The character of migrants, too, is changing. The costs of traveling north result in a de facto selectivity; the rural poor are no longer the majority. Currently, more than two-thirds are city types who look for jobs in hotels, restaurants, and bars and as maintenance workers, and the Valley of Mexico is the biggest supplier.

Regardless of that, however, life goes on as before: In California, for instance, according to statistics by the California Labor Department, illegal workers account for 90 percent of the labor force in agriculture, the garment industry, and day labor, as well as 80 percent of restaurant employees and 70 percent of domestics. Even the rural poor prefer jobs in factories or the construction industry or in private homes as nannies, maids, or gardeners. The increase in the number of urban migrants brings north a better-educated lot; never has the schooling level been higher. A majority of adult migrants have at least eight years of schooling, and some attended *prepas* (high schools); their ranks include technicians and professionals left out of the job market. According to the Mexican Ministry of Foreign Affairs, twenty thousand primary schoolteachers labor in the United States, some even in the agricultural fields. Urban women are also arriving in bigger numbers, again because they cannot find work at home and not, as formerly, simply to join husbands. By 1990, women represented up to 30 percent of the total volume of migrants, and they tended to have more years of schooling than men. "I worked alongside of teachers, physicians, and office clerks," recalled one undocumented woman, "persons with university titles." The newcomers tend to be young, the majority under thirty years old. Many of them are first-time border jumpers; this is their first experience as illegals in the United States.

Until recently, most Mexicans who ventured north stayed temporarily but then went home. Every year during the early 1920s, between one-half to three-fourths of the Mexicans who came to Texas returned to Mexico. Some never went back to the United States. Whether in Texas or California, few became American citizens; they remained loyal to their mother country. That delighted Mexican officials. Money sent home by Mexicans working in the United States was Mexico's fourth-largest source of national revenue. In 1993 alone, Mexican migrants sent back $3.4 billion. One observer believes that perhaps more than one-fifth of Mexico's population depends, to some extent, on income from family and neighbors laboring in the Unites States. To the chagrin of Mexican nationalists, the loyalist habit has weakened since the 1980s. Mexicans increasingly stay in the United States, and larger numbers of them become American citizens. Apparently, anxiety over Proposition 187, the California initiative, frightened some, fearful their children would be denied schooling, into applying for American citizenship. As the *New York Times* pontificated, "This . . . calls into question . . . the belief that non-white immigrants lack the will to adopt American values."

○　○　○　🏵　○　○　○

How many illegal immigrants are there? Answers abound, but they tend to be highly political; in a debate on the merits of illegal immigration, they generate more heat than light. Officials of the U.S. Immigration and Naturalization Service (INS) claim, as of 1997, that over 5 million illegals were residing in the United States, with more than 2 million of them in California, or 6.3 percent of that state's population; they accounted for only 3.7 percent of the population in Texas, the state with the next-largest total. Mexico is the birthplace of 54.1 percent of all the illegal immigrants, followed by El Salvador, with just 6.7 percent.

These figures, as we shall see, merely confirm what many suspect: Nobody knows exactly how many clandestine visitors there are. However, the Binational Study on Migration of 1997, cosponsored by the Mexican and U.S. governments, perhaps the most authoritative study, calculates that the Mexican-born population in the United States numbers between 7 and 7.3 million and, of that figure, from 2.3 to 2.4 million reside in the country illegally. Yearly, just over 100,000 undocumented Mexicans settled in the United States during the past decade, far fewer than once thought. But, as a Mexican demographer who participated in the study concedes, since "no controversy ever ends, so it would be ingenuous for us to think this will resolve all the disputes over migration."

Clearly, estimates vary widely. Still, INS figures raise more questions than they resolve; the agency simply lacks the resources to keep tabs on who enters clandestinely. Its figures, Bustamante believes, distort reality, since they represent the number of detentions at the border, overlooking the obvious fact that the same individual can be detained numerous times. Also, by exaggerating numbers of illegals, the figures exacerbate anti-Mexican sentiment in the United States. Instead of counting INS-style, Bustamante urges using a method he calls "circular migration," which recognizes that countless individuals alternate stays in both countries until either age, success, or failure determines where they will live. If that theory holds up, it substantially reduces the INS count of crossings and stays in the United States. Whether a migrant decides to make a home in the Unites States also depends on the relatives the person has there. The fewer family members there are, the more likely a migrant is to return home. Nearly all INS apprehensions are of temporary labor migrants caught more than once. Only about one in three are from Mexico. Canada provides the largest number of immigrants to the United States; however, the biggest pool of illegal immigrants comes not from Mexico or Asia but from Europe.

Until the 1930s, Ciudad Juárez was the principal port of entry for Mexicans. Today, it is joined by Tijuana, Mexicali, Nuevo Laredo, and Matamoros. The San Ysidro border accounts for over half of illegal entries, followed by Ciudad Juárez. Matamoros, with only 5 percent of illegal entries, has the least. After the Hong Kong–China border crossing, San Ysidro is the busiest in the world; in 1992, it also had 43 percent of all apprehensions along the border. Volume of illegal crossings fluctuates: Nogales, in 1994, ranked second only to San Ysidro in numbers of detentions, followed by McAllen-Reynosa.

To emphasize this point again: Migrant Mexicans enter the United States because Americans hire them. In the words of one El Paso employer: "I do not care whether I hire a green carder, orange carder or wet—anyone will do so long as he is warm." By 1907, nearly six thousand Mexicans were being admitted monthly to El Paso. Until 1950, the number was relatively small; then their number rose, until a record high was reached from 1980 to 1990. Over these years, a rosy myth evolved in Mexico, about an uncle or cousin who struck it rich in the United States by dint of hard work, a story that encouraged others to hazard the adventure. Late in the nineteenth century, the Mexican tide swept in from the border states, for Texas from Tamaulipas, Nuevo León, and Coahuila; the Mexicans who arrived in California hailed from Sonora; and those in New Mexico from Chihuahua. Today, their origin is usually farther south, principally from the Federal District, Guanajuato, Jalisco, and Michoacán, but also from Zacatecas and Chihuahua. It is not uncommon in Southern California to find Mixtecos from Oaxaca, who often speak in their native tongue. In Guanajuato, Jalisco, and Michoacán, one encounters families that have sent migrants to the United States for four generations. Unable to offer jobs and plentiful economic opportunities, these states have traditionally expelled their workers.

In recent years, the use of Mexican labor has assumed greater importance. Even in times of economic disequilibrium and high unemployment, U.S. society is profoundly dependent on it. With unemployment in the United States today officially hovering around 5 percent, and certainly higher in reality, Mexicans still find jobs. The hiring of Mexicans has increased in such sectors as agriculture, construction, domestic work, small industry, and the food services. Nor are domestic labor shortages the answer; as labor economist Harry Bernstein argues, "Americans do the same hard, dirty jobs that illegal immigrants are willing to perform." The explanation, Arturo Santamaría Gómez writes, is globalization, which prizes pools of low-paid and vulnerable workers. The use of undocumented workers, he goes on, "is emerging as a pillar of the reconstructed economic order." The United States benefits most from the labor of Mexican workers, but the Mexican state, by ridding itself of a jobless hangover, profits as well. The United States enjoys the enviable position of having at its gates an endless supply of cheap labor. The overwhelmingly temporary commitment of these workers meshes neatly with the kind of jobs they perform, essentially low-wage occupations shorn of job security, benefits, and hope of advancement. Since most Mexicans do not initially plan to stay in the United States, these drawbacks trouble them little.

Do immigrants, legal or otherwise, take jobs away from Americans? The answer must be ambivalent. Immigrants may take jobs from lowskilled workers, particularly in areas of a weak economy with an abundance of cheap migrant labor. African Americans are rarely hurt by migrant competition, although they can be in regions of high migration in recessionary years. Migrants hurt the job chances of other migrants, specifically those who arrived just before them. On the whole, it is other Mexicans who are adversely affected. No strong evidence suggests that immigrants lower wages. As Fix and Passel point out, the growth and decline of wages appear unrelated to immigration: "Indeed, wage growth is no slower and may be faster where immigration rates are high than where they are low." On balance, migrants do lower the wages of the unskilled, especially those of recent immigrants. As Fix and Passel say, "A 10 percent increase in the number of immigrants reduces other immigrants' wages by 9 to 10 percent." The lack of English-language skills, lower levels of schooling, and unfamiliarity with the kind of work performed by U.S. workers, particularly in a highly industrialized society, insulates immigrants from head-on competition with American workers.

Immigrants may create more jobs than they fill. According to one estimate, if they had not settled in Los Angeles County between 1970 and

1980 "53,000 production jobs, 12,000 high-paying non-productive jobs, and 25,000 jobs in related industries would have been lost." Undocumented Mexican workers, one sociologist found, explain the rapid growth of the apparel and other poorly paying industries in Los Angeles. With the influx of Mexican immigrants, there arose a demand for bilingual schoolteachers, lawyers, physicians, and plant managers. The beneficiaries are middle-class Mexican Americans, born in the United States and sometimes partly fluent in Spanish. They enjoyed only limited opportunities until the migrants arrived. Immigrant income, calculated at $89 billion in 1989, spurs retail sales in stores of every type.

Commuters, Mexican migrants of another sort, bestow benefits on both sides of border. They are the men and women—of whom there are at least 1 million, according to estimates—who go back and forth every day of the week or come and go on Mondays and Fridays. Living on the Mexican side, they commute to work on the other. At San Ysidro, they make up the bulk of border crossers. The *Los Angeles Times* reports that commuters contribute over $4 billion annually to the economies of San Diego and Tijuana. As much as 60 percent of the income of Juarenses stems from jobs in El Paso; up to 80 percent of it is spent in El Paso.

Those holding green cards, which grant legal residency in the United States, are the best off among commuters, as they are residents of Mexican cities who lawfully have the right to work on the other side. Another type of commuter uses border-crossing cards issued by the U.S. Immigration Service for visits of up to seventy-two hours in a zone not more than twenty-five miles from the border; the purpose of these permits is to stimulate tourism and shopping by Mexicans. More than 1 million Mexicans possess them and nearly 100,000 of them, women particularly, employ them to work clandestinely as maids, sales clerks, busboys, waiters, gardeners, janitors, and day laborers. Tijuana has the largest number of commuters, labeled *transmigrantes* by Mexican scholars, because better jobs can be found in San Diego. With the exception of Ciudad Juárez, as one travels east along the border, where the disparity in wages is less sharp, the number of commuters falls off. Difficult times in Mexico, especially peso devaluations, increase their numbers.

Under the green card program, foreigners, who are allowed to hold jobs in the United States, share the best of both worlds. Their advocates in the United States are farmers, businessmen, and factory owners, usually with political clout in chambers of commerce, farm bureaus, and employer associations, who desire a dependable supply of cheap labor. American union leaders charge that commuters depress wages and generate unemployment in border cities, where union influence is weak, partly because commuters make labor organization difficult. Most commuters hold jobs in Texas, a state with right-to-work laws and no state minimum-wage statute. Commuters, it is argued, serve as strikebreakers, and they work for lower wages, which harms American labor.

o   o   o   ✿   o   o   o

The United States is not the mecca of every Mexican who travels north. Some Mexicans settled on the border and became the pioneer fathers of cities such as Tijuana. The lure of jobs in casinos and bars of the 1920s enticed them north to seek their fortunes. During World War II, Mexican border cities grew by leaps and bounds, almost solely because of heavy influxes of migrants, drawn there by dreams of jobs, whether in Mexico or across the border. They came from everywhere in the republic, although each city drew its newcomers largely from certain states. Those who arrived in Matamoros were mainly from San Luis Potosí, Veracruz, and Zacatecas, but the population of Ciudad Juárez multiplied with people from Coahuila, Durango, Zacatecas, and southern Chihuahua. Tijuana drew its settlers mostly from the Northwest, from Jalisco, Nayarit, and Sinaloa.

After the end of World War II, thousands who departed for work on the other side returned to make their homes in border cities, attracted by relatively higher wages and, at times, by the hope of again finding a job in the United States or at least the ability to supplement income by occasionally working there. Mexicali, for one, has a high percentage of migrants; perhaps fifteen thousand Mexicalenses labor in the agricultural fields of the Imperial Valley, but few await the opportunity to dwell in the United States. Of border cities, Mexicali has a uniquely stable situation.

The big influx occurred at the end of the bracero program in 1964; some 5 million Mexicans were hired to work in the agricultural fields and industries of the United States during the war, and an unknown number of others joined them. When they were no longer needed, they were sent packing. How many got home is unknown, but hundreds of thousands remained in border towns, perhaps over one-third of them. Ciudad Juárez grew rapidly because of them; despairing of finding work again across the border, they took up residence there. Between 1942 and 1952, the populations of Tijuana and Mexicali grew by 250 percent. All told, between 1940 and 1960, while the national population multiplied by 67 percent, that of the border states grew by 91 percent, and most of that growth was in their cities, which became springboards and receptacles for migrants on their way to or returning from the United States. With the arrival of the *maquiladoras* in the late 1960s, another human wave swept north. With family members putting down roots along the border, relatives joined them; the family is pivotal in the process of northward migration. The result is border cities made up of migrants. By 1970, they made up nearly one-half of Tijuana's inhabitants and nearly one-fourth of the population of Ciudad Juárez. Over 70 percent of Tijuana's economically active sector is made up of migrants; the figure for Ciudad Juárez is 34 percent.

The immigrant flow has slowed; since the 1980s, net migration is down, both in relative and absolute numbers. This is especially so in Nuevo Laredo, Matamoros, Reynosa, Ciudad Juárez, and Mexicali. The border cities are no longer the most dynamic in Mexico; people are leaving them. Yet given the current Mexican economic debacle, that may not hold true much longer. The *Diario de Juárez* states that an average of 6.5 families arrive daily in the city from Coahuila, Durango, and Zacatecas, fleeing from situations of despair. That adds up, the newspaper concludes, to nearly twelve thousand new immigrants each year. "It used to be," recalled the mayor of Praxedis G. Guerrero, once a town on the outskirts of Ciudad Juárez and now a suburb, "that for generations everyone knew everyone"; but that changed. "With all of the arrivals from other states, most planning to work in the United States, we who were born here are the strangers."

8

La Migra

Mexicans and their progeny in the United States, who cut their teeth on Anglo skulduggery, know a thing or two about the border patrol, today part and parcel of life on the borderlands; on both sides of the international line, its agents and vehicles are seldom out of sight. Mexicans allude to the agency as *la migra*. For Mexicans, *la migra* is an unflattering reminder of how their Anglo neighbors look upon them. For some Mexican Americans, this federal agency is "public enemy number one," an unwelcome celebrity in the community, not merely because its agents round up ancestral kin but because that routine keeps alive memories of police harassment that they know firsthand, as well as for its historical notoriety. As J. T. Canales, a Mexican-American lawyer from Brownsville, testified in 1919, the killing of Mexicans by Texas Rangers, the forerunner of *la migra*, was rampant. They "had established a precedent," he complained, "that . . . whenever a suspect was arrested they would unceremoniously execute him. . . . Frequently we would find dead bodies. . . . That condition existed until it was nauseating." The suspects Canales referred to were invariably Mexicans.

And so it follows, hardly astonishingly, that one border patrol agent, whose father arrived from Mexico and who lived in a Mexican-American community, had this prosaic comment to make about his neighbors: "They always had their rallies, saying, 'We have got to get *la migra* out of our neighborhood.'" Given that sentiment, the agent never wore "his green . . . uniform when traveling between work and home." It "could be dangerous." To quote a veteran border patrol supervisor in Douglas, Arizona, a heavily Mexican-American town: "Agents aren't necessarily the most popular people around here."

∘ ∘ ∘ 醤 ∘ ∘ ∘

Smuggling, what the border patrol and customs, a sister agency, are supposed to prevent, whether of human beings or just goods, is an old habit along the border. As one official in Arizona acknowledges, "The business is one that has been handed down from one generation to another." The smuggling trails used by Mexicans, he explains, go back years, "inherited and handed down to the children." On the Arizona border, some trails are rented out for up to $1,000, trails that have been worn down by the footprints of a legion of smugglers, men who adopted the trade in the days of New Spain, then a colony, whose territories abutted the French and British empires in America. In Texas, after the Treaty of Guadalupe Hidalgo, countless Mexicans, formerly relatives and neighbors, now found themselves legally in two distinct countries, separated only by a river. The law told them that they could no longer visit each other without going to the ports of entry, often miles away. The response was to ignore the law, to boat or swim across, just as they had in the old days, often taking gifts along. As Américo Paredes says, "Legally, of course, this was smuggling, differing from contraband for profit only in volume." Until enforcement became stringent, small-scale smuggling of goods was a generally accepted custom, often by respectable citizens. It is said that some of Brownsville's fortunes hark back to these early smuggling days. Again, during the heyday of Prohibition, both Mexicans and Americans, often in broad daylight, moved countless barrels and bottles of liquor across the border.

At the start, the routes went south, from the United States into Mexico. Contraband goods, mostly manufactured products, seemingly entered at will, largely because of corrupt Mexican customs agents and the inability of their bankrupt country to seal its borders. Roma, Texas, where hundreds of thousands of dollars in contraband passed into Mexico, was one of the favorite routes for smugglers, particularly for cotton textiles; today, Roma is a narcotics hub. Smuggling, which is the concern of customs officials, is still a thriving business, and not just along the Texas border. The goods may be different today, but the southbound traffic persists. Evidence indicates that in the San Ysidro–Tijuana area smuggling may be the fourth- or fifth-largest industry in terms of dollars. Until recently, millions of dollars' worth of contraband goods, especially electronic components, were flown to Mexico from the Brownsville airport, on World War II aircraft—without a single cry of alarm from U.S. customs officials. Every night, reports Alan Weisman, other planes bound for Mexico and loaded with contraband "television sets, Sony VCRs, and microwave ovens," took off from Miller International Airport in McAllen, Texas.

Less grandiose is the smuggling of *ropa usada*, used clothing, whether pants, skirts, jogging suits, swimwear, sweaters, or lingerie for women, purchased on the U.S. side for sale in Mexico's black market. This business thrives in Brownsville, Texas, where smugglers range from major racketeers who deal in truckloads to mom-and-pop operators who circumvent Mexican law by taking south only a bundle at a time, explaining to customs agents that the items are for personal use. Other petty contrabandists pack their goods in old suitcases and pose as vacationers when going through customs or carry soap and bleach so as to suggest a trip to a laundromat in Matamoros. The big operators, Mexican and American merchants alike, in Brownsville handle tons of used clothing; they are legitimate businessmen. One of them, a former tire salesman, parlayed a tiny investment into a multimillion dollar business that employs 350 people and processes over fifty tons of clothing daily, discards bought for pennies from the Salvation Army and Goodwill Industries. These merchants sell their wares to small-time entrepreneurs who, not infrequently, hire *pasadores*, runners who smuggle clothes into Mexico for $20 or so. Judicious bribes to customs agents clear the path south, despite cries of alarm by Mexican merchants and textile manufacturers, who loudly bemoan the flow of contraband *ropa usada*.

One nefarious item of smugglers is guns, from pistols and rifles to assault weapons, nine out of ten of them either manufactured or imported from the United States and taken into Mexico by dealers who sell their illegal wares at huge profits. Mexico does not manufacture firearms and its gun laws are strict, though one can, through the judicious use of money, acquire weapons from corrupt police. The customers of this illegal weaponry are killers, bank robbers, drug lords, and rebels, particularly since the economic crises of 1995 that threaten to destabilize the republic. For Mexicans, this is the reverse side of the American complaint about the flow of drugs that seeps into the United States across the border. Mexicans even argue that the gun smugglers travel the identical routes of the drug lords. As a deputy attorney general says, "The drug route goes north, and the arms route goes south."

Meanwhile, *fayuqueras*, small-time Mexican smugglers, dispose of their often clandestine ballpoint pins, women's panties and brassieres, pencils, and sundry articles in open-air markets from Ciudad Juárez to Mexico City. They get them home, but the corruption of yesteryear dogs their every step; it is the nemesis of every *fayuquera*. Rosario, one of them, told an American writer that paying for the used clothing she bought in Laredo for resale in Mexico City was the least expensive part of her business; the nightmare began when she entered Mexican customs, where bribes, labeled "duties" by customs agents, are demanded, first at the *aduana* (customs), then at the bus station, and finally at the inspection stop twelve miles down the highway. "Can you imagine," she asked, "how many people cross the border in the space of an hour? Every one of them pays *mordidas* (bribes) many times the price of the goods they are carrying." The writer then asked whether free trade wouldn't end this extortion racket. Rosario explained: "You have to understand, thousands of people at the border live from collecting bribes. The entire economy of cities like Nuevo Laredo rests on the money people extort from others. It's a way of life." NAFTA, Rosario remarked, "isn't meant to rescue people like us; it's meant to help the rich." Customs and police, who live off the *mordida*, "are not going to stand around with their arms folded while their main source of income disappears."

○ ○ ○ 🀄 ○ ○ ○

However, since the early days, the human traffic flows north. Until 1924, a handful of immigration agents, aided by local police and Texas Rangers, kept a watchful eye out for border jumpers. The border patrol stepped in to fill the shoes of these early watchdogs; from the time the border patrol was placed under the U.S. Immigration and Naturalization Service (INS), an agency of the Department of Justice, it was the watchdog at the border and, for some Anglo-Americans, the guardian of American culture. In Texas, many of the original members of the border patrol were former rangers. However, the Texas Rangers, with whom Mexican Americans tend to identify the border patrol, have a nefarious past. Paredes argues that the word *rinche*, taken from "ranger," means every mounted and armed American, looking for Mexicans to kill. In the Mexican-American folklore of Texas, border patrolmen are not infrequently *rinches*. The crimes against Mexicans by rangers, Paredes recalls in *With a Pistol in His Hand*, "created in Border Mexicans a deep and understandable hostility for American authority." Their shootings and lynchings cowed the weak but, at the same time, swelled the ranks of Mexican bandits and raiders who, if treated fairly, would have been "peaceful and useful citizens." Admired for their courage, their neighbors composed *corridos* (heroic ballads) commemorating them, songs of men who defended themselves with a pistol in their hand.

The origins of the border patrol go back to 1924, when Congress passed the exclusionary Immigration Act, designed to enforce the wishes of xenophobic Americans bent on curtailing the entrance of newcomers, especially Eastern Europeans and Asians. However, during the hard times of the Great Depression in the 1930s, Mexicans were the one group singled out. With the rightward shift in American politics of the late 1970s, part and parcel of the severe recession of that era, Mexican immigrants again became, in the words of the media and politics, a major problem. Thus, the border patrol grew by leaps and bounds, both in personnel and budget, particularly during the Reagan years. Jimmy Carter, whose administration saw the heady influx of immigrants partly as a threat to national security, even vowed to double its size. Reagan and his cohorts went further, warning of "tidal waves" of unwanted immigrants and railing against "terrorist infiltration" across the border, alarmist rhetoric related to Washington's aggressive meddling in the affairs of Central American republics. Congressional funding for the border patrol, meanwhile, jumped nearly 150 percent.

For people who live on the border, particularly in Mexican-American communities, the green and yellow four-wheelers of the border patrol are salient features of daily life, as are the wide-brimmed hats of their occupants. They are seen everywhere in the cities and towns north of the international line, in Brownsville, early in the morning, five or six of them on horseback, guns at their side. Oddly, many of them look Mexican, but it is agents of Mexican descent who fill the ranks of the border patrol. They are rarely out of sight on the highways that rim the border from California to the Gulf of Mexico; and they are no less visible at the checkpoints, where agents decide whether to allow you to drive on or furnish proof of legal residency in the United States.

o   o   o   🏵   o   o   o

Mexicans who work in the United States are big business on both sides of the border. No one disputes that they fill uncounted jobs in agriculture, industry, and the service occupations in the United States, laboring throughout the Southwest, up and down the Pacific Coast, in Chicago and the Midwest, and on the East Coast, in places such as Florida and New York City: They are ubiquitous. For Mexico, the exodus means foreign currency, dollars that are hard to come by. By 1991, they had mailed home approximately $6.2 billion a year, more than Mexico earns from tourism; only petroleum and the *maquiladoras* provided more hard currency. Mexicans cross everywhere along the entire two-thousand-mile boundary, but at some places more than others. The most-traveled region is the seventeen miles from the Otay Mountains to the Pacific Ocean, just south of San Diego, California, the busiest stretch of human traffic across an international line in the world. As early as 1991, millions of crossings occurred yearly, slightly more than half by Mexicans. The rate of increase in border crossings surpasses rates of population growth in Tijuana, among the highest in Mexico. The fashionability of gates of entry, all the same, shifts from time to time. Crackdowns at San Diego and El Paso, customary routes for illegal crossings, encourage border jumpers to try their luck elsewhere, one alternative being Agua Prieta, Sonora, a fence away from Douglas, where fourteen-year-old *coyotes* were getting $20 a head early in 1996. Some who formerly entered the United States at San

Ysidro, such as a group from Baja California on its way to jobs in Illinois, detoured in 1996 through Agua Prieta, where the border patrol during January and February detained almost 35,000 Mexicans, 25 percent more than the previous year. When George Lopez, now the assistant chief of the border patrol, arrived in Douglas in 1981, there were only two agents; today, 127 of them man the battle stations, aided by tower-mounted cameras, night-vision scopes, ground sensors, and helicopters. Countless crossings are made surreptitiously but are known about and condoned by American immigration authorities. These are the commuters who, using a shopping card given to them by American authorities, illegally work in the United States. Officials of the INS know this situation exists but explain that, for lack of personnel and funds, they cannot keep track of them once they enter the United States.

The effect of the border patrol, in this charade, is like using a Band-Aid on a hemorrhage. No one is wholly happy with its performance. The border leaks; according to Ronald Reagan, then president of the United States, "We've lost control of [our] borders." Or, in the words of Fernando Quiroz, an earthy, mustachioed agent in the Brownsville corridor, no matter how many he caught, others "were probably making it across the river." The blame for the leakage cannot, in all fairness, be placed at the feet of the border patrol. The reasons are far more complex. NAFTA, to begin with, opened the doors wide to the flow of capital across borders but left untouched the barriers against transnational flows of workers. Stopping the influx of illegal entries requires Herculean measures as well as facing up to political demands in both Mexico and the United States. If the border patrol can be faulted, perhaps its underlying trouble is "its muddled mission," as the *Los Angeles Times* put it. National legislation calls for controlled immigration; you need permission to enter the United States. Nonetheless, Congress never provides funds to hire sufficient agents to truly guard the border. At the same time, a majority of the public clamors for "a crackdown on illegal immigration, while employers welcome the cheap labor."

Conflicts also flare up between the INS and the U.S. Customs Agency, the other bureau on the border. The clash is over budget and jurisdiction. Customs, charged with collecting duties and interdicting contraband, is one of the oldest federal agencies, originating in the days when the Customs Mounted Patrol rounded up horse thieves, cattle rustlers, and smugglers from both Mexico and the United States. Its border headquarters are at Laredo and El Paso, both in Texas, and Nogales, Arizona, and San Diego, California. As one writer comments, customs is caught in an untenable position, asked to help stem the influx of narcotics and, simultaneously, to encourage commerce between the two countries by speeding up the flow of border traffic. Unhappily for the architects of this scenario, bor-

der crossings as well as the traffic of drugs are on the increase. For those
who study the agency, this should come as no surprise: Commercial traffic
multiplies by leaps and bounds, but the number of customs agents increases at a snail's pace, with the subsequent result that overworked
agents are unable to properly inspect vehicles or speed up crossings. On
some days, customs delays at ports of entry stack cars for hours at a time,
as commuters at Tijuana, Mexicali, and El Paso know from experience.

The border patrol works closely with the Drug Enforcement Agency
(DEA). This extra duty has its naysayers. The use of the border patrol in
the war against drugs injects, according to one study, a "higher level of
paramilitary readiness in immigration control . . . and confuses the Patrol's mandate." This involvement comes by way of the Anti-Drug Abuse
Act, which entrusts to the patrol the job of helping to intercept drugs and
arrest these smugglers. Drug control is not the primary mission of the
border patrol, yet its involvement widens the gap between its muscle
power and the ability of border residents, often under suspicion by the
patrol, to defend themselves; of course, many of these residents are of
Mexican extraction. The study finds that there are "serious implications
in the fusion of the two tasks which require such diverse dispositions."
This is especially so because the national hype confers on the interdiction
of drugs the sound of war drums—dangerous rhetoric, as the American
Civil Liberties Union recognizes: "When war is declared on drugs, the
implicit message is win at all costs." Yet, as we all know, in war, probable
cause and reasonable force become luxuries. Equally disturbing, labeling
"entire groups of people as enemies" leads to the use of "tactics and ac-
tions that are disturbingly racist."

From the start, the border patrol's primary purpose has been to deter illegal immigration. In the early 1930s, its agents also helped carry out the
forced repatriation of Mexicans; according to one report, only 17 percent
of them voluntarily went back to Mexico. Many of them, as was explained earlier, were born in the United States, whereas others, though
natives of Mexico, had lived in the United States since the 1890s. In Texas,
as a result of this massive deportation program, the Mexican-born population dropped by 40 percent. The border patrol has also participated in
shutdowns of ports of entry as far back as 1929, when the administration
of Herbert Hoover placed a 6 P.M. curfew on Americans who visited Mexican border towns. During Richard Nixon's stay in the White House, Operation Intercept, an antidrug campaign that drew on the border patrol
for enforcement, backed up Mexican traffic at ports of entry for hours on
end from September to October 1969. The operation antagonized Mexicans up and down the border but proved a colossal failure.

The Immigration Reform and Control Act of 1986 (IRCA), hailed as a
milestone, had as its principal goal "to take back the border." The law

granted amnesty to approximately 2 million people but simultaneously promised that the flood of illegals would be curtailed by imposing sanctions on employers who knowingly hired them and through better policing at the border. Congress gave the patrol more funds and doubled the number of agents. San Ysidro and El Paso, where two-thirds of illegal entries occur, got the lion's share of resources, including the latest technology. The erection of steel fences followed. Until 1986, American courts had upheld the right of undocumented workers to the same labor standards as U.S. workers; the IRCA canceled this protection.

That Mexican aliens climb over the international fence or wade across the Rio Grande is hardly newsworthy. The activity has old roots. In the past, there were few ranches on the Mexican side of the Rio Grande that did not keep a rowboat to ferry people across, as did their Texas neighbors. Now the border patrol annually apprehends over 1 million people trying to enter illegally; of that total, 95 percent come from Mexico. San Diego, Nogales, El Paso, and the Lower Rio Grande account for a majority of the detentions. Of the clandestine entries, over two-thirds take place in San Ysidro, the favorite door among immigrants, followed by El Paso. The Matamoros region is where most Central Americans enter.

Just the same, counting the number of illegal crossings is a risky endeavor. The legislation of 1986 only briefly slowed the flow of the undocumented; their numbers soon began to climb again. The same person, furthermore, may be caught more than once. Five detentions of the same person in one day may be uncommon, but this does occur. Most likely, the person caught gives different names. Deception is a high art among border jumpers. A San Ysidro woman explains how she and her friends evade INS vigilance: "I lend my birth certificate to the Mexican women who want to cross, and once in the United States they return it to me. If they are caught, they simply say they found the certificate." In the Pico-Union area of downtown Los Angeles, where Mexicans congregate, dealers do a wholesale business peddling fake green cards and social security cards. Los Angeles is considered the capital of the multimillion-dollar fraudulent document trade. "You can get almost anything you want out there," said an official of the INS. What then do the statistics of the border patrol tells us about border jumpers?

The game of hide-and-seek between agents of the border patrol and Mexicans waiting to illegally enter occurs daily. The drama never ends. Job-hungry Mexicans risk being caught day and night, but most are nocturnal adventurers, awaited by border patrol agents on four-wheelers, horses, and helicopters. At San Ysidro, they gather at dusk, either on the Otay Mesa or at the *bordo*, the Tijuana River Valley, where stadium lights set the sky afire. The "invaders" almost always outnumber the agents, usually by ten to one. As in war, the patrol stations its forces to cover as much area as possible. Migrants and *coyotes* huddle together around bon-fires to shield themselves from the cold or climb atop a ten-foot steel bor-der fence, watching for the chance to make a run for it and evade border patrol vehicles parked across the away. *La migra* corrals only a few when groups of ten, twenty, or more at a time dash for the American side.

An identical drama unfolds up and down the border. Only the stage varies: bluffs at Matamoros, where the border patrol stations itself, or flat land up the river. At El Paso, where the Rio Grande meanders through a broad valley, four-wheelers silently keep vigil, their noses pointed in the direction of Mexico. The challenge for the border patrol is just east of La Hacienda Cafe, where the waters of the Rio Grande are shallow. A re-porter who observed the ritual had this to say: "In an hour, about thirty people slowly make their way down from the hillside shacks of plywood and tin, onto the Mexican levee," then down to the river's edge. Once there, "they scan the U.S. side for the Border Patrol's . . . vans, then, see-ing none, navigate some exposed rocks . . . to reach the El Paso bank." They are young couples, some with children, or old men with bags of used clothing to resell, "and several jobless, sullen young men." One of the young couples with a child told the reporter that they get stopped by the border patrol about twice a month, but they "cross several times a week." They were "looking for yard work, anything. We need food for the boy." Agents are not insensitive to the hardships that drive Mexicans out of their country. Asked why he released a man headed for a visit with a sick relative in the hospital, an agent replied: "One alien isn't going to change the immigration problem."

Leonel Castillo, a man of Mexican extraction who was INS chief during the administration of Jimmy Carter, described how this scenario ap-peared to him. He had gone to the San Ysidro border, as he said, "to see everything that I could." Concerning the use of the helicopter to track aliens, he said: "You're supposed to take the helicopter's spotlight and find Mexicans. . . . It's like herding. It's a weird sensation when you get that spotlight and start looking for people under bushes. In effect, you're stalking human beings." The Mexicans caught were put in vans and then deported. He related that shortly after that "they're trying to cross again . . . its all an unbelievable exercise." As Castillo recalled, "Sometimes when you apprehend all these people you really manage to make your-self feel like a real shit." You are deporting, he concluded, "young men and women" whose "sole reason for coming is work."

Of late, the Immigration and Naturalization Service, parent of the bor-der patrol, has taken to building fences, the bigger the better. In 1979, a chain-link fence, labeled the "tortilla curtain" by Mexicans, was erected in El Paso and San Ysidro, California. In a short time, the fences became vic-tims of Mexican vandals, or "hole cutters," who wanted to enter the

United States and got tired of climbing over it. For a while, the INS repaired them, then gave up in frustration. Then, in 1992, U.S. Navy Seabees and the army reserves built a mightier fence in San Ysidro, of surplus corrugated steel sheeting left over from the Vietnam War, about ten feet high and fourteen miles long, to bar vehicles from crossing into the United States. To close off a gap at the Pacific Ocean, the Army Corps of Engineers erected a barrier across the sand and into the ocean, built of steel pilings that extend 340 feet into the surf. "With the newly installed floodlights that run nearly the entire length of the fence, the wall resembles," the *Los Angeles Times* reported, "the edge of a prison camp." Without the lights, says Gustavo de la Viña, border patrol chief in 1992, "illegal immigrants basically own the night . . . We own the day. But we are hampered by darkness." Border patrol officials claim the fence works; no longer do smugglers drive truckloads of drugs into the United States, and detentions of immigrants are down. Apparently, however, it does not work well enough: The INS has now put up a three-tier fence at San Ysidro.

The latest of these fences, in reality a concrete wall fourteen feet high but euphemistically referred to as a fence by its American patrons, stands at Nogales, built according to specifications to be "forbidding yet friendly." The latest in a collection of steel walls, chain-link fences, and barbed-wire barriers, this particular monster boasts something novel. Although made of reinforced concrete and steel, it is painted in salmon colors, inlaid with bright stone chips and decorated with tiles. The structure, the pride and joy of the Americans, sports large windows so that Mexicans can peer through them and see Nogales, Arizona, and, when necessary, talk to people on the other side. The idea, say its architects, was to build an "impenetrable barrier" that was still "open, airy, and friendly." Mexicans, unimpressed by American claims of artistic aspirations, ask a most logical question: Why build barriers in a time of free trade?

The evidence, furthermore, indicates that the undocumented circumvent the fences. At San Ysidro, for example, they head east to make their entry; fences turn the tide to the lonely canyons of the backcountry, where the border, once a "geographic abstraction" now becomes a "living, breathing force that changes after the sun goes down" and countless Mexicans furtively enter the United States. As a cattle rancher on the outskirts of Boulevard, a hamlet east of San Diego, put it, he used to check his fences twice a year but now does so twice a day. Were he not to do that, he said, "you could lose your whole darn herd through one of those gaps" left behind by Mexicans. Farther east, detentions multiply in the Imperial Valley, where the undocumented increasingly brave the hazards of the hot desert. As one agent at Calexico said, "They just keep coming. . . . A first-grader could have predicted what was going to happen—the buildup there is sending everyone here." Yet the border patrol has built similar walls at El Paso and Nogales, Arizona. Fences, whatever their value, are most clearly not a final answer. Many illegal crossings at San Ysidro, for example, occur at its gates, with Mexicans using fake documents.

If they are given the resources, claim spokesmen for the patrol, "they can stop unlawful crossings right here at the border." However, complete control, experts acknowledge, is impossible, given the length of the border, the topography, and the economic disparities between Mexico and the United States. Nonetheless, more can be done. The first response, Operation Blockade, occurred in 1993 at El Paso, where a beefed-up patrol of hundreds lined the shores of the Rio Grande for twenty miles. The Clinton administration thought the blockade so successful that it became the model for a new $386 million master plan. Operation Gatekeeper, the second shutdown, went into effect a year later at San Ysidro, with border patrol agents, "using horses, bicycles and small high-speed boats," according to the *Los Angeles Times*. Following in the footsteps of El Paso, "200 agents . . . deployed in a three-tiered formation along fields, canyons, riverbanks and beaches." Operation Hardline, which snarled traffic entering Brownsville, followed in those footsteps.

Critics of sham Berlin walls are unhappy. As they rightly point out, walls are not monuments to international goodwill: To the contrary, fences and blockades set off waves of outrage and threats of economic boycotts. Mexicans, obviously, never applaud their appearance. In a protest at an international bridge in Ciudad Juárez over Operation Blockade, they burnt an American flag before a phalanx of heavily armed border patrol agents. Reaction also included boycotts of El Paso business, as well as of San Diego merchants. While paying lip service to a country's right to guard its frontiers, Mexicans, in the words of one of its congressmen, believe that walls and shutdowns "merely tarnish diplomatic relations between two countries." For Jorge Bustamante, the fence at San Ysidro tags Mexicans as a danger, as the enemy. It "was built . . . on the assumption that there is a drug trafficker behind every undocumented migrant." One needs "to believe in magic," he adds, "to believe that . . . a . . . fence . . . can stop the forces of evil."

Yet not only are fences becoming ubiquitous but, on occasion, so are soldiers, called on to help stem the immigrant tide and stamp out drug smuggling. During the last seven years, according to spokesmen for the military, soldiers from the army, marines, and national guard conducted over three thousand missions along the border. Many Mexican Americans who reside there think this is dangerous nonsense; to quote Roberto Martinez, director of San Diego's American Friends Service Committee border project, use of the military is "warmongering gone amok." Even Silvestre Reyes, a Democratic Party congressman from Texas and formerly border patrol chief in El Paso, has qualms about the use of soldiers unless accompanied by agents of the border patrol; the job of patrolling, he says, "is tough enough when you're a professional. . . . Don't make it tougher by putting people out there who aren't bilingual or familiar with the culture and customs of people they observe." Unlike police and other civilian law enforcement agents, who are required by law to take into account the civil rights of a suspect, soldiers, untrained to deal with civilians, are free to act on their own. Although a congressional act of 1878 prohibits their use for police duties, soldiers not infrequently serve as watchdogs, at times, strange as that may be, unbeknownst to the border patrol, an activity Reyes criticizes. The Clinton administration, partly to assuage these critics, says it plans to make reliance on soldiers unnecessary by beefing up the border patrol, thus ending what critics call the "militarization of the border," a decision also partly encouraged by the public outcry over the killing of a high-school student who was grazing his goats on the outskirts of Redford, Texas, by four marines, on a covert mission to watch out for drug smugglers.

Ambivalence characterizes American reaction. For years, countless migrants had floated across the Rio Grande to toil in El Paso. As the *New York Times* reported, "Illegal immigration became a symbol of tolerance, even brotherhood, between the two cities." The border patrol stopped few maids, busboys, nannies, or gardeners, which the *Times* saw as "a sign" that El Paso and Ciudad Juárez understood each other's needs. Then came the fences and the tightening of border crossings, to the delight of most Americans, but not all of them. The mayor of El Paso, for one, spoke up to proclaim that he did not want to see another Berlin Wall go up. Dissenters argue that the results of the shutdowns do not justify the efforts. They believe that it is a "confrontational waste of money and energy that would have unintended social and economic costs." Their fears include long-term damage to commercial and diplomatic relations between Mexico and the United States. As a spokeswoman for the chamber of commerce in Brownsville explains, commenting on Operation Hardline, "While we agree that we want to stop drug trafficking across the border, the Brownsville business community can not afford to go broke in the process." Its sister chamber in Douglas, Arizona, anticipated the erection of a local steel fence there, in the manner of San Diego and El Paso, as harmful to business. Similar complaints are voiced nearly everywhere along the border.

Blockades, critics believe, may be ineffective. According to one University of Texas study, though Operation Blockade makes illegal crossings more difficult, "it has done little to prevent undocumented Mexicans from living and working in the United States." As the chief of the border patrol at El Paso admitted, perhaps 60 percent of the people apprehended cross on a daily, weekly, or monthly basis. The rest simply circumvent the blockade. Sealing the border, by the same token, not only keeps Mexicans out but also keeps them in: The undocumented who work in El Paso simply stay there rather than try to go home to Ciudad Juárez, for fear of being caught by the border patrol. One study also found that illegal immigrants bound for faraway places, such as California, simply bypassed El Paso and took a different route. Nor did crime rates abate, which some Americans blame on illegal immigrants. Human rights activists also charge that crackdowns encourage mistreatment of immigrants awaiting deportation. Since the start of Operation Gatekeeper, they insist, insults and physical abuse are on the rise. Claudia Smith, regional counsel for the California Rural Legal Assistance, alleged, "It is part and parcel of the strategy . . . to make things as miserable as possible for those detained by the border patrol to deter them from coming again." Despite years of monitoring "physical abuse by border patrol agents," she wrote the attorney general, she "was surprised by how often detainees deported . . . told of suffering or witnessing acts of border injustice."

o   o   o 🏵 o   o   o

Border jumpers or "wetbacks," as they are called along the Rio Grande, risk life and limb. It is dangerous business to attempt to enter without documents. No obstacle, perhaps, looms larger than wading or swimming the Rio Grande, a polluted and muddy moat. Some who try, often natives of rural villages who never learned to swim, slip or panic and pay with their lives, victims of the river's erratic currents and the catfish and turtles that feast on the soft meat of eyelids and lips. Every year, 270 would-be migrants drown in the shallow waters of the Rio Grande, their bloated corpses rising to the surface after a day or two. Nearly all unidentified, they are buried in an unmarked plot in a pauper's cemetery. The deserts of California and Arizona claim others, sometimes entire families. Just north of the border, high-speed chases on freeways are not uncommon, as *coyotes* driving truckloads of border jumpers try to evade capture by border patrol vehicles or police cars. Some end in death for the helpless migrants; in one such chase, seven died when a pickup carrying them careened off the highway near Temecula, a town just beyond San Diego.

Violence, as these events demonstrate, is no stranger to the no-man's-land of the border. Thieves prey on migrants—on both sides of the international line. Beatings, rapes, and muggings occur. Early in April 1996, for example, sheriff's deputies beat a man and a woman after overtaking a truck loaded with undocumented migrants in Riverside County; television cameras from a hovering helicopter captured the scene in vivid color. "You have to be careful," a man warned Ramón Pérez, the author of *Tian-*

guis, Diary of an Undocumented Immigrant: "You can't cross the river by yourself and there are thieves on both banks, and you're lucky if they only rob you." Accidents happen, as in "the loss of limb or life when trying to board or leave moving trains." In vans or trucks, death from suffocation stalks the unwary; in 1995 at the Harlingen railroad switchyards in Texas, the *Brownsville Herald* reported the rescue of over one hundred "undocumented aliens . . . from a sweltering Southern Pacific boxcar." The danger of dying of thirst confronts those who challenge the desert, as the story of one immigrant tells. Caught by the border patrol and sent back to Mexico by way of Arizona, he decided to try again, this time traveling by way of the desert. On the second day, the water supply gave out, and to avoid dying of thirst, he "drank from a pool of slimy, greenish water, among bones of dead animals." In the cold of winter, others freeze to death, more than a dozen of them in just ten days in the mountains east of San Diego during January 1997. Trying to escape *la migra*, others are run over on interstate highways this side of the border.

On the Mexican end, an army of parasites waits to exploit border jumpers. Chief among them are the *coyotes*, also called *polleros*, who are paid to take immigrants across. They charge what the traffic will bear. In 1994, at Laredo, *polleros* were asking as much as $500, explaining that the added vigilance of the border patrol made the crossing riskier. At El Paso, before the border patrol shut down, *polleros* received between $20 and $30; after Operation Gatekeeper went into effect, the fee jumped to $300, and $100 more if it meant going to the airport.

Currently, smugglers of Mexicans are roundly denounced by American authorities, but whatever their degree of guilt, I confess that their crime is old hat to me. I have known *coyotes* since the late 1920s. One episode always reminds me of them. I vividly recall one day when my father received a surprise telephone call from a *compadre* ("godfather") who, embarrassingly for him, was locked up in the San Diego county jail, a stately building on Broadway, now demolished in contemporary California manner. He told my father that he had been caught bringing other Mexicans into California and needed bail money. I went with my father to see this *compadre* and recall seeing him in a dark room behind a window with bars. In the course of the visit, during which my father expressed regrets at seeing his *compadre* locked up, *papá* spoke no words of condemnation. He just thought it was rather dumb to risk jail for the few bucks a *coyote* might earn.

La Jornada reports that corrupt Mexican police, meanwhile, extort migrants and *polleros* alike. To quote the Pérez *Diary*, "He who's going to be a wetback, if he has money, will have trouble with the police, and if he doesn't have money, he'll have even more trouble." During lean times in the United States, as in the early 1990s, the *mordida* exacted from *polleros* by police ran between $15 and $30 a month, but according to *El Mexicano*, with plentiful jobs on the other side, *polleros* give the *jefes judiciales*, the police commanders, up to $10,000 a month. When migrants refuse to pay, extortion consists of threats of beatings or jail time. Scholars at the Colegio de la Frontera Norte calculate that police extortion runs as high as 50 million pesos a year. "If you want to know how much money there is in the *mordida*," to quote one source, "go look at the home of the former head of customs in Mexicali. He's retired and dwells in the most fabulous house in town." The principal victims are Mexicans of Indian appearance, natives of Oaxaca, a form of racial prejudice that exploits the most vulnerable in society. Of late, just the same, statistics indicate that border crime is down here and there. In San Diego, officials of the patrol attribute safer conditions to bigger fences and lights and to better communication with Mexican police, especially the Grupo Beta, a unit organized to combat violence against immigrants that has the respect of Mexicans in a country where police corruption is as common as the tortilla. Yet, where corruption is endemic, few escape its tentacles, including members of the Grupo Beta, whom *polleros* say "are on the take." Yes, the border zone is safer, but in the words of one *pollero*, corrupt Beta agents "come around to your house and either you pay or they expose you to their buddies, the *migra*."

Entrepreneurship, because of migrant demands, also flourishes along the border. Some diligent individuals dig holes under the steel fences, then charge Mexicans heading for the other side a dollar to crawl through; others place stepladders on the fences and demand a fee for their use. At San Ysidro, along the fences there are "sidewalk" *fondas,* concessions that sell food to the men and women on their way to the United States; industrious Mexicans collect sweaters, shoes, and blankets abandoned by migrants fleeing from the border patrol and then sell them to others waiting to make the dash. Smugglers of illegal aliens are also increasingly creative; as the border patrol tightens its vigilance, they develop new tricks, getting their "customers" across through inland checkpoints in ingenious ways, for example, by hiding them under a truckload of potting soil or painting trucks to look like telephone company vehicles and having the driver wear a blond wig.

∘ ∘ ∘ 🏵 ∘ ∘ ∘

Abuses by agents of the border patrol pose yet one more danger. In 1992, the National Commission for Human Rights highlighted violations committed against undocumented workers, placing the blame on law enforcement officers who "at times . . . exercise discriminatory practices and on other occasions foster such practices." Most interactions between agents and migrants, the commission acknowledged, ended without violence, but because incidences of mistreatment and brutality were not un-common, "the probability of an encounter with the Patrol is a frightening prospect." Americas Watch, another human rights group, concluded in its 1993 report "that serious abuses by U.S. immigration and law enforce-ment agents continue," charging that "current mechanisms intended to curtail abuses and discipline officers are woefully inadequate." The largest number of abuses, the American Friends Service Committee main-tained, involved "verbal humiliation and intimidation."

Anti-Mexican prejudice tends to color border patrol behavior. Americas Watch noted that race dictated which autos were stopped for inspection, especially in South Texas. Under the pretext of looking for illegals, patrol agents overran the campus of El Paso's Bowie High School, arbitrarily de-taining individuals because they looked Mexican, on the assumption that they were illegally in the country. The school lies next to the Rio Grande, and its student body, youngsters from the Segundo Barrio, is virtually all of Mexican origin. In the course of these raids, agents dealt harshly with faculty, staff, and students. In 1992, seven plaintiffs filed a class action suit in federal court seeking an injunction to restrain agents from entering school grounds unless they had reasonable cause. Faculty, students, and staff testified to abuses by the border patrol. One young woman re-counted how on her way home from school, an agent stopped her and asked if she was Mexican. Although she answered all questions in En-glish, the agent, for no apparent reason, knocked her to the ground and kicked her. Another agent stopped the assistant football coach at Bowie when he was driving to a game with two students and pointed a gun at his head. When he asked that the weapon be holstered, the agent told him "to shut your mouth and get out of the car." Although the coach com-plained to the border patrol chief, nothing was done. When the Bowie case came to trial, the judge ruled in the school's favor, admonished the patrol for violating the civil rights of the plaintiffs, ordered it not do so in the future, and warned that mere Hispanic appearance did not provide justification for hassling individuals in the belief that they were violating immigration laws.

One of the most damning indictments of border patrol misbehavior can be found in a series of articles published by the *Los Angeles Times* in April 1993. "From California to Texas," the paper documents, "agents of the Border Patrol . . . have crossed the line into lawbreaking and disorder." Agents were guilty of "unjustified shootings, sexual misconduct, beat-ings, stealing money from prisoners, drug trafficking, embezzlement, per-jury and indecent exposure." The authors argued that skyrocketing illegal immigration, the increase in the number of agents, and a "front-line role in the drug war" had exacerbated the problems of the border patrol. In one-third of sixty-six incidences studied, a Justice Department audit found that agents violated firearms rules. The *Times* reporters told of a Mexican crippled by an agent's shotgun blast who, when he sued in court, won nearly $1 million in damages. In Imperial County, not far from San Diego, an agent shot a twelve-year-old in the back who was standing on the Mexican side of the international boundary; a U.S. district court judge awarded the victim $574,000. The border patrol never disciplined the agent, although the judge called his defense "incredible." A report by Federal Defenders in San Diego listed 331 cases of "severe beatings at the time of arrest by Border Patrol and Customs officials from 1985 to January 1991"; in many instances, the beatings occurred when the suspect was in custody and handcuffed. At the San Clemente checkpoint some fifty miles north of San Diego, a young woman from Tijuana told the Mexican consulate of having the finger of a border patrol agent shoved up her vagina as other agents laughed. The American Friends Service Committee told of a woman accused of smuggling drugs; when she denied it, the male agent told her to pull up her blouse and then stuck his finger under her bra because, as he explained, "girls like to hide things there." He then asked her to pull down her trousers, then her panties, then stuck his finger into her vagina. Early in 1996, an agent raped a young woman he found hiding in the bushes just this side of the San Ysidro border.

The border patrol, in the opinion of its detractors, is a "rogue agency," and "the most renegade branch" patrols the Arizona-Sonora desert. During 1993, the *Times* documented, convictions for drug smuggling were meted out to an agent and a former agent; another went on trial for murder; and another was jailed for perjury; the former head of the detention office was on probation for stealing money from Mexican prisoners. On the solitary stretches of the Arizona desert, illicit shootings and cover-ups are a particular failing. One agent testified: "You hear shots every night. If you report that, you will be in the office every day for at least two hours completing paperwork." Drugs lie behind much of the turmoil; the lure of easy money proves too tempting for some. One agent even carried loads of marijuana in his border patrol four-wheeler and, with profits from its sale, bought jewels, boats, and motorcycles for himself and breast implants for his wife. Another may spend the rest of his life in prison for selling cocaine stolen from smugglers. An agent acquitted of murdering a Mexican in a sensational trial heard by an almost all-white jury, admitted using an unauthorized assault rifle, firing when not threatened, failing to report gunplay, dragging the dead man's body into the brush to conceal the remains, and not telling superiors that he had killed someone.

Why these transgressions of the law? The causes are multiple. An agent's job is risky; there is danger involved. Criminals and troublemakers frequent borders; in the fiscal year ending in 1992, there were 167 alleged assaults that injured forty-nine agents, four seriously. On occasion, drug smugglers shoot at them. In January 1996, they shot to death an agent on routine patrol in Eagle Pass, Texas; while at Tijuana, others, perhaps also drug mafiosos, used high-powered rifles on three occasions to shoot at border patrol officers. Agents in Eagle Pass now patrol in bulletproof vests. Since 1980, ten agents on patrol died in auto and aircraft accidents. A prevailing view among immigrant-rights groups is that the INS cares more about protecting its image than getting to the bottom of complaints. They point out that of 436 complaints filed in fiscal year 1992, the Department of Justice held formal investigations in just thirty cases; only a fraction of them survived a preliminary check. The others were deemed unsubstantiated.

The low complaints to arrest ratio, which the bureau trumpets as a sign that abuse occurs infrequently, actually indicts investigative procedures and results from sundry mechanisms adopted to dissuade victims from filing complaints. Unless safeguards are taken, expanding the size and scope of the border patrol will surely exacerbate abuse. Testifying before a congressional committee, an official of the Justice Department blamed misconduct and corruption on poor management. That is partially true. Not long ago, the chief border patrol agent in El Paso admitted in court that "he had not read a previous federal court order forbidding dragnet sweeps in which agents illegally targeted Latin bar patrons." In the matter of shooting incidents, the department's report cited the failure of review boards to scrutinize findings independently of local officials and the absence of a uniform policy of punishment for violations.

Critics also think that the quality of the personnel is to blame. Anyone can join without a college degree or prior police experience. The job, lamentably, is boring, demanding long hours, usually seated in a vehicle waiting for Mexicans to climb the fence or patrolling the streets of border towns day and night. How many men and women would enjoy doing that kind of work? No psychological exams are asked of applicants, who are not screened for signs of racial prejudice. One agent, unbelievably, when asked in court how he could distinguish Mexican nationals from Mexican Americans, replied, "By their darker skin . . . because they don't bathe every morning." One reason for misconduct is poor training and supervision.

The articles in the *Los Angeles Times* go further; they argue that due to flawed screening "the Border Patrol ends up with agents predisposed to criminal activity or not psychologically suited for the job." For others— the Friends Service Committee for one—the absence of an "adequate system, either internal or external, to review complaints and officer accountability," lies at the heart of the problem. In the opinion of Americas Watch, the secrecy of the investigative process and the excessive discretion in deciding the degree of punishment "foster cronyism in the application of sanctions." "I don't think we can have law enforcement that separates it-self from the people," said Bob Burgreen, former police chief of San Diego. A coalition of elected officials and citizens even asked Washington to establish a civilian review commission to investigate allegations of abuse, an unprecedented step for a federal law enforcement agency. In El Paso, the city council organized the border patrol Accountability Com-mission and, in San Diego, a blue-ribbon panel, at the behest of Burgreen, urged civilian involvement. Representative Xavier Becerra of California introduced a bill in Congress to set up an independent review system; however, the INS, which opposed the measure, instead organized the Cit-izens Advisory Panel, which meets irregularly and merely makes recom-mendations on general policy.

∘ ∘ ∘ ❁ ∘ ∘ ∘

In recent years, the formerly hunted have become the hunters. More than 40 percent of border patrol agents, two thousand out of five thousand, are Hispanics, Mexican Americans by and large. They are the children or grandchildren of immigrants, of Mexican nationals who, in most cases, il-legally entered the United States. "How ironic," Oscar Martinez com-ments, a scholar of border affairs, "that Mexican American agents now apprehend people with whom they share an ethnic affinity." The need for Spanish-speaking agents opens doors for them, and nearly all of them are from working-class backgrounds and achieve a form of upward mobility with a job in the border patrol. This is especially so in the Lower Rio Grande Valley, where poverty locks doors to Mexican Americans. Yet for decades, heads of the border patrol resisted hiring Mexican Americans, arguing that they would not police Mexicans. The few allowed into the ranks were usually assigned duties as interpreters or detention guards.

Leonel Castillo, a Mexican American from Houston, best personified this seeming contradiction of the hunted turned hunter. Other Mexican Americans increasingly hold down key agency jobs. The highest ranking is Gustavo de la Viña, once station chief at San Diego and since summer 1997 assistant INS commissioner, that is, chief of the border patrol. Earlier, he was a regional INS director and oversaw border patrol operations at the Federal Law Enforcement Training Center in Georgia. He is the grandson, he says, of "Mexican and Spanish immigrants." A native of the Lower Rio Grande Valley and folksy by nature, he wears cowboy boots and speaks with a Texas drawl. Critics say he does not countenance criticism and dis-counts most complaints of abuse. During his stay in San Diego, Mexican-American activists, as well as Mexicans in Tijuana who dealt with him, of-ten found him insensitive. Operation Gatekeeper, the blockade at San Ysidro, as well as the buildup of border fencing, came during his tenure.

Silvestre Reyes, now a Texas congressman but earlier El Paso's sector chief, is the grandson of a Mexican immigrant. He grew up in a Canutillo farm family, where he helped harvest melons. One of his chores as a boy was to watch out for *la migra* on his father's farm. "My job when I saw the agents was to blow the truck horn and get all the aliens to scatter and hide." One of ten children, he fought in Vietnam and has one semester of college. Before coming to El Paso, he headed the patrol office in McAllen, Texas, where he earned "a reputation for fine-tuning enforcement practices to national political agendas." One of his policies led to the virtual imprisonment of Central American refugees in the Rio Grande Valley. Author of the controversial blockade at El Paso, he holds immigrants responsible for crimes from car thefts to transvestite prostitution and believes members of Mexican gangs terrorize South El Paso. For him, Mexican beggars and freelance window washers "are a terrible nuisance." David Aguilar, another Texano (a Texas Mexican American) and the station chief at Brownsville, displays more compassion toward border jumpers: "What's driving these people," he has told a reporter "is human needs."

From the start, Mexican-American border patrol agents have come under heavy fire from relatives, friends, and neighbors; they are "trusted in their country but reviled in their neighborhoods," as the *New York Times* put it. The accusation is that they betray their own people. While head of the INS, Castillo had to fend off Chicano activists, hardly impressed with his highly visible appointment. But, like Juan Zavala, an agent in Laredo, most of them scoff at the criticism: "They are not my people," Zavala said of those he arrests daily. "I'm an American. They're here illegally." Or to quote Haydee Carranza, who followed in the footsteps of two brothers who joined the border patrol, "People ask me: How can you do that to your *raza* [people]? . . . I say: They're breaking the law."

Many Mexican residents of border communities label the Texanos, both those in the border patrol and customs, as the toughest and meanest of the agents. They are legendary for their aggressive behavior. No one of Mexican extraction has not had a run-in with these customs agents when coming across the border. To quote a music teacher from Tijuana, in the early 1940s and 1950s, visits to San Diego were trouble free, "until they sent the *texanos* who do not care for us. They are despots, especially those with names such as González, Ramos, or Pérez." For another Mexican woman, "These agents ask more questions of us than Anglo-Americans." One Mexican complained to Mexican consulate authorities that a border patrol agent named Sotelo had pulled him by the hair, kicked him, and then kicked him again until he was unconscious. A migrant from Guerrero recounts how four agents caught him when he attempted to enter at Tijuana; one of them, a "tall, well-built Latino . . . kicked him with the point of his cowboy boots, breaking a rib . . . then pushed his head into dirty water" and forced him to drink it, while calling him a "Mexican dog and pig." A Mexican American, the patrol head at Imperial Beach, a suburb of San Diego, referred to Mexican illegals, according to the *Los Angeles Times*, as "Tonks," slang for the sound of an agent's flashlight striking an immigrant's head. At Tijuana in 1989, a Texano agent nearly caused an international riot when he parked his four-wheeler at the bottom of the Tijuana River channel, a stone's throw from the fence, whence he used his loudspeaker to harangue people on the other side, cackling "maniacally," playing "taped ranchero music," and calling "Mexicans whores."

Hispanic agents, paradoxically, complain of racism in the border patrol. In the words of one of them, "A lot of these people [referring to Anglo-Americans] still hold a lot of hate against the Mexican people." As one agent in El Paso charges, "discriminatory attitudes pervade the organization. . . . It carries out into the field. . . . What you see is what you get." That Hispanic agents seldom get promoted is a common complaint. Mexican-American agents, they say, must show "toughness," which may explain some of their arrogance with Mexicans. For them, so goes a saying in the patrol, no neutral ground exists: "You're either a hard-ass or a bleeding heart." As one Hispanic psychiatrist who frequently treats border residents explains, these agents behave that way because they want to identify with the Anglo boss, believing it pays dividends.

9

La Maldición

For an irate Francisco Barrio Terrazas, the governor of Chihuahua, the drug trade is a *maldición* (curse) on the Mexican border. Or to quote the lament of the despondent mayor of Ciudad Juárez, "I feel so helpless when I grasp its magnitude." The culprits responsible for this calamity are a binational bunch: Americans, for their sickly habit and for the money they flaunt before traffickers to feed it; and Mexicans, their sense of right and wrong eroded away by centuries of corruption in public life, some of whom, as a result, succumb to the lure of dirty money even when it jeopardizes their morals as well as the fabric of family and society.

When you ask them, Mexicans on the border complain that they pay the piper for the sins of these culprits. They also ask why so much ado in the United States about Mexican mafiosos? Are there none across the border? Are we to believe, so goes the Mexican reply, that ghetto blacks, barrio Hispanics, and Anglo-American addicts, whom police catch on street corners and in drug busts, are the sole culprits? Who distributes the narcotics once they enter the United States? Are there no American drug rings? Is it true, as Carlos Fuentes has an American character say in *Frontera de Cristal*, that only Mexicans and Colombians are drug lords, never gringos? Border Mexicans will also tell you that except for the traffickers—the major mafiosos come from states to the south—and the usual homegrown rogues and rascals, law-abiding men and women make their homes on the northern rim of Mexico. Some were friends of my parents; others are now friends of my own family.

Drugs are hardly a recent phenomenon in Mexico. Archives document that the ceremonial use of marijuana among indigenous peoples dates from the eighteenth century. The use of heroin and cocaine, the hard drugs, arrived late to the border, as well as to the rest of the republic, but not the *mota*, as marijuana is known, particularly in the military. I recall my father, who grew up in Mexico, talking about a grandfather I never knew who, as a soldier, had served Porfirio Díaz and, to add to his meager pay, peddled *mota* in the barracks. He was never disciplined for doing so. During the Revolution of 1910, the men and women who soldiered under General Francisco Villa popularized *La Cucaracha*, a simple ditty that hails a good marijuana smoke. It is still heard wherever a mariachi band plays. The lament, which makes merry of a cockroach unwilling to move, goes like this:

> *The cockroach, the cockroach,*
> *No longer wants to march,*
> *Because it does not have,*
> *Because it needs (le falta),*
> *A marijuana joint to smoke.*

In any event, untold tons of narcotics enter by way of the border, to be injected, snorted, or smoked by Americans. The *narcotráfico*, a political quagmire for Americans and their spokesmen in Washington, is increasingly a border spectacle. One cannot bring to life the reality of the borderlands without reference to that nefarious activity. Because the trade turns cities such as Ciudad Juárez and Tijuana into a no-man's-land, people disappear overnight; drug lords, who are often one's next-door neighbor, buy off police, bribe politicos, browbeat and terrorize journalists, and wantonly torture and kill; and as a poor *maquila* worker mugged in a rat-infested slum in Tijuana said, gangs of wastrels sell dope and prey on the poor. At the same time, drug traffickers, in their haste to ferry their goods onto the other side, tear down fences and rumble through the land of American cattle ranchers, from time to time with vehicles of the border patrol in hot pursuit, while the bullet-riddled bodies of drug peddlers regularly turn up on city streets from Brownsville to San Diego.

∘　∘　∘　❁　∘　∘　∘

Near the end of Albert Camus's *The Plague,* signs appear to indicate that, just maybe, the worst is over; the horror that befell society is on its way out. Ultimately, conditions change, but not everyone can adapt because the horror has imbued many with a skepticism so deep that it is now part of their personality. They have lost hope of ever seeing better days. When dealing with the narcotics epidemic, a similar paranoia afflicts American society. Despite statistics that show illegal drug use is on the decline, the latest of which is by the 1996 National Household Survey on Drug Abuse, few Americans believe that the poisonous nightmare, akin to the plague in Camus's novel, has run its course. Mexicans, made cynical by centuries of chicanery by the powerful, merely shrug their shoulders when asked to explain why their compatriots engage in this dirty trade.

Among Americans, that proclivity lingers on, because on urban streets, narcotics are plentiful, offenders fill prisons to capacity, and drug abuse ravages cities and devastates lives, while many of the well-off snort or inhale their favorite drugs apparently safe from the vigilance of the police. The costs to society—in jails, police, murder, and violence—are enormous. Each year, women addicts give birth to 200,000 babies, nearly half of them crack babies. Drug-related violence is endemic in the inner cities, and the cost of policing their streets rises by leaps and bounds. The campaign against illicit drugs, in its blind quest to stamp them out regardless of the consequences, weakens the Bill of Rights and corrupts the law; in the words of the *National Review*, hardly a leftist journal, this encourages "civil, judicial, and penal procedures associated with a police state."

Yet stopping the drug trade is, increasingly, a daily feature of American policy, as the money spent on enforcement testifies. Fifteen years ago, federal anti-drug expenditures cost just $1 billion; currently, the annual cost is sixteen times more—and the end is not in sight. Since narcotics enter the United States from Latin America, and increasingly often from Mexico, sealing the southern border is a major preoccupation. Countries in Latin America produce or transship all but 20 percent of the cocaine as well as nearly all of the marijuana that flows north. Along with Guatemala, Mexico also produces a small fraction of world opium, enough to supply perhaps one-third of the demand in the United States. No wonder, therefore, that diplomacy between Mexico and the United States often revolves around drugs.

o　o　o　✦　o　o　o

Washington's formula since the 1970s has endeavored to eradicate the use of illicit drugs and, in order to do so, has worked to suppress their production in the Western Hemisphere. The more they cost on the street, the less the consumption, so goes the logic. Supply determines demand. To accomplish this goal, White House czars devised a blueprint that rests, first, on choking off the supply by burning crops and destroying laboratories and, second, on closing the border to drugs. This approach depends, in the jargon of the drug enforcers, on the "interdiction" of supplies bound for the American market by patrolling the Mexican border and the high seas. The "war on drugs," as Washington politicos baptized it, seeks to reduce the flow of narcotics into the United States, hike their price, punish drug traffickers, and drive users out of the market.

This formula, basically an American invention, dates from 1931, when an international meeting in Geneva declared control at the source—in other words, the country of origin—the best way to stamp out the illegal trade. This interpretation puts the blame for drugs on those who cultivate them and on those who smuggle them into the United States. Since supply leads to addiction, the responsibility lies with the countries of the peripheral world that produce drugs, not with consumers in the wealthy nations.

Drug use remained more or less limited for some time after that, so little was done to implement this formula. Then, with the rise of the drug culture of the 1960s, Washington put into action Operation Alliance, its official goal being "to interdict drugs" and, for good measure, weapons, currency, and illegal aliens. Along the Mexican border, where the Southwest Regional Command was established, agents from customs, the Federal Bureau of Investigation, the Drug Enforcement Agency, the border patrol, and police from the four border states were called upon to carry out policy.

Interdiction started out modestly; only two federal agencies existed, with a total budget of less than $10 million. By 1993, over fifty agencies were involved, including every branch of the military, and the budget had ballooned, with the DEA spending over half of it. Yet money and beefed-up patrols failed to halt the traffic or reduce use. The *Los Angeles Times* called the war a failure, of no "noticeable impact on drug importation . . . or consumption." To the contrary, the tactics of "war" led to a shift from the smuggling of bulky and, perhaps, less harmful bales of marijuana to the far more dangerous cocaine. Currently, drug enforcers seize over 100 tons of cocaine yearly, but its price and availability remains virtually unchanged, with the Texas city of Houston a major hub for Mexican traffickers. Experts estimate the worth of the illegal market at $38 million a year. Also, as one Mexican observer noted, despite the money spent and the technological innovations introduced by Americans, little has been accomplished because the drug traffickers have updated and streamlined their operations. On the Texas border, for instance, they employ night-vision equipment, cellular telephones, sentries, and an intelligence network of their own, "outmanning, outgunning and out-planning," as the *Los Angeles Times* noted, "the U.S. Border Patrol, Customs Service, and DEA at strategic points on the Rio Grande."

Mexicans offer a more logical explanation for the booming trade: It flourishes because of consumer demand in the rich nations of the Western world, specifically the United States and Europe. Already by 1989, as the State Department acknowledges, Americans consumed 60 percent of the illegal narcotics in the world. One report by the National Institute on Drug Abuse (NIDA) claims that approximately 37 percent of Americans, age twelve and older, use illicit drugs at some time in their lives. About one-third try marijuana and up to 12 percent sample cocaine. Potheads, the fans of marijuana, account for 90 percent of people who regularly use drugs. Six out of every ten Americans, say officials, have smoked "joints," as marijuana cigarettes are known, among them Bill Clinton, currently president of the United States. Interestingly, at a time when Prohibition forbade the consumption of alcohol, marijuana was legal in the United States; not until 1937 was it banned.

Interdiction, as we shall see, carries pernicious sequels. It is of itself contradictory: As the price of narcotics rises in the black market, consumption may hold steady or even occasionally drop; however, the profits for Mexican growers and traffickers spiral upward, as does the incentive to smuggle drugs into the United States. Because of interdiction, a gram of cocaine costing about $15 to legally produce sells for $150 on the black market. This turnabout invites ever more corruption in Mexico since drug lords enjoy healthy profits and are thus able to lavish bribes on politicos, police, and soldiers, some of whom are grossly underpaid. As one official concedes, when demand runs high, *narcotraficantes* wallow in money, allowing them to buy nearly everyone.

Today, although drug use appears on the decline, the number of devotees holds steady. The consumption of cocaine, a favorite of the better-off in society, shows no signs of decline, and heroin use is rising sharply. Drug abuse among teenagers has doubled. Documents from the Department of Health and Human Services reveal that the use of drugs by adolescents has been on the rise since 1992, after a welcome drop during the preceding ten-year period; in 1995, nearly 11 percent of young people between the ages of twelve and seventeen used drugs at least once a month, up from 5.3 percent in 1992. The rate of narcotics abuse among young Americans ranks among the highest in the world.

Given the rapid urbanization of American life, and no concomitant increase in jobs or opportunities for schooling, the scenario is a logical outcome. The poverty belts of American cities encourage antisocial behavior, including the use of drugs, by those left out of the American dream. The report of the NIDA, furthermore, explores narcotics abuse only among "relatively stable family situations," forgetting that the most likely users are the downtrodden of society: young minority men in inner-city ghettos, the homeless, and men and women in prison. When people are denied jobs and white racism is their daily lot, they tend to stray from the norms established by society. But there are also pot-using college students in dormitories and the well-off, the yuppies of American society, who snort or inject cocaine. In the land of Lincoln, ghetto dwellers and barrio gang members are hardly the sole consumers of narcotics.

Notwithstanding current talk of new policies, only the rhetoric of the Clinton administration differs from those of its predecessors. Despite claims of a shift in national priorities, only one-third of federal drug funds find its way into treatment and prevention: Two-thirds of this funding goes into law enforcement. The Clintonites are Mugwumps, to recall a term from United States history: Politicians with their mugs on one side of the fence and their wumps on the other. As before, the goal consists of pouring money into the military coffers of countries that produce drugs; this money is earmarked to be used in crop eradication, in attempts to break up drug cartels, and to apply diplomatic muscle to compel international cooperation. The war on drugs in Latin America has led to hilarious and tragic consequences, such as the unholy alliance of Washington policymakers and military thugs who boast atrocious human rights records. Part of the help sent south ends up in counterinsurgency wars, as with the use of American anti-narcotics helicopters by the Mexican military to kill peasant guerrillas in Chiapas.

One hand often appears not to know what the other does. NAFTA advocates in the administration call for a speedup of truck traffic at the ports of entry, but customs officials, no less eager to promote international trade, also insist that less thorough searches provide smugglers with easier ways of transporting cocaine into the United States. These critics in customs dub NAFTA the "North American Drug Trade Agreement"; enforcement, they say, has taken a back seat to trade. As they point out, when you wave trucks through, you weaken searches; as if to confirm that, the *Los Angeles Times* reports that 2 million trucks rumbled through the three busiest ports of entry in 1994 "without a single pound of cocaine being seized." At Otay Mesa, a major highway for trucks entering from Mexico, only 13 percent are thoroughly inspected, a figure actually slightly above that for all ports of entry under the controversial "line release program," which allows trucks to enter free of inspection.

The result is, according to newspaper accounts, that *capos*, the smugglers, move more of their wares through legal ports of entry. An undercover agent at El Paso estimates that during his tenure only 4 percent of the smuggled dope was intercepted. A rule a thumb is that no more than 10 percent of narcotics is detected at border crossings; by this measure, when agents in the San Diego District confiscate 63 tons of cocaine, much more gets through undetected. Smugglers, to avoid detection at one heavily watched entry point, also reroute shipments through others that are more lax. To quote a customs official, "We may have a great record of seizures in one" place, "only to find that the amount of drugs" actually smuggled "was nothing to brag about."

Dealing with drug smuggling is like trying to compress a rubber tube without first deflating it. When you press one end down, the other pops up. For example, when Washington's policymakers deploy more border patrol agents to San Diego and other troublesome crossings, they open the door to traffickers at other "soft spots," the Eagle Pass region of Texas that fronts on the Mexican state of Coahuila for one, where gangs of smugglers, relying on bribes, intimidation, and even murder, ship marijuana, cocaine, and heroin to cities in the United States.

Another unforeseen result, as a former White House drug czar admitted, is "oversights" in the formulation of national drug control strategies. For instance, zealous attempts to stem the cocaine epidemic of the 1980s may have hastened the switch to crack, a cheaper form of the drug. Nor are congratulations in order when statistics show declines in drug use. After a period when the use of cocaine and heroin seemed to be tapering off in the late 1980s, their use spiraled upward again in the 1990s.

The enforcement net leaks at other places. Zealous American agents are not immune to the temptations of money. As Michael Bromwich, inspector general for the Department of Justice told Congress, "It has been said that wherever drugs exist, corruption exists," and he added that "while I would like to believe that this bit of conventional wisdom is untrue, our experience tells us otherwise." A byproduct of the narcotics trade is the corruption of federal, state, and local law enforcement agents, which, as Bromwich admitted, is a "serious border problem." Once it was thought that this problem only afflicted remote border counties; now the evidence indicates that they are not alone. The lure of easy money seduces agents no matter where they work. During the last three years, no fewer than forty-six agents—federal, state, and local—have been indicted or convicted of some form of drug-related corruption up and down the border.

The following story illustrates the severity of the problem. The office of Daniel Knauss, the chief assistant U.S. attorney in Tucson, was investigating corruption among agents of the border patrol, customs, and the INS at Douglas in late 1996. When asked to give an opinion on the scope of the problem, Knauss refused to say how many agents were under scrutiny but insisted that "more [were] . . . honest than dishonest." A Douglas city councilman replied, "It's pretty sad" when a U.S. attorney believes "he may be sticking his neck out to declare that a majority of these guys working this border are not corrupt." But, then, Knauss had memory on his side. From 1991 to 1996, five border agents at Douglas were caught bringing cocaine into the United States, and more are now under federal investigation. In 1990, federal authorities came across a concrete-lined and lighted tunnel connecting a warehouse in Douglas and a home in Agua Prieta. Douglas, a town of fifteen thousand, has long been known as a smuggler's paradise, ever since Arizona rangers chased horse thieves and gunrunners there in the early part of this century. Residents admit that the local economy is linked to black markets controlled by families with ties to both sides of the border. With one out of five members of the labor force jobless, Douglas, to the chagrin of city fathers, has gained notoriety as "the most corrupt town" along the border. As Miguel Moreno, a convicted drug dealer now out of prison and author of the popular *Ballad of Joe Cocaine*, says, "Smuggling is part of our way of life."

Nor do Texas border towns fare any better. At El Paso, in May 1995, two customs inspectors who were in league with drug smugglers were arrested for allowing the importation of a ton of cocaine in return for a $1 million payoff. Dope smugglers infiltrate the ranks of the police, county sheriff departments, drug task forces, and federal agencies. Since 1992, the FBI has helped convict 79 local, state, and federal officials, over half of them on counts of narcotics corruption. They include the sheriff, court clerk, and presiding judge in Zapata County; a mayor and police commissioner in Hidalgo County; in Maverick County, where Eagle Pass sits, a sheriff's deputy was caught at a border patrol checkpoint smuggling marijuana while on duty, in full uniform, and driving a squad car. "They're good guys," says one local rancher, "but they see all this money, they lose their morality, and they just become part of it."

Similar accounts surface repeatedly on the California side. At San Diego, federal prosecutors indicted two agents of the INS for permitting drug traffickers to drive more than six tons of cocaine into the United States. One ten-year INS veteran, convicted of helping to smuggle narcotics at Calexico, in two years received over $350,000 in bribes. For each load of narcotics that passed through his inspection lane at the border gateway, a Mexican smuggler paid him at least $5,000 in cash. As he explained during his trial, he "allowed forty to fifty vehicles carrying narcotics . . . to enter the United States." A Mexican smuggler called him in advance with a description of the drug-laden car. On a single day in 1992, he told the court, he had permitted four vehicles, loaded with a total of over one ton of cocaine, to pass through in just half an hour. Corrupt customs agents also tip off smugglers when vehicles are targeted for inspection, and it is suspected that others remove intelligence files from computers. The desert region of the Imperial Valley, through which drugs enter Los Angeles, is called the "cocaine corridor" of the Southwest border. Perhaps as much as 80 percent of the cocaine from Mexico enters California by way of this pipeline; of the total consumed in the United States, 75 percent comes from Mexico. Gatekeepers, who earn approximately $45,000 a year, double their salaries by looking the other way when drug lords send their trucks through Calexico. Two agents there used cellular telephones and spotters to coordinate their operation with the traffickers. The conspiracy, which began in 1987, lasted until 1992 and let into the United States about $78 million worth of cocaine.

From time to time, demands for a real change in policy surface. For critics, interdiction, which costs billions of dollars, has no observable impact on drug prices, nor does it reduce abuse. According to Anthony Lewis, a political analyst for the *New York Times*, an "honest appraisal would have to conclude that 80 years of prohibition have been a disastrous failure." Prohibition is not the solution; it is the problem—the policy has no clothes. To quote the *National Review*, the war on drugs diverts "intelligent energy away from how to deal with the problem of addiction . . . that is wasting our resources." Critics of interdiction are cropping up even in the ranks of the narcotic cops. Some veterans of the narcotics war now advocate a shift from interdiction to reducing demand through education and treatment programs. To quote one of them, "If 70 percent of the cocaine goes through Mexico and 95 percent of that gets through, then stopping the flow is a failure." After three decades on the drug battlefront, this man was emphatic: "I can tell you that law enforcement is not the answer. You've got to reduce demand." Some analysts also argue that neither cocaine nor heroin sustain the drug war; the culprit is marijuana, the drug of choice. According to this viewpoint, since only 2 million Americans are hard-core addicts, a number too small to justify the upkeep of the inflated interdiction budget, the dope warriors insist "on keeping marijuana criminalized, thereby magnifying the scope of the problem."

Mexicans rightly say that pointing the finger solely at the producing countries shows only one side of the coin. Production, distribution, and consumption are, in reality, integral aspects of the same problem. As *Zeta*, the Tijuana newspaper, explains, without demand there will be no supply, whereas with demand there is always a supply. The responsibility for the affliction, the newspaper concludes, lies with the United States, the biggest consumer. In the opinion of Gustavo de Greiff, a fellow Latin American once in charge of Colombia's anti-drug campaign, efforts to rid nations of the trade seldom pay dividends. He urges a change in course, saying in no uncertain terms that the war is lost. Drug trafficking is big business, he adds, and more land than ever is planted to coca, from which cocaine derives, in spite of U.S.-assisted efforts to rid civilization of drug lords and end the flow of narcotics.

Accumulating evidence documents the interdiction is merely a stage show because it does not go to the heart of the problem, mistakenly placing the cart before the horse. Consumption drives the trade. Like the Prohibition attempt, which outlawed the manufacture and sale of alcohol but forgot that Americans drink beer and whiskey, the drug war invites massive police corruption and a rise in street crime with no discernible drop in consumption. An alternative, as critics say, would be treatment programs for addicts. But Washington, which claims to sponsor such programs, sets aside paltry sums for them. Others advocate the legalization of drugs in the pattern of Holland, which in their opinion would rid the country of dealers and place addicts under public supervision.

What is blatantly clear is that the nefarious business also corrupts the society of the exporting nations. Along the entire Mexican border, but particularly from Matamoros to Nuevo Laredo, *el contrabando hormiga*, the small-scale trafficking by local Mexicans, increasingly flourishes, especially since the collapse of the republic's economy in 1995. With the advent of the drug trade, violence is endemic not only in Colombia and Peru but is also on the rise in Mexico, where killings by drug gangs are now commonplace.

In Baja California Norte, drug-related violence accounts for 40 percent of the thirty-five homicides reported monthly on the average. A spokesman for the Baja California state attorney general's office reports that in Tijuana, "these kinds of killings have become so frequent that it's almost a normal occurrence." The *Los Angeles Times* says that "the violent score-settling between drug lords—and between traffickers and police or anyone else who gets in their way—has left behind a trail of corpses, often with signs of torture, sometimes blindfolded or with their hands tied behind their backs." Soldiers and police routinely use cigarette lighters and electric shocks to eyelids and testicles to wring confessions from their prey. "Torture," according to the National Network of Civilian Human Rights Groups, a Mexican coalition, "continues to be practiced systematically." One recent victim was a state judicial agent who had complained of corruption in police ranks; his body was dumped on an isolated stretch of beach by thugs who "meticulously broke most of his bones." As one young Tijuana mafioso confessed, "Killing is a party for them, it's a kick." There is "no remorse at all. They laugh after a murder, and go off and have a lobster dinner." These killings prompted one American prosecutor to compare Tijuana to Chicago in the 1930s, when gangsters mocked the law.

Thugs, moreover, come in all shapes and forms. Not long ago in Tijuana, *narco juniors* (young drug traffickers) shot a journalist and his son in broad daylight, and despite the known identity of the assailants, the police, who were cowed by the political clout of the families and cartel connections, failed to make an arrest. The suspects in the ambush, who have criminal records and a warrant out for their arrest, are linked to killings in both Mexico and the United States. These *juniors*, agents for regional mafias, are hardly the offspring of the impoverished families that supply most of the soldiers of the trade. To the contrary, from the day of their birth, they have had everything handed to them on a silver platter—trendy clothes, fancy cars, and schooling in Catholic institutions in San Diego. Boredom, the arrogance of wealth, and the chance to pick up $15,000 or more for a quick run across the border have perhaps led them to embrace the trade; they are "crossing the line," according to police, "from wanna-be gangsterism into cross-border smuggling, mid-level dealing, and murder." As the son of a Tijuana civil engineer and a devoutly Catholic mother testified, he started on his life of crime first by using cocaine and running errands for drug traffickers, then by helping smuggle rifles into Mexico and, eventually, as he became a full-fledged mafioso, by moving tons of cocaine and marijuana across the border. His brother, who also joined the activity, went even further, becoming a cold-blooded killer.

For outsiders, that behavior appears abnormal, and in certain ways, it certainly is, but it is also understandable and even tragically logical. For years now, the young reside in a society where avenues for social mobility are often closed, particularly since the advent of neoliberal policies that periodically plunge the economy into crisis. Promising careers become increasingly difficult to come by, and education, once seen as a panacea, rewards only a lucky few. Given this picture, the drug business becomes an alternative, a way out of the economic doldrums. The young, too, daily bear witness to the depravity of their leaders, their cohorts, and frequently their parents. Corruption, moral and otherwise, is endemic, as old as the Spanish conquest, when the first viceroy of New Spain, the colonial name for Mexico, made money off shady land deals. Independence and the Revolution of 1910, whatever their other accomplishments, have done nothing to rid the country of the moral turpitude that is rampant in politics and business. When possible, everyone gets a share of the graft. Public and private shenanigans seldom raise eyebrows, even when cabinet officers, in cahoots with businessmen, make millions—witness President Carlos Salinas's sale of the public telephone system to a business crony.

Until recently, political fraud was openly practiced by the PRI, the reigning party. The thin veneer of democracy, mainly for foreign consumption, fooled only American scholars; Mexicans, a cynical lot, were not persuaded. A study of public opinion published in 1987 revealed that nearly 80 percent of all Mexicans had no faith in either the chief executive or the Congress. Most distrusted the courts, judges, and the entire legal network. Equally telling, less than one-third of them had any faith in private enterprise. As Heberto Castillo, an honorable Mexican politico and writer, declared, "In government there is obvious dishonesty, as much as or more so than in the private sector—which is to say a lot." The *mordida*, the bribe exacted by police, is merely the tip of the iceberg. The aberrant behavior of privileged Mexican youth, whose only goal in life frequently seems to be to spend lavishly and to frolic, is thus explained by the general corruption in society and the inclination of bourgeois families in Mexico to spoil their offspring rotten.

The rot in business also corrupts their elders, who, according to the journalist Francisco Ortiz Pinchetti, suffer from moral amnesia when they knowingly accept tainted money. How many Mexican businessmen have not clasped the hands of dope dealers to open a new venture, to sell an established one, or to dispose of property for a price far beyond its value? Country clubs open their doors to *capos* so long as they pay their dues and eagerly host the lavish weddings of their sons and daughters, while narco pesos replenish the pocketbooks of owners of auto agencies, restaurants, and hotels. Ortiz Pinchetti even recounts how a group of Catholic seminarists, at the invitation of a *capo*, spent their vacation on the *capo*'s estate.

Beyond that, the sins of the traffic sully the social fabric, including popular culture. Take *corridos*, for example, the ballads that, in the time-honored tradition, tell of heroes and legendary deeds and bemoan the tragedy of death through betrayal. More recent *corridos* tell of immigrants and their run-ins with the *migra* and voracious employers in the United States. But they also dramatize the escapades of *capos* and their cocaine empires and peasants who grow poppies and marijuana. The *narcocorridos*, by glorifying drug traffickers and their money, say the critics, exalt a nihilistic cult that leads young Mexicans astray; authorities in Tijuana and the state of Sinaloa apparently agree, because both localities banned them from the airwaves. Yet narco ballads are still sung—because, to quote the Tigres del Norte, a popular *norteño* musical band, "that is what the people want to hear." One such *corrido* tells of campesinos who cultivate marijuana:

> *What I planted up there in the mountains,*
> *The Federales burn.*
> *But this time they failed*
> *Because they arrived late.*
> *All they found was the tire tracks of a trailer.*

Some on the border believe that these ballads mirror the violence so common in the American movies and television that Mexicans of all ages watch. Thus, the corruption that the ballads introduce is also felt to be of American manufacture. José Manuel Valenzuela, a Mexican scholar of border culture, believes these ballads help to perpetuate macho attitudes by reproducing sexist stereotypes of women who invariably appear as mothers, lovers, or dutiful and faithful wives: "Women are invisible, or make their bows as foils to spotlight the virtues of the men." A boast in one verse of a macho ballad encapsulates this attitude:

> *Speaking of the mother of my children,*
> *I do not have to look for women.*
> *On the contrary, there are times when I have to hide.*
> *They flock after me like bees to a honeycomb.*

∘ ∘ ∘ ❈ ∘ ∘ ∘

From the start, perhaps because of geographical proximity as well as weakness, Mexico has shared Washington's interdiction philosophy, whether willingly or not. Since 1912, when Washington convinced President Franciso I. Madero to adhere to the 1912 Hague Convention, Mexico has toed the American line. Narcotics violations are federal crimes in Mexico, and the responsibility for prosecution rests with the attorney general. The army and the navy, as well as elements of the judicial police, collaborate with the office of the attorney general in the Mexican version of the narcotics war. A permanent campaign against the traffic dates from the 1970s. The results, enthusiasts of the effort say, are impressive, and they point to the eradication of plants, the confiscation of cocaine supplies, and the jailing of traffickers. Among those who often praise the Mexican response are officials and diplomats of the United States, who, for a variety of reasons, including the wish to sell NAFTA to the Mexicans, gloss over failures. According to the *New York Times*, when Mexicans did nothing to stop the laundering of money from narcotics, Washington's officials, rather than protesting, "usually wrote off such episodes as unavoidable bumps in a long, bumpy road."

The sale of Mexican marijuana in the United States for medicinal purposes began during the nineteenth century and survived even after the Mexican government banned it in the 1920s; Washington largely looked the other way, since this marijuana was consumed mostly by Mexicans living in the United States. Until the 1960s, Mexico supplied marijuana for nearly the entire American market; the weed is cultivated in eleven states, four of them along the border, partly in response to the successful campaign Colombia waged in the 1970s to stop its production. Today, however, Americans grow approximately two-thirds of the pot they smoke.

Chinese traders, it is asserted, planted the first opium poppy seeds. As early as the turn of the twentieth century, Chinese opium dens were fixtures of such border towns as Mexicali and Ciudad Juárez. The critics of Esteban Cantú, the military governor of Baja California, say he had a hand in this nasty development; even after General Abelardo Rodríguez replaced him, opium dens survived in Mexicali. In 1923, when Mexican authorities carried out an anti-drug campaign, among those arrested for drug abuse were 184 Americans, as well as 182 Chinese. Eventually, heroin, which was made by acetylation from the opium poppy seed, began to find its way to both Mexico and the United States. When World War II cut off American supplies of morphine, another derivative of opium that was needed to treat wounded soldiers, Mexico stepped in to fill the breach. After the war, the traditional suppliers of these drugs, from Asia, Europe, and the Middle East, regained the lion's share of the American market. The Vietnam War and its aftermath, a long-time resident of Tijuana recalls, injected new life into the trade; addicts would even walk across the international line to get a fix. After the breakdown of the French connection in the early 1970s, which closed off one American source of heroin, Mexican planters supplanted their Turkish rivals. This is

in keeping with the logic of the business. As a student of the traffic observes, when a source is "eliminated or substantially reduced, the vac-
uum tends to be filled by a new source."

According to some, drug abuse in Mexico is far less than in the United
States; to cite one critic, it is "one-tenth the level . . . for virtually every
drug, for every age group," a view partially supported by statistics of the
Sistema Nacional de Vigilancia Epidemiológica de Adicciones. Poverty itself, so goes this thesis, is not directly linked to drug abuse; rather, the nature of the family is the stronger determinant. A functional family environment, where parents show love and children attend school—the
Mexican model, supposedly—helps bar the door to the devil. That, in my
opinion, is a fairy tale. As spokesmen for the Sistema Nacional warn, recent trends in drug consumption are cause for "worry," though, according to national statistics, fewer than 2 million Mexicans have tried drugs
(largely marijuana). Still, in Northwest Mexico, which includes the states
of Sonora and Baja California, the use of cocaine is on the rise.

To quote one aficionado of the theory of Mexican resiliency, when Mexicans succumb to drugs, it is frequently because of their contacts with American culture. Drug use is much higher among Mexicans who have been in
the United States. This scholar stands on firmer ground when he concedes
that drug use is more prevalent among Mexicans who live close to growing
grounds and drug laboratories. The more you come into contact with
drugs, the greater the chances that you will use them. That, apparently, is
true even for Mexico's federal law enforcement agencies. Mandatory drug
tests early in 1997 turned up 424 police, prosecutors, and administrative
personnel who tested positive, nearly half of them for cocaine use. Especially targeted were agents of the National Institute to Combat Drugs, the
equivalent of the Drug Enforcement Agency in the United States.

Whatever the resiliency of Mexicans, much of their country is turning
into a funnel for narcotics, and diverse regions are becoming drug haciendas. The evidence also shows that easy availability encourages use. One
Mexican border official, for example, believes that drug-related crimes are
on the rise partly because of a growth in local drug sales and consumption.
If this is true, the official American interpretation for drug abuse is not entirely mistaken: Supply encourages demand. As one person who succumbed to the wiles of heroin confesses, "You grow up watching your
friends use it, and then one day you're fixing too." Conversations with affluent yuppies along the border, whether in Tijuana or Matamoros, confirm that the use of cocaine, which is easily obtainable, is on the rise, and
statistics of the Sistema Nacional prove this; the newspaper *El Zócalo* concedes that 500,000 young men, principally in the border states, are addicted, and their numbers are growing. *Cuadernos del Norte* reports that
residents of Chihuahua are among the chief users of cocaine; of every

thousand people, one out of ten smokes marijuana. Drug use among students of the secondary and high schools of Ciudad Juárez is climbing at an alarming rate. Police in the city can tell you the location of *picaderos*, private galleries where aficionados buy and shoot heroin. They stay open, so goes one local complaint, because of bribes given the police. On some mornings, it is not uncommon for Juarenses to stumble upon bodies of people dead from overdoses. In the secondary schools of Mexicali, *El Mexicano* reports, police take into custody dealers selling heroin to students. Among the poor of Mexico, according to *Diario 29*, more than three out of four drug abusers between the ages of fifteen and seventeen, most with less than a secondary-school education, were unemployed. This clearly refutes the belief of some that poverty plays no significant role in Mexican drug abuse. Witness to this tragedy is a mural painted on the walls of a barrio in Matamoros, dedicated by friends to Chato Gaytón, who died from an overdose, "without ever having the opportunity to know how much the *chavos* [slang for "companions"] of his *barrio* loved him."

As recent events in the Western Hemisphere document, drug cartels, through the use of bribery, intimidation, and murder, undermine already weak political and legal institutions. That is the experience of Mexico, now confronted by the deadly mixture of politics and drugs that characterizes Colombia. To emphasize this again, in Mexico the traffic is ever more profitable. American officials calculate the yearly earnings of the Gulf cartel that operates from Tamaulipas at between $10 and $20 billion; a DEA and FBI study of the Ciudad Juárez cartel talks of weekly $200 million transactions. In the Ciudad Juárez–El Paso region, the report charges, no less than two thousand individuals are involved in the business. In 1994, according to some estimates, Mexico earned between $10 and $30 billion from the trade, while oil exports, the country's chief source of outside income, netted just $7 billion. Recycled narco dollars propel much of the country's private investment, turning tourism, which ranks third on the list of money makers, into a "money launderer's paradise." Unmonitored cash transactions go unnoticed in hotels, nightclubs, and restaurants, as well as at *casas de cambio* (money exchanges), many of which are havens for drug dealers. Even legitimate businessmen launder drug money. One congressional subcommittee in the United States recently heard testimony that up to $30 billion per year may be laundered on the border.

But the cancer that eats at Mexico transcends tourists and hotels, as any observer of border events knows. It embraces judicial authorities and police at all levels, as well as federal officials, as José Manuel di Bella charges in "El Madruguete," a short story about life in Mexicali, in which he writes of bribery, corruption, and sellouts at every level of officialdom. Baja California's human rights ombudsman says that confidence in the police "is very low. It is commonly known that there are criminals within the police forces." In Matamoros, to cite another report, few Mexicans believe that the police, outgunned and short on resources, can provide security. Few drug-related murders are ever solved. Or, to cite the testimony of a police commander in Tijuana who was later slain by the mafia, corrupt federal police are "not just the friends of the traffickers, they [are] . . . their servants." The angry outburst followed on the heels of a shootout on the streets of Tijuana in 1994, when state judicial police attacked federal agents trying to arrest a drug lord. The corrupt cops rescued him and whisked him away. Terrence E. Poppa, in his hard-hitting book, describes a district attorney in Ciudad Juárez who, helped by allies in the state police, ran his own marijuana smuggling operation. Poppa goes on to charge that federal and state police collect $12 to $17 for every pound of marijuana from smugglers in Ciudad Juárez. One former police officer in Ciudad Juárez admitted that he had loaded a plane with boxes stuffed with payoffs for the republic's attorney general for shipment to Mexico City. When asked what his other duties as a policeman were, he replied, "Pick up the money; other times pick up the drugs." Had he ever done any police work? "Sometimes," he replied. Another officeholder made his money by exacting bribes from traffickers who operated in Ciudad Juárez and El Paso. He kept his job until ten of his men killed a TV anchorwoman, her mother-in-law, and a third person in Ciudad Juárez; he had her silenced to keep her from revealing what she knew about his activities. The death toll from killings by mafiosos in Matamoros has recently taken a worrisome jump. Police regularly come across the bodies of men killed in gang wars, handcuffed and shot through the head—a trademark, according to authorities, of drug hits. In Brownsville, during the last six months of 1996, at least six corpses turned up, all the victims of torture.

Elsewhere along the border similar stories repeat themselves. Police corruption follows a pattern. Commanders on the take sell protection to one gang of drug merchants and attack rival ones. In Nogales, anti-narcotics police seized a repairman, drove him to the home of a cocaine dealer, and beat him—all because he had failed to pay money he owed the drug merchant. The police, the evidence indicates, were the paid enforcers of the trafficker. Mexican federal police not infrequently escort tons of illegal narcotics to the border, whence the drugs enter the United States. One agent in El Paso recalls shoot-outs with drug smugglers protected by Mexican police: "We were shot at by both the smugglers and the police." Unbelievably, after the gunfight, one of the police came over to the American side and demanded that the dope be turned over to him, claiming he had been chasing the drug dealers. "We couldn't help but laugh," the agent remembered; "What balls he had to give us that crap." Pervasive corruption in the Mexican police, as the above story illustrates, ridicules enforcement. *Boletín de Prensa*, a narco ballad, mocks the police:

> *It is said that the border*
> *Harbors nests of drug traffickers.*
> *That may be true.*
> *But who can verify what is said*
> *If not the police . . .*

Not immune, by the same token, is the military; its ranks, the Mexican bishopric reports, are "infiltrated by the traffic in narcotics." Its involvement in the sordid business dates from 1977, when it was asked to help out in the campaign against the drug traffic. As one dissident army officer told me in Michoacán, few generals in narcotics zones have not soiled their reputations. To illustrate the extent of this sordid behavior, in summer 1995, soldiers in the command of General Alfredo Morán Acevedo shot to death seven drug agents at the site of a planeload of drugs from Colombia at a remote airstrip in Veracruz. U.S. customs pilots, who had followed the agents, videotaped the shooting; the soldiers had come there to protect the drugs. The agents, autopsy reports revealed, were shot at point-blank range. Army generals participate in the protection racket. Miguel de la Madrid's minister of defense, General Juan Arévalo Gardoqui, was named in U.S. court papers as a protector of narcotics-smuggling operations. As commander of the Fifth Military Zone in Chihuahua City, Arévalo, according to testimony given by a dope dealer, had accepted a $10 million bribe from Rafael Caro Quintero, a major trafficker in the mid-1980s—in return for having soldiers stand guard over his marijuana crop in Chihuahua. In the 1970s, the Chihuahua border town of Ojinaga had a garrison of soldiers. Local inhabitants told everyone who would listen that Pablo Acosta, the town's *capo*, paid their commander in Chihuahua City $100,000 a month for protection; without it, they believed "there was no way he could do what he was doing." When planes from Colombia landed at hidden airfields near Ojinaga, soldiers escorted the shipment of cocaine to a desert ranch; Acosta rewarded each one with a $20 bill.

The most embarrassing scandal was yet to come. Early in 1997, General Jesús Gutiérrez Rebollo, two months earlier named Mexico's drug czar, was arrested for trafficking in cocaine and shielding one of the country's biggest cartels. At the time of his appointment, General Barry McCaffrey, his cohort in the United States, had called Gutiérrez "a guy of absolute unquestioned integrity." The Gutiérrez episode also reveals that drug gangs compete with one another to buy protection from the officer corps, as the arrest of General Alfredo Navarro Lara demonstrated; just weeks after the Gutiérrez jailing, Navarro Lara was apprehended for trying to buy off a top law enforcement authority on behalf of a powerful cocaine cartel that operates in Baja California.

The cancer eats away at the PRI, as yet the heart of the political system. As Ernesto Zedillo, currently president of Mexico, acknowledged after he had appointed Gutiérrez Rebollo chief of the anti-narcotics effort, the horrendous error had made him "realize that narcotics crime" had reached extremely serious levels" and brought "national shame" upon his country. Zedillos's apology to the nation was in order. A study by the National Autonomous University of Mexico estimates that drug lords spend up to $500 million annually on bribes to officials of all sorts. To quote one assistant attorney general of the republic, there are politicos tied to drug traffickers and politicos who are drug traffickers. "They are numerous," he added. Before he resigned, he named the governors of four states, one of whom, the chief of Morelos, was driven out of office because of a national uproar over charges of corruption levied against him and his underlings, including the police commander. Among those accused of complicity with traffickers were two members of the presidential cabinet. One was Manuel Bartlett, minister of education under Carlos Salinas and formerly head of the Interior Department and now governor of Puebla. Worse still, a longtime private secretary of Raul Salinas Lozano, the patriarch of the Salinas clan, not only implicated him but also named his son, Raul Salinas de Gortari, brother of the former president, and, in addition, José Francisco Ruiz Massieu, a son-in-law who was the number two politico of the PRI until he was gunned down in 1994. Salinas Lozano, the aging patriarch, had earlier earned a master's degree from Harvard, headed the Ministry of Commerce and Industry, and represented the state of Nuevo León in the senate; Raul, his brother, had held high-ranking jobs in federal agencies. Upon hearing tales of Raul's ties to the narco traffic, Salinas sent him away to the University of California at San Diego, where an American friend on the faculty found him a research fellowship. During the notoriously corrupt Salinas years, a woman on the payroll of a major mafioso was the paramour of Emilio Gamboa Patrón, a cabinet member and top security official, and at the same time, she carried on a torrid love affair with José Córdoba Montoya, Salinas's chief of staff. Drugs had, indeed, exacerbated endemic corruption in the PRI.

Official corruption, which Priistas exemplify, has been around for a long time, but the drug variety has flourished particularly since the presidency of Salinas from 1988 to 1994, when it penetrated every level of enforcement. Evidence shows that traffickers had the ear of high officials in his administration. Federal police commanders and two of the three chiefs of the enforcement campaign were taking bribes at the time. Drug merchants, according to an FBI officer, bought state-owned companies privatized by Salinas, purchased bank stock, and sought election to bank boards in order to facilitate laundering their ill-gotten money. Federal and state judicial police, although constantly announcing the capture of minor drug dealers, never seemed to get their hands on the real bosses. When these law enforcement agencies did nothing to halt the wave of drug-related assassinations in Baja California Norte, Governor Ernesto Ruffo traveled to Mexico City to complain personally to the attorney general about the inaction by federal authorities. Although he carried proof of what was going on in Tijuana, the attorney general ignored his demands that something be done to rid his state of traffickers. Fearing that the *capos* would learn of his complaints by way of informants in the office of the attorney general, Ruffo hired more bodyguards and used public taxis for transportation. Luis Gutiérrez Rodríguez, the editor of *Uno Mas Uno,* a Mexico City daily, warns that drug traffickers have made inroads into the nation's press, an indictment that has been repeated by Ruffo, who took to task certain newspaper reporters for accepting bribes from dealers in narcotics.

Yet until the embarrassment of Gutiérrez Rebollo, officials under Zedillo, the chief of the republic since 1994, appeared to close their eyes to evidence indicating complicity among high officeholders and the drug cartels. The capture of the famous cocaine smuggler Juan García Abrego and his deportation to Houston seemingly contradicts this view. Still, most Mexican analysts have their doubts; they admit it was masterful political theater and welcome the arrest as a first step, but they believe it was mainly motivated by the administration's wish to appease the United States. The *capo,* the analysts say, was already a spent bullet, his power eclipsed after the Salinistas left office and he lost his protectors, who had made it possible for him to move his cargo from airstrip to airstrip without fear of arrest. The *New York Times* editorialized that in his heyday, García Abrego reputedly "enjoyed links with the president's brother, Raul Salinas," and with Emilio Gamboa Patrón, who headed the cabinet in control of airports, highways, and seaports; an assistant U.S. attorney general has declared that García Abrego also enjoyed the connivance of federal police, judiciously bribed—as were federal law enforcement officers in the United States. Stripped of that protection, the *capo* turned fugitive. Unless more is done, a New York daily admonished, the arrest "represents no more than shallow symbolism"; alone, it "will barely slow the torrent of drugs flowing over the Mexican border." That warning proved prophetic: "With or without the *capo,*" laments a highly placed customs official in Brownsville, Texas, "the traffic in drugs continues, above all marijuana and cocaine, but today also heroin."

The execution, in 1993, of Cardinal Juan Jesús Posadas Campo at the Guadalajara airport lends weight to this skepticism. Nothing has been done to punish the culprits, though the evidence implicates the Tijuana-based drug cartel that pulls in millions of dollars handling shipments of

Colombian cocaine and heroin from Southeast Asia and Pakistan destined for the United States. The killing was initially blamed on a case of mistaken identity; Posadas, however, had earlier been Catholic bishop of Tijuana. The assassins apparently escaped with the connivance of federal police who put them on an Aeromexico flight bound for Tijuana; its departure was delayed for twenty minutes to await their arrival. This could not have occurred without the green light from a higher-up in government. A former official quoted by the *Los Angeles Times* says that person is Carlos Hank González, a billionaire speculator and secretary of tourism and later agriculture under Salinas. One of his sons, Jorge Hank Rhon, owns the Agua Caliente racetrack in Tijuana, reputedly a money-laundering depot for drug lords. According to Porfirio Muñoz Ledo, a leader of the Partido de la Revolución Democrática, Miguel de la Madrid, who preceded Salinas, thought briefly of indicting Carlos Hank for corruption but declined to do so out of fear for his life.

But Carlos Salinas, in a turnabout, named him to his cabinet. As Andrew Reding of the Pacific News Service says, this was "not an isolated case of coddling corruption." Admiral Mauricio Schleske, Salinas's secretary of the navy, had to resign when it was learned that sailors at the Matamoros naval base smuggled drugs across the border and the admiral was found to own luxury condos in Houston. Salinas's first drug chief was Javier Coello Trejo, whose tough-on-crime stance won him the accolades of Washington but the condemnation of Mexico's human rights commission, which accused him of torturing and murdering innocent citizens. Salinas turned a deaf ear to these charges, merely reassigning Coello. Yet, Coello, insiders say, was in the pay of traffickers; a relative of the chief of the Gulf cartel testified in a Texas courtroom that Coello was paid more than $1 million for protection. For attorney general, Salinas picked Enrique Alvarez del Castillo, the former governor of Jalisco, a politico with ties, so went the rumors, to the Guadalajara cartel, accused by two witnesses of taking part in the plot to kill Enrique Camarena, a DEA agent, in 1985.

Analysts doubt that Zedillo and his cohorts are truly ready to take on the mobs and their protectors and exacerbate economic and political problems. Mexico, additionally, might well be addicted to the billions reaped from the trade. A former U.S. Senate financial investigator told a House banking subcommittee that the money helps prop up the bankrupt Mexican banking system. Both marijuana and heroin, which are grown locally, provide badly needed foreign exchange, blessings to debt-burdened Mexico. They are also windfalls to campesinos, who are unable to survive by planting corn and beans and discover rewards in the cultivation of marijuana and poppies. Nationwide, it is estimated that nearly 33.5 thousand acres of the Mexican countryside are planted to opium poppies. Many of the Tarahumara Indians of Chihuahua, for example, now cultivate them rather than corn, though what money they make has yet to make a dent in their style of life. At Baborigame, a Tarahumara hamlet of no more than three thousand people, almost every family cultivates marijuana plants and opium poppies. All of the residents, declares a community leader, "eat from the profits of the drug trade." Since the crisis of 1982, these crops, as *El Financiero* puts it, are commonplace in rural Mexico, particularly in Chihuahua, Durango, and Sinaloa.

∘ ∘ ∘ ✦ ∘ ∘ ∘

Whatever the responsibility of Mexico, the border is "an expressway for narcotics," as one pundit puts it. James R. Jones, until recently the U.S. ambassador to Mexico, warns that until steps are taken to prevent it, "Mexico will take over from Colombia in a few years as the traffickers' headquarters of choice." Jones's assertion merits careful consideration. At present, Mexicans transship more than three-fourths of the cocaine entering the United States, in addition to marijuana and black heroin, their traditional products; they now handle quality white heroin from Colombia and Southeast Asia and virtually run the profitable and growing market in the United States for methamphetamine, or "speed."

In his book titled *The Life and Death of a Mexican Kingpin*, which concerns the activities of a *capo* in dusty Ojinaga, Poppa describes the border as a "two-thousand mile sieve" where traffickers "operate from towns and villages behind the security of an international line." In the East County of San Diego, where seizures of cocaine have risen tenfold, the border is a barbwire fence, openly inviting drug smugglers to drive through it. Most seizures take place between Tecate, Campo, and Boulevard, communities of retired people, small-scale ranchers, and goatherds, all of whom have to contend with drug drop-offs and vehicle chases by the border patrol, according to one account. One veteran of World War II, who owns thirteen acres of land facing on the border, has had smugglers drive though his gates with the border patrol not far behind. Until the drug epidemic, the only crime in the rural expanse had been a stolen goose at Christmastime. In the Del Rio sector of Texas, just across from Piedras Negras and Ciudad Acuña, ranchers cannot rely on local authorities to protect them from narcotics smugglers who traverse their lands, seemingly at will. One frightened rancher, whose house was shot at by them, now will not even give his name to reporters; in his view, since the dope traffickers know where "we live, my wife and I aren't safe." Another rancher stumbled upon armed smugglers on pastureland on the shores of the Rio Grande. He was told to clear out; he related that one smuggler holding a rifle said if he didn't, "he was gonna kill me." Now when this rancher rides the range in his pickup truck, he carries a "shotgun, an assault rifle, and a .45 automatic." Poppa recalls that in Matamoros, dope dealers were brought to justice "only after fifteen people were kidnapped and hacked to death," and in Ciudad Juárez, a drug dealer had the run of the city until he kidnapped and then tortured a freelance photographer from El Paso because of stories he published about him. The "bodies of police informants still turn up" in Ciudad Juárez, the *New York Times* reports, "their mouths sometimes stuffed with one of the fingers they might have pointed at drug traffickers."

From what is known, three mafias control the trade. Their *capos* come and go. But their demise sets off turf wars, as rivals fight to supplant them. These are bloody encounters, where hired gunmen go after rival kingpins, killing at will whoever stands in their way. The death of Amado Carrillo Fuentes on July 4, 1997, then boss of the Juárez cartel, is a case in point. His departure set off a wave of killings, the first just nine days after his demise, followed by another wave three days later. On a Sunday evening early in August, as was the custom in Ciudad Juárez after the curtain had fallen on the last of the bullfights at the Plaza Monumental, an ally of Carrillo Fuentes sat down to eat at the restaurant Max Fim. Suddenly, two gunmen armed with AK-47s entered from the street, firing off 102 shots and killing five people, among them the drug lord, his girlfriend, and their bodyguards, and wounding six others. That same month, local residents came upon the bodies of four physicians who were slain, police believe, because they treated the wounds of a rival gunman. These executions and others that regularly occur have hurt the tourist industry, particularly the business of downtown hotels, because fearful Americans stay away in droves and many Juarenses stop patronizing restaurants. They have also led some Juarenses, long willing to close their eyes to the cancer, to hold a march against violence. "I know the narcos won't hear us," a Catholic priest lamented, "but maybe God will."

The state of Chihuahua, the headquarters for the mafia from Ciudad Juárez, sits between Durango and Sinaloa, and the three are known as the Golden Triangle. According to the newspaper *El Bravo*, this is the most active drug zone. One of its hot spots is the town of Ojinaga, a smuggler's paradise, during Prohibition for bootleg liquor and *sotol*, a form of tequila, and after World War II a hub for heroin from poppies planted in the mountains of Sinaloa, turned into heroin in clandestine laboratories on the outskirts of Parral. From Ojinaga, the drug goes to such places as Odessa, Texas, and Hobbs, New Mexico, at times flown there by airplanes that take off from hidden airstrips. Some of the traffickers are Mexicans, but others are Americans. By 1984, the drug dealers of Ojinaga were also transshipping Colombian cocaine, smuggling some of it into Texas and selling to dealers as far away as Matamoros and Tijuana. By 1987, as much as five tons a month of Colombian cocaine entered Ojinaga. Drugs altered life in Ojinaga. "We have shoot-outs at any hour on our major streets," a schoolteacher lamented. No one touches those responsible, because as the locals say, "the police and the army are all involved." Across the border, life also changed. Before the advent of drugs, Presidio, Texas, in the heart of the Big Bend country, was merely a dot on the map, a place where summer temperatures seldom dipped below 100 degrees Fahrenheit and where border patrol agents who lived in Alpine, sixty miles away, served on temporary duty. Drugs transformed Presidio into a key post for U.S. customs.

On the Gulf side, Matamoros shelters another cartel that got a heady push in the 1980s with the U.S. crackdown on Caribbean mobs, which transformed the Lower Rio Grande Valley into a smuggler's haven. The cartel handles cocaine, worth as much as $20 billion a year, shipped north from Colombia. Residents say that Mission, one of the towns in the Valley, boasts of having twenty-five drug millionaires. In Starr County, where almost half of its residents receive welfare checks, contraband is referred to as *mercancía noble*, or noble merchandise. Nearly one-third of its population makes its "living from contraband." Fronting on the Rio Grande for fifty miles, property along the river belongs to families of Mexican origin with ties to both sides. As Alan Weisman writes, "Floating contraband from one relative's front yard to another's backyard is a sure way to combat poverty." One story in the *Brownsville Herald* on these family enterprises describes how Artemio Belmontes and his three sons transported marijuana out of the valley, as others in the family had done before. Hidalgo and Cameron, though lagging behind Starr, are drug counties, too. Almost daily, the *Herald* reports on seizures of drugs from Mexico, mainly marijuana but also cocaine.

Smuggling "is a way of life," *U.S. News and World Report* concludes. On the outskirts of Matamoros and Brownsville, smugglers fill rubber rafts and float their goods across the Rio Grande. If smugglers need a "mule," they find a teenager who wants to earn a buck driving a truck from the river to Rio Grande City, one of Starr County's towns. After a while, the unemployed young man begins wearing fancy cowboys boots and driving a new pickup, which means profits for car dealers, sales for clothes merchants, more gasoline pumped, and, ultimately, profitable times for the community. Money laundering, a mushrooming industry up and down the border, marches hand in hand with the operations of cartels. In 1994, one officer of the American Express International Bank office in Beverly Hills, California, was sentenced to ten years in prison for laundering $30 million of cocaine money for García Abrego, who was then able to finance the development of a country club in Harlingen, Texas. The bank paid a fine of $7 million for its role in this scheme. But violence, too, accompanies drugs; murders are up in the Rio Grande Valley, statistics of local police testify, the result of expanded drug trafficking in Cameron and Hidalgo Counties. In July 1994, Los Texas, a drug mob, killed the Nuevo Laredo commander of the federal police; the gang had been a fixture in the border city since 1980.

Another cartel runs the trade in Northwest Mexico. The traffickers make their homes in the best *colonias* of Tijuana, the Chapultepec and Bolaños Cacho, in million-dollar mansions flanked by swimming pools. The *capos*, natives of Sinaloa, manage a multimillion-dollar empire; they own warehouses, hotels, pharmacies, and nightspots. Drugs, *El Mexicano* writes, revive the black legend of yore, but this time, the locus is tawdry border cities, the sites of murders committed by state and federal police in league with drug dealers. The resurrected legend is not entirely false, as Governor Ruffo admits. In Tijuana, according to *Zeta*, chiefs of the federal police use payoffs from traffickers to buy office buildings and restaurants and to go into legitimate business themselves. In 1994, a state prosecutor was arrested on suspicion of shielding the assassins of Cardinal Posadas, and a crusading police chief was gunned down. In that same year, a shoot-out between special agents from Mexico City and the state police, who were shielding traffickers, killed both the federal commander, who was visiting Tijuana to investigate the death of Cardinal Posada, and two state officers. At the center of this traffic are Tijuana and Mexicali, but Sonora, the neighboring state, is also notorious for drugs. A good part of the cocaine entering the United States, says *La Jornada*, comes through Nogales and its desert hinterland, some of it transported on horseback. For "$500," the newspaper explains, "any *chavo* will take one or two kilos, whatever you want, over the border." As José Luis Ibarra, rector of the University of Sonora, laments, the trade has led to ties with traffickers from Colombia, to violence, to corruption in politics and business, and, equally devastating, to drug addiction and juvenile delinquency.

Drug smuggling along the border, as the above discussion demonstrates, has regional foci. One is Baja California Norte, where the traffic has increased because drug traders, faced with mounting surveillance in South Florida, have also shifted their operations to Imperial County, on the edges of Baja California. In this isolated land, filled with barren hills and canyons and sparsely populated, airplanes land that take off from clandestine airstrips hidden in the mountains and deserts of northern Mexico. The *San Diego Union-Tribune* asserts that at "any given time . . . 20,000 to 30,000 pounds of cocaine are stashed in warehouses, truck trailers and underground bunkers or sitting in clandestine airstrips around Mexicali." American neighbors complain that Mexican authorities do too little to combat the traffic; one angry county official even demanded that marines be employed to patrol the border. Yet these people forget that San

Diego is the amphetamine capital of the world, which creates, in the opinion of Mexicans, a serious problem for Tijuana.

The business flourishes by auto, truck, and airplane. Smugglers are an ingenious lot when it comes to getting their goods into the United States. One way is to build false bottoms in tanker trucks or double walls in big semitrailers or to put special traps in the fenders of cars, under the fenders, in the door panels, or in the body itself. They stuff drugs into the butane tanks and refrigerators of campers, and they entice every type of person into being a "mule," a petty smuggler. A young woman driving a car with her two children told customs inspectors at the port of entry that she was going home to Los Angeles, but something seemed fishy. Sure enough, when the agents searched her car they found fifty-four pounds of marijuana. On another occasion, an elderly man who gave no sign of being a smuggler patiently waited his turn to drive past customs, but a package of marijuana caught the attention of a dog trained to detect drugs. As one agent acknowledges, the smugglers "are extremely cunning. . . . Rather than bringing one tanker across with 10,000 pounds of pot, they hire one hundred poor people to each bring one hundred pounds of pot."

Smugglers rely on up-to-date tools of the trade. One is the airplane, whether small or large, old or new. Authorities constantly report finding hidden airstrips, on one occasion nineteen of them in the backcountry of Mexicali. One wonders how these airstrips, which at times receive drug shipments every two weeks, operate without being detected. Planes from Colombia ferry the cocaine to Central Mexico, whence smaller planes or trucks carry the merchandise north to cities such as Mexicali, where smugglers package it in small parcels and conceal them in passenger cars that will carry the drugs over the border.

10

Man Against Nature

Whatever else might be said about the borderlands, one truth is indisputable: Ill fares the land. For this crime against nature, Americans and Mexicans share equal responsibility: The ongoing abuse is a binational enterprise, at times part and parcel of the global economy. As Peter Steinhart warns in his book *Two Eagles,* the "fine ecological balance is tipping," plunging toward its "complete destruction, until there will be nothing left but those new steel fences the U.S. Border Patrol is erecting to keep Mexicans out." Man has laid waste to a remarkable region, where plants, animals, and the land interblend in a wondrous, strange symbiosis.

The landscape of the borderlands is hardly static. West of Del Rio, a town not too distant from Laredo, Texas, as miles are reckoned in this vast territory, Nature rarely beckons with open arms. Only the Lower Rio Grande Valley, which lies on the Gulf of Mexico, sometimes provides lush, green havens, where Mexicans and Americans, with only a river to separate them, have lived, if not always in the friendliest of fashion, side by side since the middle of the nineteenth century. A discordant borderlands awaits to the west. In this belt of striking diversity exists a landscape seldom imitated—a jumble of craggy mountains, expansive valleys, riverbeds, grasslands, and deserts. Yet judged by its natural resources, it is a stingy land; poverty is more at home here than abundance.

• • • ✦ • • •

From El Paso to San Diego lies a harsh landscape, of mesquite and prickly pear cactus; in one author's view, this is "brush country . . . ugly in summer, drought-stricken, dusty, glaring." Heat pervades the landscape; it is relentless, but nowhere more so than in the Pinacate Desert of northern Sonora, named after a volcano. Wild and untamed by humans, the Pinacate sits forty miles west of Sonoita and just south of the international border. Called the "harshest desert in North America," the Pinacate goes years without tasting a drop of rain. Still, it is a land of beauty, where plant life, a riot of color during the spring, welcomes adventurous travelers. Julian Hayden, an anthropologist, tells a story that sums up what this desert means for humans. The story is about a mechanic in the 1930s who traveled the Pinacate on the lookout for abandoned cars. He slept under his truck during the day and conducted his search at night, once or twice coming across travelers dying of thirst. One day he stumbled upon an empty car, and when he opened one of its doors, the skeleton of a baby who had died of thirst fell out.

Most of the border cities sit where the climate is dry and the winds gusty; the soil, rarely very fertile, sustains desert or semidesert vegetation. The mesquite of Mexicali survives in a virtual desert, but in Ciudad Juárez, where the rains fall late in the summer but winds blow constantly and dust storms are commonplace, as they are in El Paso, the natural vegetation is mesquite and yucca. Cities like Ciudad Juárez and Mexicali, where demographic growth sabotages even the best-laid plans, are not known for their lush green parks.

On the shores of the Gulf of Mexico, the climate and landscape change. Mild, almost frost-free winters and moderate rainfall as one approaches the coastal plain are its attributes. The banks of the Rio Grande River, which winds its way to the ocean through dense thickets of carrizo cane and sabal palms, shelter endangered species of flora and fauna under the protection of the U.S. Fish and Wildlife Service. At the mouth of the river, not far from Brownsville, fishing buffs cast for redfish and flounder. However, the dry surrounding countryside is slowly engulfing much of what was once marshy woodland, though it still continues to lure migrating birds not found anywhere else. This riverfront refuge is one of America's chief bird-watching outposts. Upstream dams proved unfriendly to the old *resacas*, natural canals filled with flood waters. When they dried up, the forests that fed on their waters perished, too.

Despite the harm that man has wrought on the ecology, the borderlands, fifty miles on both sides, are richly biodiverse. Pronghorn antelope and long-nosed bats, animals uniquely adapted to the waterless world, live in the Pinacate. Bighorn sheep, their numbers decimated by hunters and diseases domesticated cattle and sheep carry, are also found. Reptiles, the natural offspring of the desert, are commonplace inhabitants of the border—lizards, particularly—as are roadrunners, ravens, coyotes, bobcats, and mountain lions, who somehow manage to evade hunters and cattlemen. Water, the key to their survival, hangs in the balance; as "water goes," predicts Steinhart, "so goes the wildlife. . . . At stake is the survival of its distinctive landscape and the living things that make it unique."

Unless man takes heed, disaster looms ahead. Today, environmental degradation is the name of the game, so long as individual gain dictates behavior. Even setting aside issues of social justice and quality of life, border cities, if judged by water purity, solid waste disposal, and clean air, measure up poorly. The cities grow rapidly, in helter-skelter fashion, particularly on the Mexican side, their demographics driven by *maquiladoras*. The first to suffer is the physical environment, as the smog from cars and industries pollutes the air, and simultaneously, the exploding population drains the countryside of its water, uproots its vegetation, and drives off its animal kingdom.

Once upon a time, a mighty river ran through nearly half of the borderlands, before man chose to build big dams, once the icons of progress but now symbols of waste and inefficiency that wreak havoc on ecosystems. On crossing the river, the Spaniards baptized it the Rio Bravo, later renamed the Rio Grande by the American conquerors of Texas and New Mexico. Cora Montgomery, an adventurous woman from upstate New York who lived in tiny Eagle Pass in the early 1850s, recalls in her memoirs a Bravo "about as wide as the Hudson at Troy" and passionately argued that it was most "navigable," since three successful attempts had already been made. The first party, which sailed from the Gulf of Mexico, reached Eagle Pass; the second party crossed in a keel boat fifty feet long, sixteen wide, and drawing eighteen inches of water and came to within two hundred miles of El Paso; the last party got one hundred miles beyond the mouth of the Pecos River, "at the very lowest stage of water." All that must be done, Montgomery concluded, so that light-draft steamers might journey up the river was to clear a channel, and that could be done for just $50,000. This was the Rio Grande, or Bravo, until man radically altered its character.

Yet, until the twentieth century, when Americans poured tons of cement and sand to build monster dams such as Elephant Butte, the "big river" was still capable of overrunning its banks. Americans and Mexicans, eager to further exploit its waters, tamed it even more in the Texas region of the river when they built the Amistad and Falcon dams, joint reservoirs and, supposedly, flood-control projects. A statue of Tlaloc, the Aztec rain god, on the Mexican side overlooks Lake Amistad, a reservoir that never seems to fill up. Falcon Dam, which lies to the east and is perpetually near empty, is also a hydroelectric plant, as well as a haven for fishermen, boating enthusiasts, and gangs of international smugglers.

Man, nonetheless, discards past ideas, no matter how dumb, only slowly, and so at times narrow ends prevail over wiser counsel. Wildlife on the banks of the "big river," having somehow survived man's missteps, for example, may yet face extinction from what he does, as the current behavior of the border patrol at Brownsville vividly shows. There, political expediency threatens to destroy a river that is still flanked by some of the most ecologically important lands left in the United States. At Brownsville, agents of the patrol who are intent on stopping the flow of illegal migrants bulldoze virgin lands for roads, erect fences, and nightly light up the banks of the Rio Grande, thus jeopardizing the ecosystem. Although helping them to spot men and women hiding in the brush, the glow from the high-intensity floodlights disrupts the life of cherished ocelots and jaguarundi, rare bobcats that hunt rodents in the dark, so say the men and women who run the U.S. Fish and Wildlife Service. For their part, these environmentalists dream of a refuge for birds and animals on the banks of the "big river" and, for that purpose, buy up abandoned farmlands and restore them to their natural state. But, as a local hunter and fishing buff says, "If the Border Patrol had its way, this place would look like the moon." To call up an astute observation, this episode juxtaposes, on the one hand, a river that is an ecological marvel against a politically charged international border, on the other.

The patrol is merely a recent sinner. For decades, man's antics have threatened wildlife and virtually killed off some species. Nearly all of the native habitat lying on the U.S. side of the Rio Grande is gone because of the spread of farming, cattle ranching, and urban sprawl. In this region, the World Environment Center affirms, over one hundred vertebrate species are "listed as endangered, threatened, or at the periphery of their range." Downstream from the Brownsville area, in the tidal basins and subtropical marshlands, the destruction of the oxbow lakes has led to the potential disappearance of the *chachalaca,* or Mexican pheasant, and the alligator gar, or *catán*, both now considered endangered species; the dumping of raw sewage and toxic industrial wastes from Eagle Pass to Brownsville hastened the demise of the alligator gar, as did the construction of dams and reservoirs such as Lake Amistad. DDT spraying that contaminates a vital habitat puts the horned toad of South Texas on the brink of extinction. Once a common sight, the Mexican gray wolf survives merely here and there, the victim of federal policies that labeled it a livestock predator until a few years ago, and of course, it falls prey to random shooting by ranchers and farmers.

No river basin, as the harm done to the native habitat illustrates, is safe from man's paradoxical behavior. Colorado River water that reaches Mexicali is so contaminated with the raw sewage of Yuma, the chemical fertilizers and insecticides used by farmers in the Imperial Valley, and salt, above all, that because of international agreements, the U.S. Bureau of Reclamation had to build a desalinization plant so that downstream Mexican farmers could use the water. The state of California and county officials in the Imperial Valley label the New River, which arises in the United States and then flows through the sprawling city of Mexicali before dumping its polluted water into the Salton Sea, "the dirtiest river in America." One official of the Environmental Protection Agency (EPA), claims that the New River "contains every disease known in the Western Hemisphere." The culprits are binational: millions of gallons of raw Mexican sewage and the toxic wastes of *maquiladora* plants. "It runs through the heart of our city and makes it a no-man's-land," laments the mayor of Mexicali. As the "New River sloshes across the international line," a reporter for the *San Diego Union-Tribune* wrote, "with a scummy green color, detergent foam and repellent odors of sewer and slaughterhouse, it is difficult to remember that its main ingredient is a precious resource—water." According to the local sheriff's office, the river carries the germs of polio, hepatitis, encephalitis, and typhoid, nor is it difficult to find carcasses of dead animals in its waters.

The tribulations of the New River testify to the difficulties of coping with the pollution of the border's water resources. As Mexicali grew by leaps and bounds, largely because of the arrival of the *maquiladora* industry, the old sewage treatment system that dumped its refuse into the New River collapsed, so that today it treats merely one-third of the city's waste. Now, to save money, a "quick fix" is on, calculated to eliminate one-third of the raw sewage discharge of older *colonias,* but while this goes on, raw sewage from the newer ones increases. Plans are also afoot to build a second treatment plant, but the clean water will belong to Mexico and no longer flow north into the Salton Sea, which, in the opinion of environmentalists, will hasten the salt buildup to the point where the sea's fish and birds will no longer be able to reproduce.

This sorry picture is hardly unique. In 1993, the *Journal of American Rivers*, a prestigious publication, put the Rio Grande at the top of its list of the "most endangered rivers." Because of its heavy pollution, as anyone who sees it can verify, its "rehabilitation" requires "a level of cooperation and zealous law enforcement never before witnessed in the often contentious history" of Mexico and the United States, to quote the *Los Angeles Times*. At this juncture, that warning will likely go unheeded, despite efforts by the well-intentioned in both countries.

The Rio Grande is the second-longest river in North America, surpassed only by the Mississippi. It drains over 355,000 square miles in Colorado, New Mexico, and Texas, as well as Durango, Chihuahua, Nuevo León, Coahuila, and Tamaulipas in Mexico. At the federal prison of La Tuna just below El Paso, the river starts on a 1,200-mile journey to the Gulf of Mexico, its course marking out the international boundary line between Mexico and the United States. Daily, it seems, people on both sides of the border abuse its waters, either sucking them dry or dumping pesticides or carcinogenic and industrial solvents into them. According to one report, nearly 100 million gallons of raw sewage from the Mexican cities of Ciudad Juárez, Nuevo Laredo, Reynosa, Ciudad Acuña, and Matamoros flow into the river; none has a waste treatment plant. Toxic-waste dumps can be found along the edges of the Rio Grande, and farmers, by siphoning water and adding to the concentration of toxins, exacerbate the problem. The sorry plight of its waters bodes ill for the survival of the once great river.

Along the border, water is the indispensable commodity. Without it, life dies. Yet by the time the Rio Grande reaches El Paso, it is more creek than river; that occurred, say Mexicans, when growing populations in New Mexico and Colorado began to preempt water for downstream users, bringing ruin to the agriculture of the Valley of Juárez. Not until the Río Conchos, which flows down from the Western Sierra Madre through Chihuahua, and the Río Salado and Río San Juan, both Mexican waterways, enter the Rio Grande just above Ojinaga does it again become a river. This runoff from Mexico provides more than 70 percent of the Rio Grande's downstream water. The Amistad and Falcon dams, both in Texas, divert more of its water to American farmers, city dwellers, and industry, leaving only a trickle (just 15 percent of its original volume) for the Mexicans of Matamoros.

Farmers on both sides of the river pay the price for a river made unfit for irrigation. On the American side, they sell their land to speculators, and the poor build homes next to the river, where the absence of zoning laws permit them to dump raw sewage and garbage into its waters. The result is contamination, which, combined with erosion and air pollution, destroys plant and animal life and endangers human health. It was not always this way. Before the upriver irrigation projects, the Lower Rio Grande, in the manner of the Nile, watered and made fertile the lands on its banks.

This scenario unfolds over and over again, from one end of the borderlands to the other: streams and creeks damaged or destroyed; or dammed and diverted for use by farmers; and the pumping of groundwater for urban landscaping and agriculture that lowers water tables and sucks springs dry. Some rivers, the lucky ones, went underground, but others— the Gila, the Santa Cruz, and the Lower Salt in Arizona, to name three— died of thirst.

Water, more and more, becomes an issue of life or death for one and all, whether American or Mexican. Always, the theme overlaps or takes on ancillary significance with problems of diverse hues. Existing treaties invariably favor the United States; but Mexicans demand more of the waters they share, namely, the Rio Grande and the Colorado. Agricultural and municipal wastes endanger marine life in the estuaries and coastal belt on the Gulf of Mexico. Raw sewage dumped by Nuevo Laredo into the Rio Grande jeopardizes the health of both Mexicans and Americans. Failure to enforce the water emissions standards of the federal Clean Water Act led the U.S. Justice Department to file a suit against the City of El Paso in 1989. From Del Rio to Laredo, Texas, bulldozers level the land for industrial warehouses and border patrol roads, upsetting the habitats of wildlife, inviting erosion, and sowing salinity in the Rio Grande.

Water pollution, of course, is a major international problem. The 1991 report of the National Campaign Fund labeled the border region as a "2,000-mile-long Love Canal"; one-third of the sites tested by the group contained levels of toxins "20 to 215 times higher" than those allowed by laws in the United States. Two of the worst offenders were close by the Ford plant in Nuevo Laredo and the General Motors plant in Matamoros. On both sides of the border, water contamination causes intestinal diseases; they kill more Mexicans, especially children, than any other disease, and they are rampant among the poor who dwell on the American side. Even poor Mexicans, when they can afford it, drink bottled water, a universal practice in the region. In Ciudad Juárez, university scientists urge people to boil their water or buy it bottled. In Brownsville, waiters may serve you tap water, but they drink bottled water. There may be, according to one author, a link between high cancer rates and drinking water from the Rio Grande. Some thirty-three counties that draw their water from the river show rates of cancer above the national average. Groundwater contaminated by American assembly plants on the Mexican side may be responsible for a cancer cluster in Nogales, Arizona.

The availability of water will likely determine the scope of future border development. Supply falters and quality is poor. That international metropolises thrive under these circumstances hardly justifies their existence. Neither the urban complex of El Paso–Ciudad Juárez nor that of Mexicali-Calexico possesses sufficient water for current populations, "let alone future ones," as Richard C. Bath argues. As *El Continental* of Ciudad Juárez puts it, "The lack of water is frightening . . . the majority of the people are dying of thirst." To quote *El Diario* of Nuevo Laredo, "We have more people than water." The situation of Nogales, Sonora, is, if anything, more critical. For the border cities, the challenge of the future is the supply of water, a headache that worsens in accordance with population growth and industrial use.

The problem includes groundwater, especially for "metroplexes" such as El Paso–Ciudad Juárez, which rely heavily on subsurface aquifers. The principal water reserve for both cities is the Hueco Bolson, a large subsurface table that extends for miles that is predicted to dry out, according to Sito Negron of the *El Paso Times*, no later than the year 2020. Of the big population clusters in the Lower Rio Grande Valley, only Matamoros and

Reynosa do not face a groundwater shortage, but this is of little consolation since their supply is too saline for most uses. Although there are international agreements for surface waters, there are none covering underground deposits, which is likely to stimulate more disputes between Mexico and the United States because both compete for the same water. This appears to be almost certain for the Hueco Bolson, which provides about 65 percent of the total water for El Paso and is the chief source of well water for Ciudad Juárez. Its use, however, differs from one side of the border to the other. El Pasoans use a goodly portion of their water for lawns, gardens, and air conditioners, but in Ciudad Juárez most of it goes for human consumption. "I was probably one of the guilty ones," José Madrid of West El Paso confesses. "We just got a house and it takes a lot of water to put in a nice lawn."

For cities on the shores of the Rio Grande, the supply of water is also drying up. Stream flow is below normal, especially when the rains do not fall, making for periodic and lasting droughts. For similar reasons, groundwater levels drop, causing wildlife, fish first of all, to die out. Droughts, it should be remembered, plague the borderlands. In New Mexico during the drought of 1902, cowboys told of being able to "step from one dead animal to another and not touch ground around the dried-up water holes." During the 1934 drought, one rancher recalls, "federal officials came onto [my] father's ranch, paid for the cattle, shot every one, and left them dead on the ground."

The current drought exemplifies the calamities that befall border communities when Mother Nature withholds her blessings. According to the *El Paso Herald Post*, this is the worst drought in over half a century to hit Northeastern Mexico. So desperate are Mexican farmers on the outskirts of Matamoros that they take water from an old drainage ditch saturated with salt; when told of the danger of doing it, they reply that "water from the polluted ditch . . . is better than no water at all." Near Mission, Texas, other Mexican farmers clandestinely pump water from the Rio Grande; one Texas official said he blamed Mexicans "when we couldn't get water down to users in Brownsville because of the water pumped illicitly." He forgot to add that American farmers were doing the same. Mexican reservoirs in Tamaulipas, Coahuila, and Chihuahua are largely depleted, threatening 2.5 million acres planted to corn, sorghum, and cotton. Even water set aside for drinking by human beings is being used for irrigation. The lack of rain and the ravenous use of water by city dwellers and farmers depresses levels of water in both the Falcon and Amistad dams.

This situation, not illogically, encourages international bickering. "Texas should not be punished for conserving their Rio Grande water reserves," Governor George W. Bush declared, opposing any concession of water rights to Mexicans. At issue are the low reserves of water in the Falcon and Amistad reservoirs; the Mexicans, in the opinion of the International Boundary and Water Commission, have used up all of their allotments. As Bush says, any loan of water to Mexico "would jeopardize the welfare of many of our citizens." Four straight years of below-normal inflows into the reservoirs, the result of a prolonged drought, led to this sorry state of affairs.

○ ○ ○ 🏵 ○ ○ ○

Long, long ago, grass carpeted much of the borderlands. Cattlemen on both sides of the border are responsible for its disappearance. The demise of the grasslands started in 1540, when Coronado, the Spanish explorer, introduced livestock. Eventually, a ranching lifestyle, which relied on vast grasslands to feed cattle, took over. The cattle clustered around water holes and streams, where they ate the grass, made the soil hard with their hooves, and eroded the land. The rains that fell washed away the topsoil. Eventually, mesquite, a bush-tree that had not previously grown near cottonwoods or willows, borrow weed or snakeweed, replaced grass. The results were disastrous; in the years from 1870 to 1886, when cattle freely roamed the New Mexican range, the grasslands declined from 90 percent to 25 percent, but mesquite, which thrives on little water, increased its domain tenfold. We have become, writes Guillermo Bonfil Batalla, a perceptive Mexican anthropologist, "amazingly adept at creating deserts, raping the land, exhausting water supplies and polluting the air." This is especially true for the borderlands, where humans and cattle have transformed grasslands into deserts; the devastation includes a 50 percent drop in the ability of the land to sustain crops or natural vegetation. In some places, the land has been made useless forever. In the Lower Basin of the Rio Grande Valley, man's antics destroyed nearly all of its ecosystem, a pattern repeated along the entire Rio Grande, where native habitat was cut, burned, and cleared for agriculture. During World War II, the fever to plant cotton wiped out acre upon acre of native vegetation; today, little remains of the Texas thorn forests. Not to be outdone, Mexico played copycat, setting fire to the brush and plowing the land of the Tamaulipas plain for cotton fields, driving birds and animals away.

Charcoal, one of the oldest fuels, provides a living example of the human propensity to cut off the nose to spite the face. Boxcars full of charcoal bound for northern markets cross the border at Nogales, and local consumption in Mexico keeps pace. For centuries, Chihuahuenses cut mesquite to make charcoal, but ultimately they cut so much of it that they now buy it from their neighbors. A similar tragedy is unfolding in northern Tamaulipas, where deforestation follows the drive to cut and burn mesquite in order to make charcoal. To quote one American observer,

"The topsoil layer is not very thick, so they're not going to get many years out of it." When they cannot plant crops anymore, they "run cattle . . . then goats." Once the land is exhausted, the people who lived on it "become refugees and move to the poorest areas of Matamoros or Tampico." But then, why should this tragic drama come as a surprise: No country on the face of this earth outdoes Mexico's rate of deforestation.

The culprits in this drama of man's folly are Americans and Mexicans. In the lexicon of Southwest-style cookery, it is taken for granted that charcoal enriches the flavor of beef and chicken, a belief that leads backyard barbecuers and restaurants to demand more and more of it. That demand spurred a flourishing mesquite charcoal industry in Tamaulipas, where cutting and burning mesquite for export to markets across the border occupies many natives. Steinhart describes this activity: "A dealer in Matamoros buys the charcoal "from Mexicans on impoverished ejidos" and "trucks it across the border to Brownsville," where others "repack it and ship it to American restaurant suppliers and supermarkets." By 1993, one such businessman, the proprietor of an enterprise in Donna, Texas, was selling nearly $700,000 worth of mesquite annually, mostly to Wal-Mart. He paid his Mexican suppliers $.06 a pound for their charcoal, which he also exported to Germany, England, Japan, and Belgium.

○ ○ ○ 📧 ○ ○ ○

The rape of the land goes hand in hand with the pollution of water and air. The pollution, as with everything else, is a joint affair. Economics partially explain Mexico's tardiness to safeguard its domain from polluters. To cite the official justification, "When we have jobs for everyone, we will worry about the physical environment." Or, to cite a Mexican representative for the *maquiladoras* of Tijuana, "We don't have the necessary infrastructure to destroy our toxic wastes." Growth, for the San Diego–Tijuana area, as for other regions, poses diabolical ecological challenges, which require regional planning to circumvent national constraints. If enlightened cooperation is not forthcoming, Alan Weisman says, "the border could deteriorate into a refuse heap, with each side blaming the other for what occurs."

Tijuana, along with Ciudad Juárez and most other communities, already has a problem with toxic wastes, particularly the contamination of its drainage system by deposits from *maquiladoras* and paint shops. As in most Mexican cities, unscrupulous land speculators and impoverished home owners ignore building codes, especially those covering the disposal of raw sewage. Neither are local officials free of responsibility for this neglect. Residents of the *colonias* Niños Heroes, Arboledas, and Constitución say, "For the past fifteen years, we have complained of the raw sewage that runs down our streets," but "neither municipal, state, nor federal authorities respond."

Tijuana has a celebrated case of international water pollution. Millions of gallons of raw sewage flow into the Tijuana River and then into the Pacific Ocean, where wastes drift onto Imperial Beach, an estuary in San Diego County. The water contains, according to San Diego health authorities, bacteria for amoebic dysentery, cholera, hepatitis, encephalitis, and polio. "The water's real dirty, and it stinks. . . . This is the most polluted beach in the nation," said one lifeguard. In 1961, Tijuana built a treatment facility to dump waste into the ocean, but its inadequacies and frequent breakdowns compelled reliance on San Diego's system. By 1975, twenty tons of raw sewage from Tijuana were daily piped for treatment to the San Diego Metro Sewage Authority. Tijuana inaugurated a new plant in 1987, but events since then do not show different results; untreated sewage still flows into the Pacific Ocean, while breaks in the rotting pipes of the city spill more of it into canyons that cross over into San Diego.

That situation, naturally enough, angers San Diegans. When raw sewage again seeped onto the beaches of his city, a local congressman dispatched a nasty letter to Mexico's president: "The transmission of sewage endangers the health of thousands of Americans, is destroying the economy of the border community, and represents a serious obstacle to building closer United States–Mexican relations." The "Mexicans can't act like we're their private toilet," a spokesman declared in the name of Citizens Revolting Against Pollution, which represents Tijuana River Valley homeowners. The director of the Imperial Beach Chamber of Commerce told the *Los Angeles Times*: "This sewage stuff has been devastating to Imperial Beach. . . . Mexicans get caught red-handed dumping sewage onto us and nobody does anything." A Mexican solution was not, just the same, on the horizon, as the chairman of the Ecological Committee of the Baja California state congress confessed: "We have no money to solve the problem, because we have no legislation or projects for laws to regulate pollution." Ultimately, the United States had to take it upon itself to build a treatment plant for Mexican sewage in the Tijuana River Valley.

Tijuana is not alone in this race to pollute. The cities of Nogales, Agua Prieta, and San Luis Río Colorado, Sonora bailiwicks, do their share. A member of El Colegio de Sonora, a think tank in Hermosillo, classifies the three cities as "notorious polluters of the urban environment." One woman resident exclaims that "we are sitting on a time bomb," but there is scant public awareness; nothing will be done "until we see people die off like flies." Yet hope exists: Joint financing built a waste treatment plant for both Nogales.

The scene repeats itself in El Paso–Ciudad Juárez, where both cities are supplied by the waters of the Rio Grande. Lawrence Nickey, director of the El Paso City-County Health District, who once swam and fished in the Rio Grande, says, "I wouldn't put my big toe in it now." He tells anyone who will listen that the two cities are, for public health purposes, one community; what affects one affects the other. "We share the same pollution, the same diseases, and water." Up to 400,000 people in Ciudad Juárez lack running water or a sewer in their homes, and 68,000 in El Paso County lack both. There are thousands of illegal septic tanks that contaminate river and underground water when it rains. The shallow wells of the poor on the shores of the Rio Grande are easily contaminated by sewage. There is no waste treatment plant in Ciudad Juárez, so each day up to 55 millions gallons of raw sewage pour into an irrigation canal that has been baptized, most appropriately, *aguas negras* (black waters); the waste, a reporter was told, irrigates cotton and alfalfa fields. But Nickey maintains that it also waters chilies and vegetables: "They say it doesn't go into the Rio Grande, but we hear that it does," and this view dovetails closely with that of the *Diario de Juárez*, a most-Mexican newspaper.

Farther down the river, at Ciudad Acuña, Piedras Negras, and both Laredos, residents worry about water quality. Neither Ciudad Acuña nor Piedras Negras has treatment plants, and the one at Nuevo Laredo treats no more than 60 percent of that city's water. Leslie Kochan, an American writer, maintains that "levels of bacteria along some points between Nuevo Laredo and Lake Falcon," because of the dumping of raw sewage into the Rio Grande, "are so high that it makes the lake one of the largest sewage ponds in the United States." Matamoros and Reynosa have no treatment plants, so their discharge of raw sewage and toxic wastes from *maquiladoras* also pollute the Rio Grande. In Brownsville, an inexplicably high incidence of babies stillborn without brains, the *New York Times* has reported, leads "people to suspect contamination from industries across the border in Matamoros, where the same phenomenon has appeared." At Brownsville, to paraphrase *El Mexicano*, where the Rio Grande is virtually a toilet for untreated human waste as well as a receptacle for waste from *maquiladoras* in Matamoros, María Guadalupe Esparza, one of sixteen mothers, won at least $100,000 in a court settlement of $17 million from forty *maquiladoras;* in a lawsuit filed in 1993, the mothers accused the firms of killing or deforming over a dozen newborn babies with factory emissions and the burning of toxic wastes at the dump in Matamoros. Esparza's child, who suffered from anencephaly, a birth defect that the lawsuit linked to toxic emissions, "died the moment they cut the umbilical cord," she explained. In one heavily Mexican-American *colonia* of South Texas, a study discovered that 90 percent of its residents had contracted hepatitis before their thirtieth birthday.

Illegal dumping of hazardous wastes exacerbates the problem. American companies by the hundreds ship their wastes to Mexico for disposal. As landfills and incinerators at home come under stiffer regulations, the cost of disposing of toxic wastes escalates, making disposal cheaper in Mexico. In 1989, authorities in El Paso found four abandoned trucks loaded with barrels of hazardous waste; the trucks belonged to a Mexican waiting to drive them to Ciudad Juárez for disposal. A subsidiary of General Motors was caught dumping barrels of toxic waste at a site less than two miles from a popular beach in Matamoros.

Tijuana, meanwhile, records case after case of illegal dumping. In one of them, a U.S. ink manufacturer shipped toxic chemicals to a phony Mexican recycler, who then mixed them with paving asphalt in a poor *colonia*, where residents took sick with lead poisoning. For years, an article in the *Nation* reports, trucks from Los Angeles unloaded used-car batteries at the Alco Pacífico plant near El Florido and a dairy farm, both just east of Tijuana, where their lead was supposedly melted down. During the congressional debate on NAFTA, when environmental concerns appeared to threaten its approval, Mexican authorities finally decided to investigate what was going on. They discovered fourteen acres contaminated by 31 million pounds of lead waste. At Mexicali—"the most polluted city in Baja California," according to the newspaper *Zeta*—13,500 tons of toxic waste arrive daily from the United States. Less than half of the six thousand tons of trash and garbage generated by Mexicali's inhabitants is collected either by the city or by private agencies; the rest rots on abandoned lots or on the outskirts of the city. Despite NAFTA, U.S. courts have charged few companies with illegal dumping in Mexico, and none have been prosecuted in Mexican courts.

o　o　o　🔲　o　o　o

Residents on both sides of the border share the same air quality needs. What endangers one side endangers the other. The problem, which covers the entire border, arises from population growth, autos, and industry. There are three especially contaminated areas: San Diego–Tijuana, the twin cities of El Paso and Ciudad Juárez, and the copper-smelting zone of northern Sonora and southern Arizona.

San Diego's air basin fails to meet state air quality standards for smog. Some of Tijuana's smog is locally generated, but much of it comes from San Diego and Los Angeles, both exporters of smog, especially from April to September, when the prevailing winds blow from north to south. Voluntary cooperative measures ameliorate the problem, but only temporarily. Only one monitoring station, an American gift, operates in Tijuana, making it difficult to measure the dispersion of smog. Most of it, Tijuana experts say, derives from automobiles. Smog control devices are not required of cars, many of them old and leaking fumes; most autos use regular gasoline, not unleaded.

The El Paso–Ciudad Juárez air basin is increasingly dirty. The cities do not lag far behind Los Angeles in the manufacture of smog. The pollutants are not necessarily the same on both sides of the border: Different levels of economic development dictate that. Ciudad Juárez's smog results primarily from poverty, and that of its neighbor, from industry and higher levels of consumption. Of the two cities, Ciudad Juárez is the bigger culprit; to quote *El Mexicano*, "The metropolitan area of El Paso has some of the worst air quality in the United States because of its proximity . . . to Ciudad Juárez."

Geographical contours partially explain the poor air quality. The cities lie between the Franklin Mountains to the north and the Sierra de Juárez to the south. Both share one airshed. Smog is an old problem; as early as 1915, inhabitants of El Paso complained about the smoke that enveloped their city. Air inversions afflict the basin, especially during the winter months, when geographical contours trap air pollutants until the sun burns them away or the winds sweep them out. That aspect of Mother Nature has remained constant, but the character of the pollutants has changed. The old pollutants derived mainly from smoke, much of it from coal or wood fires used to heat homes, from dirt streets in both cities, from cement plants and rock quarries, and from blowing dust. That is no longer true. The chief pollutants are automobiles and photochemical smog.

High levels of air pollution, basically from motor vehicles—82 million cars and over 3 million trucks cross each year—endanger public health everywhere on the border. They are particularly acute in the El Paso–Ciudad Juárez metroplex because of its location. Neither city meets federal standards for carbon monoxide. Residents of El Paso lay much of the blame for their plight on their Mexican neighbors, whose smog originates from multiple sources, including the ovens of 250 brickyards that frequently use discarded tires for fuel, the open burning of trash, and the dust of unpaved streets. There are over 180 miles of unpaved roads in Ciudad Juárez, but only 18 in El Paso.

Above all, old autos are responsible for the smog. Cities on both sides of the border are hardly wealthy. San Diego, the one exception, is not a border city. Low levels of income mean worn-out autos, especially on the Mexican side, where they are poorly maintained and seldom, if ever, inspected for emission controls. Mexican cities are junkyards for older vehicles from the United States, and they are a major source of air pollution. The newspaper *Diario 29* concedes that nearly all of the autos from Mexicali that enter Calexico fail to meet California emission standards. Until recently, when nonleaded gasoline was introduced, Mexican gasoline ranked high in lead content.

The Ciudad Juárez–El Paso metroplex embodies all of these ills. Since both cities are poor, air pollution management takes second place to economic growth. Like other Mexican cities, Ciudad Juárez stockpiles old ve-hicles; used-auto dealerships selling to Mexican customers are eyesores in El Paso, as they are up and down the border. On El Paso's side, too many freeways exist; there is too much driving, too many cars. Ciudad Juárez once had fewer cars, but that has now changed. Traffic patterns, however, are different; the absence of freeways in Mexico means stop-and-go driv-ing, a heavy pollutant. El Paso's public transportation system serves some of the population, but the antiquated and ill-maintained buses of its neighbor are stinking polluters. The old trolley system, which used to carry people back and forth across the border, was dismantled in 1973, adding to the volume of traffic on the international bridges. With the coming of the *maquiladoras* and NAFTA, more heavy trucks wait in line at the international bridges, some for twelve to thirteen hours, helping to el-evate smog content.

Ports of entry are another reason for high carbon monoxide levels, and not just in El Paso–Ciudad Juárez; a major factor is the long wait for cars crossing into the United States. It takes approximately thirty minutes, and longer on weekends and holidays, for a car from Ciudad Juárez to pass through U.S. customs; since the engine is left running, it constantly emits carbon monoxide. Speeding up the inspection process, experts say, would reduce pollution. As would doubling the number of international bridges or opening more entry gates at San Ysidro and Mexicali, where long waits are also the rule.

Autos, though certainly guilty of contaminating El Paso's air, are not the lone culprit. Also responsible is industry, specifically the American Smelting and Refining Company (ASARCO) smelter, which dates from 1885, on the edges of downtown El Paso and a stone's throw away from Ciudad Juárez; until 1977, its tall smokestack, a local landmark, belched high levels of lead, zinc, arsenic, and cadmium into the air. The winds blew them over Ciudad Juárez. After long delays, El Paso finally filed a court suit against ASARCO; high levels of lead poisoning had been found in children, all of Mexican origin, living in Smeltertown, a slum in the shadow of the smokestack. Age-adjusted IQs, one study revealed, were lower for these children. The company eventually installed pollution con-trols, but that did not solve the problem; Mexicans in Ciudad Juárez claim that ASARCO's smokestack still emits lead. In 1982, the EPA faulted the city of El Paso for failing to meet air quality standards for ozone, carbon monoxide, and sulfur dioxide. The prognosis, one scholar at the Univer-sity of Texas concludes, is not promising: "El Paso's air is not getting any better and, in fact, seems to be deteriorating," and "the situation in Ciu-dad Juárez can only be expected to get worse."

For years, the smokestack of the Phelps Dodge smelter at Douglas, Ari-zona, erected in 1913, spewed its murky smoke over the international landscape, enveloping both Douglas and Agua Prieta and coloring the Continental Divide forty miles away. When the smelter closed, Mexico built its own copper refinery just north of Nacozari, installing a smoke-stack four hundred feet taller than Phelps Dodges's, but without pollution controls. Only one out of every ten streets in Agua Prieta is paved; when the winds blow, as they often do, the swirling dust combines with the haze from Nacozari to pollute the air of both towns. Respiratory infections rank high on the list of local ills. At Calexico in 1992, not until two days had gone by did EPA authorities learn of the release in Mexicali of a cloud of hydrochloric acid from a fertilizer plant that had resulted in the sudden evacuation of over one hundred thousand nearby residents. Under an international agreement, however, they should have been told immediately about the spill so as to be able to take precautionary measures.

○ ○ ○ 🏵 ○ ○ ○

The *maquiladora* industry, obviously, must shoulder some responsibility for the pollution. According to Devon G. Peña, author of *The Terror Machine*, "Maquilas generate at least one-third of the total waste discharge" flowing into the New River and the Rio Grande from El Paso to Brownsville. The more *maquiladoras*, the more the pollution, so goes a popular rule of thumb. Three decades ago, when assembly plants first appeared, no one was prepared for the consequences. The *maquiladoras* brought jobs and people, but they also brought stress on the airshed, the watershed, and the land and created new health hazards. To cite William Hobby, then lieutenant governor of Texas, "Unless the environmental problems caused by the *maquiladoras* are eradicated, they may well cause serious health hazards." They also sanctify the rationale that allows the installation of toxic and nuclear waste dumps, permitting, for instance, asbestos plants banned in Colorado to appear as *maquiladoras* in Mexicali. One reason *maquiladoras* settled along the border was to eliminate costs at home, one of them being environmental restrictions. They fled to the border, it is said, "as much for the freedom to pollute as for the low labor costs."

Mexican regulations require that *maquiladoras* return their toxic wastes to the United States. Yet, as the *Los Angeles Times* reports, when Mexican inspectors first visited one thousand *maquiladoras* in 1991, they found that one-third of them operated without the required environmental license and fewer than 15 percent of them returned hazardous waste to the United States for disposal. Eventually, more of them did, but the *Times* concluded, "the new figures . . . are still abysmal." As one Mexican official acknowledged, "it was only recently that anyone here started to care about the environment." In a study in 1988 by the *Austin American States-man*, a Texas journal, only eleven *maquiladoras* out of four hundred returned waste to the United States. The others simply flushed their waste down a drain or dumped it in remote areas. On the eve of the vote on NAFTA, when Congressman Richard Gephardt paid unannounced visits to *maquiladoras* in Tijuana, he uncovered "massive evidence of industrial pollution." Mexico, one local environmentalist concluded, is being used as a "wastebasket."

One reason is the unwillingness of Mexican authorities to enforce safeguards. As an editorial in *El Mexicano* points out, controls over the *maquiladora* industry are lax because of the local economic benefits and revenues paid to the federal exchequer. Kochan speaks of "a silent compact between many corporations and the Mexican government, which amounts to a waiver of responsibility for the safe use of toxics . . . and their careful transportation and disposal." But Kochan also believes that citizens' groups in the United States, already rebelling against expanded landfills and waste incinerators, "will not take kindly to the thought of accepting waste from U.S. owned *maquiladoras*." So far, however, their protests have not curtailed the tide of waste and trash from Mexico. Each year, *maquiladoras* in Matamoros unload ten thousand tons of paper and plastic cartons in the rubbish dump of Brownsville. As more *maquiladoras* arrive, they will surely dump more, unless existing international agreements are enforced.

Notions that industry has environmental obligations are weakly held in the probusiness border towns. For example, businessmen in Tijuana are ecstatic about the benefits of free trade, but their city, partly because of it, is one of the most polluted in the Western Hemisphere. In 1994, for example, used-car dealers in Tijuana stopped importing cars from San Diego and Los Angeles for local resale until federal authorities discontinued enforcing California emission standards. Municipal authorities may, when citizens complain, clean up trash in empty lots, but they steer clear of complaints against *maquiladoras*. Stonewalling by officials, as the following story documents, is a common practice. When residents of El Cañón del Padre, angry over the pollution on the Mesa de Otay, blamed the *maquiladoras*, the secretary of public health turned a deaf ear; during a visit to Tijuana, President Carlos Salinas, an advocate of *maquiladoras*, promised to clean up the mess, but that also was unfulfilled. Clearly, no one wanted to take on the *maquiladoras*, certainly not on behalf of a poor community.

The problem, viewed from the Mexican perspective, is twofold. On the one hand, there are the *maquila* owners, who, because their investment is highly transitory, make no commitment to the preservation of the environment. When their profits tumble, they simply move to another part of the world. "They have come here from all over, saying they are going to invest," according to Mauricio Sánchez of the Ejido Chilpancingo on the edge of a *maquiladora* park. On the other hand, there are the environmental effects. As Sánchez says, "When it comes to complying with ecological laws, [the *maquiladoras*] say they don't speak Spanish." Sánchez has good reason to complain; his neighborhood is one of the most polluted. An analysis by the Universidad Autónoma de Baja California of the water of a creek that flows through the *ejido* discovered levels of lead 11,200 percent higher than the U.S. legal limit, and according to a 1990 government report, over 16 percent of its inhabitants suffer from skin diseases, more than 8 percent from respiratory illnesses, and more than 5 percent are anemic. As El Paso's air pollution supervisor says, "We don't know what is going on over there. Emissions just go out the window. . . . Heaven knows what kinds of exotic solvents GM, RCA, and Sylvania use in Ciudad Juárez."

Maquila operators relocate in Mexico partly for the freedom from U.S. environmental legislation. The *Los Angles Times* makes this abundantly clear in a story published in 1991. It is about a Los Angeles furniture manufacture who shut down his plant to move to Tijuana. He employed six hundred people, the same number he had in Los Angeles, but wages were much lower. Best of all, in his opinion, he no longer had "to deal with the constant intrusions of air quality inspectors, emissions monitors . . . and ever-stricter rules." In Los Angeles, environmental penalties had cost him thousands of dollars. In Tijuana, Mexican laws do not limit the amount of air pollution from furniture factories. "We're trying to live with reality," the owner says. And he does. Muebles Finos Buenos, his Mexican company, pollutes freely: "Gases pour from the stacks for longer hours. Shifting winds carry the sharp tang of the solvents to surrounding homes." It bothers the owner not a bit that the foul winds make the throats of neighbors sore or that water samples of nearby *colonias* show levels of two particular carcinogens at eighteen to twenty-four times the drinking water standards of the EPA.

Then there are opportunistic Mexicans who make money by transporting toxic wastes back to the United States but, instead, dump them in Mexico. Because of them, the recycling and disposal of wastes is haphazard at best. To use a story in the *San Francisco Examiner*, unscrupulous *maquiladora* managers sell "drums of waste to small-time operators who dump the chemicals in the middle of the desert or in someone's backyard." They get away with this behavior because the original stipulations—which required that if the point of origin for *maquila* waste was the United States, it had to be returned there—were changed to permit them to be transferred to Mexico. As one observer notes, the evidence suggests that little of it actually comes home. *La Jornada* points out that "in Mexico no one knows what happens to 99 percent of the toxic wastes." Most elected officials, in reality, either distort the facts or show little concern for reducing air pollution. A Colegio de la Frontera Norte study for 1986 documents that the EPA knew that only 20 of the then 772 *maquiladoras* on the border returned waste to the United States. According to a congressional study for 1992, less than one-third of them reported on their waste disposal practices.

Tijuana exemplifies what occurs elsewhere; differences, if any, are of degree. At Agua Prieta, asbestos chemicals from the Amatex *maquiladora* spill out onto the streets, endangering the health of youngsters who play on them; tests show toxic chemicals in the drinking water and sewage. Levels of toxic chemicals are high near the *maquiladora* industrial park of Nogales. According to the *Los Angeles Times*, the residents of Matamoros, a city known for its *maquiladoras*, "are routinely exposed to chemical leaks and often evacuated," and "chemically-related births are strikingly common." A Boston laboratory, this paper reported, discovered in a canal leading from Stepan Chemical, a U.S. *maquiladora*, levels of the solvent xylene, which causes lung, liver, and kidney damage, "52,000 times the U.S. drinking water standard." Matamoros, the newspaper conceded, "is not a town that free-trade proponents rush to show off."

○　○　○　🏵　○　○　○

Mexico has environmental laws the equivalent of those in the United States. Some go back to the 1970s; later, the Ministry of Ecology and Urban Development (SEDUE) was established. Until the 1994 devaluation of the peso, environmental concerns were a priority issue; however, as Congresswoman Liliana Flores Benavides of the Democratic Labor Movement says, despite the "effort to dress authorities in green, ecological results are limited and superficial." Or as the distinguished Mexican economist Victor L. Urquidi says, until recently little has been done; to the contrary, Mexico has become inundated by fecal contamination of air, water, and land, a disaster that worsens by the day. Laws on the statute books are not adequately enforced at the federal, state, and local levels. According to Urquidi, outside of some of the giant transnationals, which tend at times to obey environmental regulations, Mexican industry rarely heeds these laws. When it comes to environmental concerns, Mexico, he concedes, "lags at least a generation behind the Western nations." Despite NAFTA, to quote Joel Simon, author of a damning indictment, "Mexico is an incompetent and wholly unreliable ally in the fight against pollution and environmental devastation."

At times this results from a shortage of funds, but not always. Until recently, few Mexicans worried about environmental issues; even now, Mexico can boast only a handful of distinguished conservationists. As late as the 1970s, Luis Echeverría, then president of the republic, saw conservation as part of conspiracies headed by multinationals seeking to set aside Third World resources for their own benefit at some future date. José López Portillo, his successor, thought concerns about pollution were "hysterical exaggerations." Environmental concerns, after all, conflict with the interpretations of economic growth and free trade currently in vogue in Mexico. Air pollution, in the view of Mexican economists, accompanies economic growth. Thus, as long as poverty is the lot of 40 million Mexicans and extreme poverty that of 20 million more, no room exists in a hungry stomach for ecological menus. The poor, whether in city or village, think survival; that is their priority. A 1991 study by two Princeton economists that is frequently cited by Mexican officials concludes that "economic growth tends to alleviate pollution problems." The takeoff occurs, according to these pundits, with a per capita income of $4,000 to $5,000. Environmentalists generally label this assertion wishful thinking. The ecological movement in Mexico, basically urban and upper-middle-class, exists, but it is barely off the ground, though it sponsored a presidential candidate in the elections of 1994, who fared badly in the voting.

"We'll make our mess now and clean it up later when we can afford it" is a standard argument in Third World countries, but it is fraught with peril, as the experience of Thailand, blessed with free-market growth, illustrates. It is in Bangkok where, largely because of free-market capitalism and the absence of governmental controls, more people per capita drive Mercedes Benzes than anywhere else in the world; but at the same time, more people per capita cannot enjoy them because they are always stuck in traffic. In Bangkok, one does not leave home in an auto without a mobile phone and a portable potty. The exhausts of expensive cars, meanwhile, turn the air into a gray blanket. The *New York Times* reports that in Thailand, private enterprise flourishes so much that it is able "to buy off every environmental regulation with corruption." The result is that canals are cemented over for new buildings, fish die in the rivers, and one of every two traffic cops suffers from respiratory infections. Until 1995, Bangkok had no wastewater treatment plant, and even today, most people throw their garbage and flush untreated toilet waste into the city's canals.

In Mexico, to dig up an old cliché, we are asking the fox to guard the henhouse. In the entire state of Tamaulipas, home to both Matamoros and Reynosa, there is only one environmental inspector, and not many more in Chihuahua. In Ciudad Juárez, only three officials were charged with overseeing environmental concerns in a city of nearly 1 million people. They lack a budget of any consequence and possess little technical training. In 1993, the city fired two inspectors because, so went the official version, they solicited bribes at an engine plant. Environmentalists told the *New York Times* that their mistake had been "to push hard for inspections against the wishes of superiors afraid of angering local businessmen." Earning no more than $150 a month, inspectors, nonetheless, can be bribed, a practice now routine among many factory owners.

The trials and tribulations of Ramiro Mendoza, a young lawyer who headed the environmental enforcement agency in Tijuana in 1992, throws light on this state of affairs. Anxious to enforce legislation, he hired thirty-three inspectors, dressed them in green jackets, and began to train them. No government agency cooperated; files on polluters remained off limits, and laboratory tests could not be carried out for lack of equipment and supplies. Then paychecks failed to arrive for five months, by which time only five inspectors remained on the job. Mendoza acknowledged: "We've been bluffing. If they knew how few people we had, they would just laugh at us." The work of environmental inspectors, in the judgment of the *New York Times*, "continues to be hampered by insufficient and un-certain resources, political considerations, and at least occasionally by corruption." Environmental agents, asked to clean up the air, were in-stead told to pass out literature, plant trees, and discuss pollution with schoolchildren. "Pollution-prevention efforts are almost nonexistent," the newspaper concluded.

With the passage of NAFTA, its supporters proclaimed, much could be done to undo the damage wrought by humans on land and water. To get the agreement approved by Congress, its sponsors established a trina-tional Commission on Environmental Cooperation (CEC), and when the unmet concerns of Americans about Mexico's commitment placed NAFTA's passage in doubt, the Salinistas quickly set up two agencies within the federal office established to carry the ecological banner. With headquarters in Montreal, the CEC supposedly keeps tabs on persistent violators of environmental laws in the United States, Canada, and Mex-ico, the three signatories to the treaty. But the CEC has no teeth; its only power is the "public shame factor." It can merely ask that sanctions be im-posed on the culprit nation. The failure of NAFTA's environmental agree-ments—if indeed ecological concerns had priority in Washington and Mexico City—should have been foreseen, as a panel appointed by Mex-ico, the United States, and Canada reported in the fall of 1997. As Joel Si-mon rightly concludes, so far as border policing is concerned, NAFTA is "almost irrelevant," particularly since Mexico, its economy in shambles, has neither the funds nor the will to carry out its promises.

NAFTA, in reality, hardly offers much hope for an ecological new day. Although its master plan requires that the United States spend over $1 bil-lion for environmental cleanup, so far only a paltry sum has been spent by the North American Development Bank, the financial arm of NAFTA—for a wastewater treatment plant in an industrial park in Mata-moros. One reason is the bank's high interest rates, which virtually exclude Mexicans. To quote the general manager of the water department of the Mexican town of San Luis Río Colorado, just across from Yuma, Arizona, "I can attest that the mutual promises made by our two governments have not yet been kept." As he explains, the North American Development Bank does not have "a single client," though its directors enjoy diplomatic status and live the good life in a Ciudad Juárez's penthouse, but "so far they have done nothing to justify their salaries." He has good cause for his anger. With 160,000 inhabitants, San Luis Río Colorado had gone begging for financial help, but to no avail. It had no waste treatment plant, although its drainage system, old and in disrepair, served only 38 percent of the population, so sewage from this border *maquila* hub spilled over the bed of the Colorado River every day, poisoning the land and leaving the air reeking of stench. Despite pleas for help, no NAFTA funds were forthcoming.

o   o   o   ◈   o   o   o

Today, as the degradation of the borderlands vividly illustrates, mankind confronts an ecological crisis that threatens its survival. Yet orthodox economic thought still basks in what the economist John Kenneth Galbraith labels the "culture of contentment," believing that the way out of the deepening global nightmare lies in the self-regulation of a market system and higher rates of economic growth—which would make less difficult paying for the costs of the ever-bigger environmental cleanup. The viability of modern capitalism, which must grow to thrive, to cite John Bellamy Foster, author of *The Vulnerable Planet*, "remains unquestioned." Yet, calling to mind the wisdom of another scholar, "anyone who believes exponential growth can go on forever in a finite world is either a madman or an economist." Despite the assurances of David Ricardo, the first of the classical theorists, nature is neither "indestructible" nor "inexhaustible." To the contrary, in order to maintain a balance between the needs of mankind and those of nature, as others rightly argue, we must build the institutional foundations for a steady-state economy and promote an equitable distribution of wealth, not only at home but between rich and poor nations.

What drives capitalism, as Marx revealed, is a money fetishism; but what is required, to quote Foster, is the "satisfaction of human needs." The regime of capital, to expand on this thesis, is inherently expansionary: "It is impossible to envision a capitalist economy operating on a steady-state basis." Capitalism, as we have known it since its inception, shows little concern for the implications of environmental degradation and its cost to society; it is essentially irrational and indifferent to ecological needs. If, as Foster maintains, capitalism is a system geared primarily toward economic growth and the multiplication of profits and rarely "directly concerned with the promotion of human welfare or the preservation of nature as such, the question of capitalism versus the earth must sooner or later occupy the central place in any ecological economics worthy of the name." As documented in the degradation of the borderlands, where the poor struggle to survive while the rich enjoy the fruits of plenty, capitalism's economic logic can only lead to increasingly more profound ecological problems. The result, as some ecologists testify, is a "huge unpaid debt to nature." The borderland's ecological crisis, as elsewhere on the face of our earth, is not merely the offshoot of technical factors but the logical result of a system that enshrines greed, overlooks basic human needs, and jeopardizes the survival of the biosphere itself.

⌖ 11

Dependency

As has been explained time and again over the course of these pages, the economy and society of Mexico's northern border as we currently know them are, in more ways than one, the progeny of their neighbor. Developments on the U.S. side, whether the consequences of a global economy or not, virtually dictate results on the other side. This may be, as sundry Americans wish to believe, compatible development but, from my viewpoint, it is hardly equitable.

Given this historical dependency—for that is the reality—can Mexicans, whether at the border or elsewhere in the republic, ever dream of a more equitable tomorrow where they wield more control over their own destiny? Or is this merely wishful thinking? Is the volatile past that marches to the drumbeat of the almighty dollar to keep on calling the tune? In this age of a global capitalism that runs hot and cold, that renders it difficult for even educated American professionals to find stable, reasonably dignified, and adequately paying jobs, is a rosy prognosis for Mexicans merely a fool's naïveté?

∘ ∘ ∘ ⌖ ∘ ∘ ∘

Pundits who wax eloquent on binational economies and what they label "interdependency," have, of course, a ready answer; but they must surely be disciples of George Bernard Shaw, who asked in *Pygmalion*: "Independence? That's middle-class blasphemy. We are all dependent, on one another, every soul of us on earth." The reply is yes—and no; not everyone is equally dependent. I say this because these soothsayers delight in predicting that a cornucopia awaits Mexicans on the border, especially with the passage of NAFTA. Since the late 1960s, they argue, dramatic economic transformations have reshaped Mexico's border provinces. These have been accompanied by a freshly vigorous commercial sector, the relentless growth of the service industry, a more dynamic role for agribusiness, and the astonishing performance of assembly plants. At the same time, the border has undergone unprecedented demographic growth, converting small towns into urban metropolises. One statistic is particularly impressive. Since the 1970s, the national economy has either stagnated or endured erratic health. On the border, in contrast, industrial production between 1970 and 1975 grew at a yearly average of 4.9 percent, then jumped during the next ten years to 12 percent; though no longer climbing so rapidly, it currently hovers at 11 percent. The principal reason for this phenomenon is the appearance of the assembly plant.

For all that, the rosy future predicted by Walter W. Rostow, mentor to Presidents John F. Kennedy and Lyndon B. Johnson, has not come to pass. In *Stages of Economic Growth*, a book avidly read by professors and their students in the 1960s, most of them boosters of Kennedy's New Frontier, Rostow chartered the path for an American-style prosperity: Shun communism, embrace capitalism, and wallow in the hedonistic joys of mass consumption. In the Third World, that vision invited disaster. Soviet communism collapsed, but much of Latin America, Africa, and Asia, where elites quaffed Rostow's tonic, harbor the injustices of yesteryear, and the gap between the haves and the have-nots grows wider. The capitalist triumph helped the rich become richer and escalated poverty in countries such as Mexico.

Yes, much has changed since the 1920s. The border towns of bars and bordellos no longer flourish, replaced by complex cities where the joy palaces of yesteryear are merely a sideshow. Industry by way of *maquiladoras* flourishes virtually everywhere. A growing middle class prospers, and the rich and well-off are numerous, and others enjoy the good life, dwell in comfortable homes, send their children to school, and raise prosperous and happy families. Numerous employees of federal, state, and even municipal governments are hardly reliant for their livelihood on their Yankee neighbors. Professionals, among them physicians, lawyers, architects, and engineers, sell their services to Mexicans and are seldom indebted to tourists or other foreigners. They make up part of what Mexican scholars refer to as a national bourgeoisie. For some pundits of border affairs, the people of the Mexican border, when compared to those who preceded them, are less dependent on outsiders for their welfare.

Yet the transformation may be more mirage than real. As the nature of the assembly plants reveals, economic growth continues to be an offshoot of American capitalism. Obviously, this troubles few Americans. Yet in the opinion of numerous Mexicans, this lies at the heart of the problem, a situation they view as an increasing subordination to the United States. This symbiotic relationship, regardless of what is beneficial about it, spells dependency. The northern edge of the border, with its far larger capital resources and gigantic markets, controls the dynamics of the southern side. In large measure, Mexicans, among them even indirectly the "national bourgeoisie," rely for their daily bread on economic ties with the United States.

That is so because of the obsequious nature of the border economy, composed of a weak primary sector, basically an agriculture and cattle industry for export; a secondary sector, swiftly climbing the economic ladder with assembly plants, but also reliant on outsiders; and a bloated tertiary sector, occupied chiefly with the handling of exports and imports and serving tourists. This occupational distribution has been formed or, as some Mexicans insist, deformed by the nature of the international ties. Because of that, Mexican border cities react quickly to modifications in their relationship to the other side. Proof of this is the assembly plant closures of 1975 that left twenty-six thousand workers unemployed, the international gasoline shortage of 1977 that abruptly reduced the flow of tourists from California and Texas, and, obviously, peso devaluations that turn economics topsy-turvy.

This is hardly a dynamic binational economy, as developmentalists would have us believe. According to them, the border represents two parts of a dual society, where the modern and backward coexist. The marginal half, in this case poor Mexicans, lies outside of the dual society, being neither incorporated nor integrated. The marginalized, so this theory goes, do not share identical values or norms, nor are they part of the division of labor. They do not contribute, either by their decisions or responsibilities, to the solution of social problems, not even when they directly affect them. For developmentalists, therefore, the solution demands the incorporation of the marginalized into the modern society. This interpretation argues that a better distribution of income and more democracy in Mexico will change the nature of the international relationship and make the two societies more equitable.

But these theorists ignore the structural causes of the asymmetrical relationship. There can be no equality between two societies so long as one, the more powerful and rich, gets the better of the other. Unless a miracle occurs, the Mexican side will always be the tail on the dog. The theory of comparative advantage, which essentially underlies the developmentalist argument, simply does not work. The abundance of cheap labor on the Mexican side does not complement the avalanche of capital, technology, and consumer power wielded by Americans. It is wrongheaded to argue that the Mexican and American economies benefit equally from this exchange. Interdependence, which American pundits eulogize, cannot be based on an unequal exchange, a relationship where the dynamics of one control the other. The reality of Mexican border life is dependency.

All the same, I am not attempting to measure the degree of dependency: As Fernando Henrique Cardoso and Enzo Faleto stress in their *Dependency and Development in Latin America*, this makes little sense. They wrote, of course, before Henrique Cardoso, currently president of Brazil, embraced neoliberal doctrines. Reliance on the other side is inevitable because of the weak Mexican border economy, the result of a structural dependency. Mexico, after all, exports over three-fourths of its national product to the United States, which in return buys only 4 percent of its imports from Mexico. Thus, the rhetoric of interdependency is more myth than fact; there is merely a deformed mutual dependency. We could, of course, play word games and call this relationship one of asymmetrical interdependency, since one country dominates the other; or we could blur the truth of the matter and explain that one country simply profits more.

An enormous chasm, moreover, has developed over the centuries between the wealthy capitalist nations and the peripheral ones. We can, if we wish, talk about "developing nations," as American economists who deal in foreign aid frequently do when referring to the world's poor (the condition of most Mexicans) as living in a "developing" country, an Orwellian term employed to describe a global spread of diverse nations united by a common history of dependency and dashed hopes. As Frantz Fanon once observed, poverty in this "developing" world is just as pervasive as ever. Between the "wretched of the earth" (the reality of Mexico) and the well-off, the distribution of wealth is more unequal now than before. At best, no matter how dependent "development" is presented, its benefits rarely trickle down to the needy. When disparate economies interact, the advanced one gets the blessings, a process that exacerbates divergences in the development of the two countries. In the border cities, the large pool of cheap labor, including many who seek jobs on the other side, serves as a brake on wages on both sides of the border and therefore has a functional role to play within the system. Nonetheless, marginalized workers, who will not be incorporated for various reasons, are dysfunctional. For them, however, marginalization is not a transitory phenomenon but a structural aspect of dependent capitalism.

o　o　o　🏵　o　o　o

On the Mexican border, industry is merely a lofty dream; more often than not, it is realized as a soft-drink or pasteurization plant, a brickyard, a small furniture factory, a bakery, or a print shop. Many are family operations. Small, medium, and microindustries represent all but a tiny percentage of border establishments, yet they employ nearly half of the industrial workforce. Until its demise, the brewery Cruz Blanca, which gave jobs to nearly four hundred workers, was the largest in Ciudad Juárez, a city known for its industry. The category "industry" includes auto and electrical repair shops as well as the maintenance and installation of heating and air-conditioning units—over 42 percent of industrial establishments in the city. Tourist demands dictate the nature of other industries: the making of colonial-style furniture, clay tiles and pots, or ornamental iron for home decoration.

The infant status of industry explains other problems. Although it does offer significant employment, it cannot provide the jobs needed in these Mexican cities. The survival rate of industries, moreover, is dismal. Of every one hundred industries launched, according to the newspaper *El Mexicano*, eighty fail within twelve months and only two operate for more than five years. The weakness of consumer buying power, the lack of starter capital, the shortage of bank credit, and the ubiquitous presence of cheap American goods, either at home or across the border, lie at the core of this depressing record. According to a report by the Colegio de la Frontera Norte, Mexican industry, excluding assembly plants, is "relatively unimportant." That, clearly, is an understatement. Even Mexican commerce, as a past president of the Tijuana Chamber of Commerce told *El Mexicano,* is 80 percent sales of American products and less than 20 percent native goods. To pinpoint this: Mexican industry supplies merely 3 percent of the products required by the people of Matamoros. As already noted, one major reason for this horrendous reality is that Mexicans easily buy what they want across the way because the United States either manufactures or sells every conceivable product. The adoption of NAFTA, which opened the gates to a host of American manufactured goods, exacerbated this unequal competition. To make matters worse, under the terms of NAFTA, by the year 2000 Mexico will open wide its doors to American agribusiness exports, which will surely drive down agricultural prices and, combined with land privatization, another neoliberal plank, will lure more campesinos into border cities. That may provide a surplus labor force for *maquiladoras,* but it will also further push down wages. Proximity to the United States actually deters Mexican industrialization. At best, proximity is a two-edged sword; the opportunity to supply labor, sell certain goods, and provide services to wealthier Americans offers advantages not shared by other Mexicans that, occasionally, translate into a higher standard of living. These border residents can, once in a while, buy cheaper groceries, clothes for the family, used autos at better prices, computers, electronic gadgets, compact disks, and the like.

The much-maligned Porfirio Díaz, who ruled Mexico with an iron fist for three decades, used to say "that between Mexico and the United States the best thing was the desert." That view makes no sense anymore; global economics dictate otherwise. Still, Don Porfirio was not entirely mistaken. The economic gap between the two countries, which he feared so much, is growing wider. In 1910, the difference in the per capita output of Mexico and the United States was $1,453 (based on 1970 prices); by 1984, it had ballooned to $6,815. Over the years, this inequality has translated into dependency and its sundry ills of recessions, financial crisis, and unemployment, in one way or another tied to the cycles of the American economy. This dependency, to cite a Mexican study, has "reached the proportions of a crisis, particularly because of the trade imbalance and because American assembly plants drain capital out of Mexico."

A contorted rule of thumb, more true than false, might be formulated. The more border Mexicans depend on location, the less well-off they are. Non-*fronterizo* activities, those not associated with location on the border, tend to reward more handsomely and offer greater stability; conversely, labor in a typical border enterprise, and the *maquilas* exemplify this, pays poorly and is highly unreliable, here today and gone tomorrow. It is necessary to separate border activities such as tourism, racetracks, and restaurants that serve Americans, which are beholden to location, from nonborder activities that are beholden to Mexican development, such as the PEMEX refinery in Reynosa or farming on the Mexican side of the Rio Grande Valley. Assembly plants are border activities because of the advantages of location; this is also true for much commerce and the service industry. These activities rely, in large measure, on decisions taken in the United States and on whether that country enjoys prosperous times or lapses into a recession. For that reason, they are less stable; they confront obstacles not of their own making, and their workers never know when their jobs will disappear. Nonborder activities are less exposed to these risks because their survival does not depend on their location; they could just as well operate in other parts of the republic.

∘ ∘ ∘ ⬡ ∘ ∘ ∘

Any relationship between two parties implies a certain interdependence. The pools of cheap labor as well as consumer markets south of the border encouraged the development of American border cities. The proximity of El Paso, by the same token, helped Ciudad Juárez. Conversely, the lack of capital and resources, in addition to the inability of Mexican industry to supply these things, and the distance from industrial centers made Ciudad Juárez a captive of El Paso. The absence of adequate transportation facilities severely handicapped trade with other regions of the republic. No wonder, then, that Ciudad Juárez developed an externally oriented economy early on, a condition characteristic of all border communities. As late as the 1930s, the inhabitants of the city imported from the United

States coal and oil, clothing, shoes, medical supplies, jellies and jams, meat, glass, cement and lumber, autos, and hardware, among other items. In the opinion of Mexican merchants, the prosperity of American border towns rested not on sales to their inhabitants but on sales to Mexican communities. Many Juarenses, additionally, traveled daily to jobs in El Paso. That picture, though modified, survives. Ciudad Juárez continues to export cheap labor, and American investments in hotels and restaurants play an increasingly large role in the tourist trade. The assembly plants, the biggest employer in the city, are foreign owned. Foreign investment, basically American, is concentrated in the key sectors of the economy—tourism and assembly plants. The Mexican cities along the border, Carlos Monsiváis writes, "tend to be, in terms of economics, satellites of the United States."

The reverse is true for El Paso, which boasts links not only with other American cities but with Mexican cities. Americans control commerce and industry, and they decide what is best for El Paso, although they may rely on cheap Mexican labor. As Lawrence A. Herzog recognizes, the big size of Mexican border cities can, "in large part, be attributed to concentrations of Mexican workers" who serve as a "reserve army of labor," to be summoned by industries and agriculture across the border when the need arises. Mexican investment in El Paso, by the same token, is negligible. It begs the question to say, as one American scholar does, that El Paso without Ciudad Juárez "would never have become a big city . . . just as Ciudad Juárez would never have been a bigger city without El Paso." True enough: The cities may be "joined at the cash register," but they are definitely not Siamese twins. Only in small border towns, such as San Luis, Nogales, and Calexico, is the principal activity serving the Mexican population on the other side. Tijuana's economy, like that of Ciudad Juárez, is even more externally oriented. Until recently, Ciudad Juárez could at least be proud of an agricultural hinterland where fruits and vegetables were raised for local consumption. Once upon a time, Juarenses dealt exclusively in pesos, paying their rents in pesos, as national law stipulates.

That is no longer so; like Tijuana, dollars decide the fate of Ciudad Juárez. That is logical. Tijuana is the progeny of American capital and, after the appearance of assembly plants, has become more so. American capital, American markets, and American tourists, as in the past, control its present and map out its future. Nothing illustrates this better than the ghastly impact on Tijuana of every California economic downturn, such as that of the early 1990s. "The situation is difficult," *El Mexicano* editorialized. "Crisis grips the border and no way out is in sight." The recession, which started in California, "requires an immediate and drastic response" for Tijuana commerce and business to survive. But the editorial concluded, "Since our economy is intimately linked to that of the other side, we can only hope that our neighbors will overcome their problems so that we may solve ours." In the year 1992 alone, thirty stores on Avenida Revolución closed, and sales in the city fell by 50 percent. Californians were no longer shopping in Tijuana, so Mexican merchants, shorn of customers, let employees go, and the ranks of the unemployed multiplied. The crisis was citywide, not just in the tourist sector. A bed "we were selling for 430 pesos until two weeks ago," a dealer in used furniture complained, "today we offer for half the price; we will lose money but we have to eat."

NAFTA, however, has somewhat altered this relationship, particularly in Texas. Today, while *maquilas* spring up across the border (517 of them alone between 1994 and 1996 in the four Mexican states that front on Texas) and the rest of the United States enjoys bonanza days, the Texas border stands still. Job flight from El Paso to Brownsville is an almost daily occurrence as employers take their apparel, auto parts, and electronic plants into Mexico, where labor is cheaper. Thus, countless workers on the Texas border live in depressed times. El Paso, a border city of 700,000, is a case in point. For years advertising itself as a haven for low-wage labor, the city, nonetheless, has lost over 5,600 jobs to Mexico; most of the jobless are of Mexican origin. In 1995, El Paso suffered a net loss of nearly 15,000 people who left in search of jobs and better wages, and the flight continues. Many in El Paso, including Larry Francis, its mayor, are angry. When he first learned of NAFTA, Francis acknowledges, he supported it, but not today, even though he once owned a *maquiladora* in Ciudad Juárez. Now he chastises the border-hopping businessmen of El Paso "for bleeding away employment and pulverizing roads and bridges with truck traffic but doing little that benefits the city." Clearly, NAFTA has hardly altered the terms of the relationship: El Paso still wields the bigger stick, while the dependency of Ciudad Juárez lingers on. However, the American city on the other side of the Rio Grande, as measured by job loss, is less prosperous.

o o o 🏵 o o o

Dependency, at least for the foreseeable future, is here to stay. These are the days of a global economy that sucks into its vortex the entire world, the Mexican border being simply one of many regions. Globalization captures the essence of capitalism, essentially the lust for profits no matter what the cost to labor. The goal of this never-ending search for cheap labor in global industries is part of a dynamic modus operandi of cheapening labor costs everywhere in order to enhance private gain. This process should alert us to the ways in which income inequality grows not just in the nation itself but between nations as capitalism becomes a truly ubiq-

uitous system. Transnational corporations, the harbingers of this omnivo-
rous capitalism, encircle the globe, as automation and a remarkable technological network invite worldwide changes in the organization of production, making possible the separation of manufacturing stages. Those
who run the huge corporations quickly learned that profits could be multiplied manyfold by using the cheap labor of Third World countries. That
relegates certain types of jobs in countries such as the United States to the
dustbin and dispatches them to countries where women and children labor for a pittance. The industrial capitalism of yesteryear has undergone a
metamorphosis, shedding its image as part and parcel of the nation-state
and acquiring the status of a nationless phenomenon, though still the
child of the capitalist economies of Western Europe, Japan, and the
United States. The movement of capital appears to know no international
boundaries; it moves freely everywhere.

Although the idea of a global economy strikes one as novel, its origins
date back to the fifteenth century and the expansion of Europe, when
Columbus's touted "discovery" of America set off the plunder of Indian
gold and silver in Mexico and Peru. There followed the era of European
colonization, when the natives of the peripheral world were put to work
raising food and extracting raw materials for the glory of the conquerors.
This was especially the case during the early years of the industrial revolution, basically the nineteenth century; later, in the heyday of capitalist
economics, European factories flooded peripheral markets, rendering local industrialization virtually impossible. After the rise in popularity in
the 1950s of the concept of erecting a home industry through import sub-
stitution, foreign entrepreneurs, who were the offspring of nationalist aspirations in nations such as Mexico and were welcomed there with open
arms by the local *burguesías*, circumvented tariff walls by establishing
subsidiaries in the underdeveloped countries to supply consumer goods.
Offshore production is the latest stage in this unfolding drama.

True, we live in an era of Homeric technological innovations but hardly
unprecedented ones, despite contemporary alarmist rhetoric warning of
dire future calamities unless certain steps are taken. Recall the pages of
history that chronicle the startling turnabouts in human life that have occurred during the last two centuries, for example, the development of the
steam engine, which opened the doors to an industrial revolution that
planted the seeds of present-day capitalism; then jump to the history of
inventions: the telegraph and telephone, which revolutionized communi-
cations, followed by the automobile, the airplane, and the radio. Did they
not dramatically alter how people live and work? Did Western Europeans
and Americans who experienced these advances and enjoyed the fruits of
this profound transformation witness less technosocial change than the
present generation?

Decades ago, with the advent of the Great Depression, much of the world, Mexico included, sought, albeit never successfully, ways to protect men and women from the ravages of free market economics, the scourge of the nineteenth century. For Mexico, these were the days of the Cardenista reforms of the late 1930s, when political leaders put social justice ahead of private gain. In the world order of global economics, these attempts are no longer fashionable. Unemployment is on the rise, but politicians compete with bankers and industrialists in the race to eliminate safety nets. The watchwords are privatization and good riddance to the government's watchdog role in the affairs of society. Although history does not repeat itself, historians will someday surely look upon this era, with its sale of national resources and labor to foreigners, as the rebirth of the nineteenth century.

In this restructuring of the Mexican border, industrial capital hunts for better strategic locations and bigger pools of cheap labor. Thanks to the *maquiladoras* and the emergence of economic blocs in Western Europe, the Far East, and the Americas, the globalized economy has pulled the Mexican border into its vortex. For Mexicans, the global tint is American; of the five hundred biggest corporations in the world, half are American, some controlling budgets far larger than those of their Third World host countries; their eighteen thousand worldwide foreign subsidiaries employ approximately 7 million workers. Increasingly, countries such as Mexico that are havens for these offshore assembly plants produce a larger share of the world's manufactures, but nearly two-thirds of these products end up in the markets of the home countries. Again and again, Americans buy factory goods made with cheap foreign labor in foreign subsidiaries of American corporations.

To march in step with this global current, Mexican elites turned their backs on national policies from yesteryear and, in the manner of Porfirio Díaz, put their faith in foreign capital. However, as border Mexicans know from long experience, the pitfalls are formidable. It is risky business to gamble your well-being on foreigners. When capital, technology, and markets are one and the same, analysts note, the result is usually an "isolated enclave of export-oriented manufacturing" without "broad-based internal industrialization." The storm clouds hover ominously nearby when one deals with foreign assembly plants. On the Mexican border, the reality that was once feared has come to pass. The *maquiladoras* are, for all intents and purposes, an industrial enclave shorn of ties to the local economy.

Whether globalization signifies progress depends essentially on where one stands in the economic picture. From the perspective of analysts in the Third World, the horizons are murky at best. As many argue, the moral content of economic relations flies out the window when commerce is unhampered by social controls, and at the same time, the need to fulfill market demands at the lowest possible price fosters a callous indifference to the conditions under which goods are produced. Historians of progressive bent see today's sweatshops, such as the *maquiladoras* of Mexico, as the functional equivalents of colonial slavery because consumer demands and the capitalists' hunger for profits shunt aside the rights and dreams of working men and women, whose labor produces the salable goods. Writing in *Proceso*, the best of the political journals in Mexico, Heberto Castillo, a senator for the PRD, put these thoughts down in plain Spanish; let it be understood, he emphasized, that those who march to the tune of global economics end up as lackeys of the imperial powers. Thanks to the General Agreement on Tariffs and Trade (GATT), a forerunner of NAFTA that the Salinistas also embraced, "Mexico now confronts the worst crisis of the century." So far, the critic Rachael Kamel adds, "economic integration has meant globalization from above," the free movement of capital across international boundaries, making "the rich richer" and "producing what has been called a global pillage." Those who spearhead the new economic order, whether as bankers or managers of transnationals, sit at desks in the European capitals or in New York or Tokyo, but the octopus they have created stands at loggerheads with a state's responsibility in the Third World for the common well-being and people's right to choose their own destiny. The fierce competition among bankrupt countries for foreign currency and jobs is partly responsible for how things stack up. The consequence is a "race to the bottom in which wages . . . tend to fall to the level of the most desperate." Globalization, by the same token, sounds the death knell of Mexico's historic struggle to build a national industry and develop an internal market. Recurrent debt crises, too, jeopardize hopes for a semblance of independence. To avoid defaulting, Mexico must beg for credit from the bankers at the International Monetary Fund who, more often than not, demand tight money policies and deep cuts in social programs.

o o o 🏵 o o o

Today, the ubiquitous *maquila* is the economic pillar of border society, defining the character and pace of life. Matamoros exemplifies this. On Avenida Lauro Villar, where *maquiladoras* beckon, one shift of workers starts in the morning, another in midafternoon, a third replaces them at midnight. The city awakens, with multitudes of people coming and going, taking buses home or to buy groceries, as others enter the workplace. At Thompson Industries, Alan Weisman recalls, "machines sweep back and forth on belts and women furiously wind and knit cables for automobile electric systems." On the muddy alley leading to the Thompson,

Fisher Price, and Zenith plants, vendors peddle tacos, tamales, corn on the cob, pumpkin seeds, Hershey bars, and cigarettes to throngs of women on their half-hour breaks. In Tijuana, as a reporter for the *San Diego Union-Tribune* notes, the dusty outskirts bulge with faceless, boxy factories that belong to such corporate giants as General Electric, General Motors, and Mattel, where women entering and leaving form a human chain.

Maquilas, true enough, are evolving. One in five no longer simply relies on cheap Mexican labor but leans more and more on advanced machinery and technology, mostly in the assembly of television sets, auto parts, and electronics. The *maquilas* hire a larger number of men. For some pundits, the new *maquilas* are proving "that they can help Mexico move to a higher level of development by fostering," in their argot, "greater technology transfer and the training of a skilled and well-educated workforce," but, they caution, "it is too early to tell" whether they "will usher in a higher state of development in Mexico."

Signs abound, all the same, that it is not too soon to offer a prognosis. As Leslie Sklair, the British scholar, points out, the hopes that Mexican planners have so far pinned on the *maquiladoras* are just pipe dreams; *maquilas,* instead, exacerbate endemic distortions in the economy. Material inputs, essential to the promotion of local industry, are negligible, as are transfers of free technology that would cost thousands their jobs if carried out. Nor have *maquilas* solved the problem of male unemployment. Concerning *maquila* workers, Sklair compares them to "landless rural laborers"—poorly paid, nonunion, and dependent on government largesse for their social benefits.

True believers predict that working conditions and wages, although poor today, will improve as they did in Western Europe early in this century. Poorly paying jobs are better than none and, in time, so goes this argument, "subcontracting" industries help poor countries to develop and eventually promote higher wages. That supposition is tenuous at best, as a recent International Labor Organization study confirms; in its opinion, this type of "subcontracting" does little for long-term economic development in poor countries, encouraging, because of competition among Third World countries to meet market demands, a downward push on wages and working conditions, leading to nefarious forms of employment, such as a rise in homework and the use of child labor, already characteristics of the Mexican scene. Moreover, not only are living standards declining for workers in such countries as the United States, but it is also true that the well-off nations have always depended for their bounty on the exploitation of peripheral peoples. Transnationals, it must be understood, rarely help raise the technical level of a country such as Mexico because the jobs such workers provide are unskilled. When advanced technology is employed, it is mostly under foreign control, not transferred to national industry.

Yes, South Korea, Hong Kong, and Taiwan expanded their own industries while producing for the global economy, but they did so behind tariff walls, through policies that compelled foreign corporations to buy a percentage of components from local manufacturers. From the beginning, goals also diverged, with the East Asian countries primarily seeking not jobs, as in Mexico, but foreign exchange to sustain their economic growth. Sources of foreign capital and export markets, too, are dissimilar; unlike Mexico, where capital and markets are American, the Asians are more diversified. They do not rely solely on one country. The Asian *maquila* industry is not the enclave model of Mexico but the more sophisticated "component supplier" type, in which the manufacture of components takes place at home, with final assembly usually in the more developed Asian nations. Yet, experts testify, poverty is rampant in these places because wealth never trickles down. Despite putting in some of the longest working hours anywhere in the world, the average Korean earns about $10,000 a year, just half of the per capita gross domestic product in the advanced Western countries.

Bear in mind, too, that labor earnings do not necessarily remain in Mexico. *Maquila* workers spend a good part of them on the other side of the border; speaking in McAllen in 1994, Senator Lloyd Bentsen, a firm believer in *maquilas,* told an audience that Mexican workers in the *maquila* industry spent 40 percent of their wages in the United States. This, Bentsen gloated, is good news for American business, but, Mexican analysts hasten to add, hardly for Mexicans. Nor have *maquilas* halted the decline in per capita income in Mexico.

Not everyone in Mexico, unsurprisingly, endorses the panacea of assembly plants. Independent labor, economists, businessmen, and people in every walk of life express misgivings daily about a policy that shamefully kowtows to the whims of foreigners, allows total outside control over a major industry, alienates the land, and endorses a quirky transformation of the border and ultimately the national economy into an export platform. Rather than integrate the economy of the border more closely with the republic's, *maquilas* link it more tightly with that of the United States. The *maquilas* take our land, use up our energy sources, and exploit our workers, so goes the Mexican litany, and then run off to another country where labor is cheaper. Excluding wages, Samuel Schmidt says, "they bring little economic benefit and limited additional economic opportunities." Or to quote Sklair, unless Mexico and the transnationals "can work out ways of transforming" *maquilas* "into a more potent instrument for the development of Mexico and the advancement of its people, Mexico is better off without" them. Yet Mexico surely sits on the horns of a dilemma; were the *maquilas* to depart tomorrow, its economy would fall into a violent tailspin.

○ ○ ○ ⬡ ○ ○ ○

NAFTA, a celebration of commercial ties between Mexico and the United States, emerges out of this global blueprint. However, the *maquila* industry, one of its cornerstones, was made possible by prior changes in Mexico's laws, not by NAFTA, which is not primarily a trade pact but rather about the freedom of capital to relocate where it chooses. After all, by the standards of the industrial powers, the Mexican economy is quite small; from January through September 1994, the *New York Times* reported, exports to Mexico represented less than 1 percent of the goods and services produced in the United States. Transnational corporations and banks are the architects of the Western Hemisphere's bloc goal, which NAFTA symbolizes, in order to "consolidate a free-for-capital region . . . to better exploit human and natural resources."

NAFTA, in fact, is a modern version of colonialism, a restatement in economic terms of the Monroe Doctrine, this time to blunt competition in the Western Hemisphere from European and Japanese rivals for American transnationals. It provides added guarantees for American investments, promotes greater integration of money markets, and opens the way for more industrial concentration. Since trade between Mexico and the United States seldom faces knotty hurdles, the novelty of NAFTA is that it opens wide the door to uninhibited investment, which, it should be obvious, limits the power of the Mexican state to oversee economic development. NAFTA says not a word about the free movement of labor and leaves the most vulnerable at the mercy of transnational employers.

To underline this again: Trade is not the issue. Free trade zones, which NAFTA purportedly guarantees, are an inherent part of the border's history. They go back to 1858, when Chihuahua and Tamaulipas established the first of them. For Juarenses, who complained the loudest, Mexican tariffs, which they labeled arbitrary as well as exorbitant, made impossible the purchase of foreign merchandise, raised the cost of living, and drove friends and neighbors to settle in El Paso, where goods cost half as much. This situation, a bonanza for El Paso, brought economic ruin to Ciudad Juárez and led, logically, to a flourishing contraband trade. The free trade zone restored economic sanity to the border, so much so, its defenders argue, that Ciudad Juárez and other towns in Chihuahua and Tamaulipas soon surpassed their American neighbors in well-being and population. The turnabout, this version goes on, led merchants in the United States to ask officials in Washington to demand that Mexico abandon the free trade zone. Washington's intervention, as well as the lobbying of Mexican merchants from the interior of the republic who imported European goods for resale, ended the experiment, but not for long. The free trade zone surfaced again in 1885, but this time lasted only until 1891, and in Tamaulipas until 1905, its demise again producing calamitous results for Ciudad Juárez. In 1933, in order to cushion the economic blows that befell Baja California because of the Great Depression and the collapse of Prohibition, Mexican authorities decreed a free trade zone for Tijuana and Ensenada and, in 1935, broadened it to include Mexicali, Tecate, and San Luis Río Colorado.

The free trade zone, a welcome remedy for Mexican store owners on the border who became free to import American goods for resale, proved no solution at all. According to studies made of the Baja California experience, the merchants failed to reinvest their profits or bring their businesses up to date and instead speculated with real estate in other parts of the republic. As a result, most were unprepared to compete under the terms of NAFTA, a kind of substitute for the free trade zone of yesteryear. Free trade panaceas, furthermore, always posed a dilemma for national authorities, caught between the need to concede greater freedom to border residents to buy articles of prime necessity not available at home and the need to integrate the economy of the republic, protect national industry, and prevent loss of foreign exchange.

In 1971, yet another effort was made to placate the insatiable appetite for American goods, this time with Artículos Ganchos, a program that allowed merchants to import duty-free basic necessities, such as cooking oils, cereals, butter, mayonnaise, fruits and vegetables, electrical appliances, hardware, and clothes. They could resell these goods so long as at least half of their merchandise was Mexican. The idea behind Artículos Ganchos was that by permitting the sale of imported goods at prices equal to or lower than those charged by stores across the border, the money would stay in Mexico. It solved nothing, because it simply fueled the hunger for American goods, discouraged their manufacture in Mexico, and kept alive the old dependency.

As this story unfolded, Mexico exported capital—through debt payments and flights of profits from foreign corporations. That left it always in hock and unable, even when it wished, to minister to the needs of its impoverished. Whatever experts might think, NAFTA will not rewrite that scenario or introduce an authentic interdependency; to the contrary, it endangers, among others, the livelihood of storekeepers, this time on both sides of the border, because neither can compete with the giant transnationals. As one former president of the Tijuana Chamber of Commerce explained, once Mexico joined the GATT, foreign goods flooded local markets, saddling Mexico with a bulging commercial deficit. According to a spokesman for CANACINTRA, no less than one hundred small industries, employing 60 percent of the local labor force, closed their doors in one year in the port city of Ensenada. Why, he asked, had small industry not been shielded from the effects of NAFTA? Regarding its drafting, the president of the Milk Producers Association in Tijuana complained, dairymen were not consulted; "incredibly, we read the text of NAFTA in newspapers," and learned that American dairies "could export . . . tons of milk powder and millions of gallons of fresh milk" but we "could only sell . . . the ridiculous amount of . . . 205 gallons per day." Later, when California dairymen were losing a critical export market because Mexican regulations limited the shelf life of milk in Tijuana *supermercados* (supermarkets) to two days, local officials, at the urging of American interests who labeled Mexican regulations anti-NAFTA, interceded to make it seven days. Since then, American milk exports to Baja California are on the rise, to the detriment of Mexican dairymen. Nor will NAFTA erase, as the performance of assembly plants verifies, the reasons poor Mexicans look for jobs in the United States. When *maquiladoras* pay $5 a day but workers in the United States earn that in one hour, "who in his right mind," the author of an article in the *Nation* asks, "would bother staying on the south side?"

NAFTA could, if Washington were to deem fit, alter the rules of this game so that workers on both sides of the border would benefit. For this to occur, the "free trade or no trade" rhetoric that dogged the original NAFTA debate, and that continues to fill the editorial pages of American newspapers, must fall by the wayside, replaced by a more responsible view. The real issue, as David Bonier, the House Democratic whip, puts it, is that trade must benefit ordinary people, a commitment that requires rejecting "trade agreements that ignore wages, labor rights, and environmental standards." Unless this is done, workers in both Mexico and the United States will carry the weight of free trade on their backs because the combination of "First World productivity at Third World pay" merely creates a windfall for corporations.

○　○　○　❀　○　○　○

This drama is unfolding on an international stage, where the almighty dollar presides, where Mexicans, unless a dramatic turnabout in the rules of the game occurs, are condemned. To fall back on a bit of English wisdom: "To each his suff'rings . . . Condemned alike to groan." Many Americans will reject this scenario and reply that border Mexicans are better off today than before or place the responsibility for local ills solely on the victims themselves. But they are surely mistaken. In this age of a global economy, all of us, whether in rich or poor nations, are in this together. As William Greider, an expert on the subject, argues eloquently, we are all "on the same runaway train." What affects one segment of the world economy eventually touches everyone. Americans can no longer take refuge behind isolationist policies or imperialistic adventures; nor will American taxpayers forever support Washington's bailouts, in Mexico or Asia, of faltering dependent economies.

Until Americans learn to think globally and reject behavior that dumps "poor people over the side," such as badly paid Mexican workers employed by American corporations, job loss and depressed wages will be their lot. Workers at the bottom of the barrel, those in the *maquilas* for one, must enjoy the right to organize and bargain for a larger share of profits or the American way of life will face a rocky road ahead. The reason seems obvious: Illogical as it may seem, well-paid American workers cannot compete with productive Mexicans driven to labor for a pittance. When potential customers are too poor to buy, markets inevitably become glutted, as the rising global overproduction of automobiles confirms. Without strong consumer demand, the productivity we covet pushes wages down, cuts jobs, and, lest we forget, hurts profits; that, along with inflated stock markets and speculating banks, leads inexorably to global depression—witness the great crash of 1929. Today, to quote Greider again, "the global economy is choking on its own productive overcapacity," victimized by the very captains of industry who, up to now, have profited most from it. As Henry Ford, never known for his largesse, once pontificated, an industrial system stagnates once its workers are unable to buy what they produce. A healthy and prosperous American economy will not forever endure if the mass of Mexicans to the south, many of whom labor for greedy American employers, live in Third World dependency.

Sources

For the Mexican side of the border, studies by the Colegio de la Frontera Norte are unsurpassed. The Colegio, a Mexican-government think tank with headquarters a few miles south of Tijuana, has offices in every major border city. Dedicated to the study of border issues, scholars at the Colegio publish articles and books on subjects ranging from immigrants to assembly plants. Virtually nothing of prime importance escapes their attention, although cultural questions, in the mold of contemporary social science research, are hardly a top priority. Together, these articles, books, and unpublished manuscripts are the single most valuable collection of materials on the life of border Mexicans, and equally important, they include sundry statistics on topics such as social conditions, immigrants' moving back and forth across international boundaries, wages and hours of *maquiladora* workers, and so forth. Every two years, moreover, scholars from every branch of the Colegio come together in Tijuana for two days of intellectual discussion, during which they present their latest findings to each other and to invited scholars from both Mexico and the United States. So far, there have been four "COLEFS," as the meetings are called. Some of the manuscripts are eventually published; but whether in print or not, they are splendid tools for students of Mexican border affairs. Following is a list of the unpublished manuscripts I have used from three meetings of Colegio scholars.

COLEF Manuscripts

COLEF I

Alarcón Cantú, Eduardo. "Evolución y Dependencia en el Noreste; las Ciudades Fronterizas de Tamaulipas."

Hernández, Alberto. "Transformaciones Sociales y Pluralismo Religioso en Cinco Ciudades Fronterizas."

Iglesias, Norma. "La Fábrica de los Sueños: El Cine Fronterizo y Relación con el Público."

COLEF II

Castro, José Luis, and Eduardo Alarcón Cantú. "Estructura Urbana de Nuevo Laredo."

Alegría Olazábal, Tito. "Estructura Urbana de Tijuana."

Barajas Escamilla, Rocío. "La Industria Maquiladora del Noroeste."

Barajas Escamilla, Rocío, and Arón Noe Fuentes. "Patrones de Competividad y Especialización Industrial en la Frontera Norte."

Barrera, Eduardo, "Reconversión Industrial y Revolución de las Telecomunicaciones en la Industria Maquiladora."

Bringas, Nora L. "El Caso del Turismo en Baja California."

Calleros, Jesús Roman, and Francisco Bernal. "México-Estados Unidos: Divergencias por el Agua del Río Colorado."

Canales, Alejandro. "Dotación de Personal en la Industria Maquiladora."

Carrillo, Jorge, and Jorge Santibañez. "Determinantes de la Rotación de Personal en las Maquiladoras de Tijuana."

Carrillo, Jorge, Oscar F. Contreras, and Miguel Angel Ramírez. "Sindicalismo y Modernización Industrial en Tres Sectores: Maquiladoras, Automotriz y Minería."

Castillo, Gustavo del. "Movimientos Transnacionales de Mano de Obra y Ciclos Económicos: El Caso de San Diego-Tijuana."

Corona, Rodolfo. "Dinámica Demográfica en la Frontera de México."

Fuentes, César, Jesús Montenegro, and Victor Zúñiga. "Institucionalización y Organización del Arte en Dos Ciudades del Norte de México (Ciudad Juárez y Monterrey, 1945–1990)."

González Ramírez, Raul Sergio. "La Evolución de la Población Económicamente Activa en las Ciudades de la Frontera, 1970–1990."

_____. "La Fecundidad en la Frontera Norte de México: El Caso de Tijuana."

Guillén López, Tonatiuh. "Cultura Política en la Frontera Norte."

_____. "El Municipio y el Desarrollo Regional."

_____. "Los Retos Sociales de la Administración Municipal en la Frontera Norte."

Hodara, Joseph. "Escritura y Frontrera Norte."

Lara, Francisco. "Formación y Estructura del Espacio Urbano de Nogales."

Lozano Rendón, José Carlos. "Identidad Nacional en la Frontera."

Mendoza, Jaime, and José Luis Castro. "Estructura Urbana de Matamoros."

Ramos, José Mariak. "El Servicio de Aduanas de Estados Unidos y la Política Antidrogas Fronteriza: El Rol e Impacto Social."

Ruiz Marrujo, Olivia. "La Mujer como Agente Transfronterizo: La Convergencia de Género, Etnia y Clase Social."

Sánchez, Roberto, and Francisco Lara. "El Manejo del Agua en la Región de los dos Nogales: Consideraciones Sociales y Ambientales."

Valenzuela Arce, José Manuel. "El Color de las Sombras: Racismo Antimexicano en la Frontera México-Estados Unidos."

_____. "Voy a dar un Pormenor: El Corrido y la Canción Norteña."

Woo Morales, Ofelia. "La Migración de Indocumentados en el Este de la Frontera Norte: El Caso de Matamoros, Tamaulipas."

Zúñiga, Victor. "La Política Cultural Hacia la Frontera Norte . . . 1887–1990."

COLEF III

Alegría Olazábal, Tito. "Geografía de la Trasmigracion: Un Modelo Simple de Estimaciones. Frontera y Migraciones."

Bustamante, Jorge. "Undocumented Migration from Mexico to the United States: A Theoretical Approach for a Research Strategy and Policy Making."

Ham Chande, Roberto. "Diferenciales de Población y Migración Internacional a Corta Distancia en la Frontera México-Estados Unidos."

_____. "Etnicidad y Estructura de Población en la Frontera de Estados Unidos con México."

_____. "Notas Estadísticas Sobre la Población de Origen Mexicano en Estados Unidos."

Heer, David M. "Values at Stake for Both Mexico and the United States."

Zenteno Quintero, René M. "Migración Hacia la Frontera Norte de México: Tijuana, Baja California."

Newspapers

Equally essential to studies on border issues are the many newspapers that cover this topic. Ill fares a study lacking a careful reading of the *New York Times* and the *Los Angeles Times*. Mexican newspapers are more inclusive, dealing with all aspects of border life, although given the dictatorial nature of national regimes, they are circumspect when reporting on political affairs. American papers, conversely, tend to favor matters of particular signficance to the United States and expend less ink on cultural or social questions. Not surprisingly, both have decidedly nationalistic bents; reporters and editorial writers, after all, are part and parcel of their country's *ambiente*.

Mexican

Baja California, Mexicali, Baja Caliornia Norte
Diario 29, Mexicali, Baja California Norte
Diario de Juárez, Ciudad Juárez, Chihuahua
Diario de la Frontera, Nogales, Sonora
El Diario de Monterrey, Monterrey, Nuevo León
El Diario de Nuevo Laredo, Nuevo Laredo, Tamaulipas
El Financiero, Mexico City
El Mañana, Nuevo Laredo, Tamaulipas
El Mexicano, Baja California Norte
El Sol de Tijuana, Tijuana, Baja California Norte
Excelsior, Mexico City
La Jornada, Mexico City
La Tarde de Baja California, Tijuana, Baja California Norte
La Voz de la Frontera, Mexicali, Baja California Norte
Norte de Chihuahua, Ciudad Juárez, Chihuahua
Valle del Norte, Reynosa, Tamaulipas
Zeta, Tijuana, Baja California Norte
Zócalo, Piedras Negras, Coahuila

United States

Albuquerque Journal, Albuquerque, New Mexico
Arizona Republic, Phoenix, Arizona

Austin American Statesman, Austin, Texas
Brownsville Herald, Brownsville, Texas
Calexico Chronicle, Calexico, California
Coastal Current, South Padre Island, Texas
Dallas Morning Herald, Dallas, Texas
El Latino, San Diego, California
El Paso Herald Post, El Paso, Texas
El Paso Times, El Paso, Texas
La Opinión, Jacksonville, Texas
Laredo Morning Times, Laredo, Texas
Los Angeles Times, Los Angeles, California
Monitor, McAllen, Texas
New York Times, New York, New York
San Antonio Express-News, San Antonio, Texas
San Francisco Examiner, San Francisco, California
San Diego Union-Tribune, San Diego, California
Valley Morning Star, Harlingen, Texas
Voz Fronteriza, San Diego, California
Wall Street Journal, New York, New York

Journals

Al Punto del Alba
Border Economy. Economía Fronteriza
Businessweek
Chamizal
Cuadernos de Trabajo
Cuadernos del Norte
Democratic Left
El Puente Negro
Esquina Baja
Estudios Fronterizos
Frontera Norte
Harper's
In These Times
La Corriente
Mayibo
Nation
National Review
New Republic
Noesis
Norte
Puente Libre
Proceso
Rutas
Social Contract
Time

Books

Alarcón Cantú, Eduardo. *Evolución y Dependencia en las Ciudades Fronterizas y Dependencia de Tamaulipas.* Mexico, 1990.

Alegría Olazábal, Tito. *Desarrollo Urbano en la Frontera México-Estados Unidos: Una Interpretacion y Algunos Resultados.* Mexico, 1992.

Allen, John Houghton. *Southwest.* Philadelphia and New York, 1952.

Anzaldua, Gloria. *Borderlands: La Frontera.* San Francisco, 1987.

Arreola, Daniel D., and James R. Curtis. *The Mexican Border Cities: Landscape Anatomy and Place Personality.* Tucson, 1993.

Baum, Dan. *Smoke and Mirrors: The War on Drugs and the Politics of Failure.* New York, 1996.

Bayardo Gómez, Patricio. *El Signo y la Alambrada.* Mexico, 1990.

Bonfil Batalla, Guillermo. *México Profundo: Una Civilización Negada.* Mexico, 1987.

Cahill, Rick. *Border Towns of the Southwest: Shopping, Dining, Fun, and Adventure from Tijuana to Ciudad Juarez.* Boulder, 1987.

Campbell, Federico. *Tijuanenses.* Mexico, 1989.

Carretero Balboa, José. *Historia de H. Matamoros, Tamaulipas.* Matamoros, 1981.

Carrillo, Jorge, and Alberto Hernández. *Mujeres Fronterizas en la Industria Maquiladora.* Mexico, 1985.

Castañeda, Jorge C. *Utopia Unarmed: The Latin American Left After the Cold War.* New York, 1993.

Castellanos Guerrero, Alicia. *La Vida Fronteriza.* Mexico, 1981.

Cazneau, Mrs. William L. (Cora Montgomery). *Eagle Pass or Life on the Border.* Austin, Texas, 1966.

Chatfield, W. H. *The Twin Cities of the Border: Brownsville, Texas, Matamoros, Mexico, and the Country of the Lower Rio Grande.* New Orleans, 1893.

Chávez, Armando. *Historia de Ciudad Juárez, Chihuahua.* Mexico, 1991.

Clement, Norris C., and Eduardo Zepeda Miramontes. *San Diego-Tijuana in Transition: A Regional Analysis.* San Diego, 1993.

Conde, Rosina. *Arrieros Somos.* Mexico, 1994.

———. *El Agente Secreto.* Tijuana, 1990.

Conover, Ted. *Coyotes: A Journey Through the Secret World of America's Illegal Aliens.* New York, 1987.

Cornelius, Wayne A., Philip L. Martin, and James F. Hollifield. *Controlling Immigration: A Global Perspective.* San Diego and Stanford, 1995.

Crosthwaite, Luis Humberto. *El Gran Pretender.* Mexico, 1992.

———. *Marcela y el Rey: Al Fin Juntos.* Zacatecas, 1987.

Cruz Vázquez, Eduardo. *Desde la Frontera Norte.* Mexico, 1991.

D'Antonio, William V., and William H. Form. *Influentials in Two Border Cities: A Study in Community Decision Making.* Notre Dame, Indiana, 1965.

Demaris, Ovid. *Poso del Mundo: Inside the Mexican-American Border, from Tijuana to Matamoros.* Boston, 1970.

Dunn, Timothy J. *The Militarization of the Border, 1978–1992: Low-Intensity Conflict Doctrine Comes Home.* Austin, Texas, 1996.

Esparza Marín, Ignacio. *Monografía Histórica de Ciudad Juárez.* 2 vols. Ciudad Juárez, 1990.

Espinosa Valle, Victor Alejandro, ed. *Don Crispín: Una Crónica Fronteriza, Memoria y Diálogos de Don Crispín Valle Castañeda.* Tijuana, 1990.

_____. *Reforma del Estado y Empleo Público.* Mexico, 1993.

Fernández, Raul A. *La Frontera México-Estados Unidos: Un Estudio Socioeconómico.* Mexico, 1980.

Fernández Kelly, María Patricia. *For We Are Sold, I and My People: Women and Industry in Mexico's Frontier.* New York, 1983.

Figueroa, Jesús, and David Piñera Ramírez, eds. *Historia de Tijuana, 1889–1989.* Vol. 2. Tijuana, 1982.

Flores Simental, Raul, ed. *Crónica en el Desierto: Ciudad Juárez de 1659 a 1970.* Ciudad Juárez, 1994.

Fowler, Gene, and Bill Crawford. *Border Radio.* Austin, Texas, 1987.

Fuentes, Carlos. *La Frontera de Cristal.* Mexico, 1995.

Gamboa, Federico. *Diario de Federico Gamboa, 1882–1939.* Mexico, 1977.

Gibson, Lay James, and Alfonso Corona Rentería, eds. *Regional Impact of United States–Mexico Economic Relations.* Mexico, 1984.

Gómez Montero, Sergio. *Sociedad y Desierto: Literatura en la Frontera Norte.* Mexico, 1993.

González, Soledad, Olivia Ruiz Marrujo, Laura Velasco, and Ofelia Woo. *Mujeres, Migración, y Maquila en la Frontera Norte.* Mexico, 1995.

Gray, Robert, Jesús Reynosa, Conrado Q. Díaz, and Howard G. Applegate. *Vehicular Traffic and Air Pollution in El Paso-Ciudad Juárez.* El Paso, Texas, 1989.

Greene, Graham. *Another Mexico.* New York, 1939.

Hall, Douglas K. *The Border: Life on the Line.* New York, 1988.

Hansen, Niles. *The Border Economy: Regional Development in the Southwest.* Austin, Texas, 1981.

Heer, David M. *Undocumented Workers in the United States.* New York, 1990.

Hellman, Judith Adler. *Mexican Lives.* New York, 1994.

Herzog, Lawrence A. *Where North Meets South: Cities, Space, and Politics on the U.S.-Mexican Border.* Austin, Texas, 1990.

Iglesias Prieto, Norma. *La Flor Más Bella de la Maquiladora: Historias de Vida de la Mujer Obrera en Tijuana,* 1985.

Jordán, Fernando. *El Otro México: Biografía de Baja California.* Mexico, 1987.

Karp, Ilián. *Movimientos Culturales en la Frontera Sonorense.* Hermosillo, 1991.

Kearney, Milo, ed. *Studies in Brownsville's History.* Brownsville, Texas, 1986.

Klagsbrunn, Victor, ed. *Tijuana: Cambio Social y Migración.* Tijuana, 1988.

Least Heat-Moon, William. *Blue Highways: A Journey into America.* Boston, 1982.

Loaeza, Guadalupe. *Las Niñas Bien.* Mexico, 1987.

López, Silvia, and Norma Ojeda. *Familias Transfronterizas en Tijuana: Dos Estudios Complementarios.* Tijuana, 1994.

Mangin, Frank. *El Paso in Pictures.* El Paso, Texas, 1971.

Margulis, Mario, and Rodolfo Tuirán. *Desarrollo y Población en la Frontera Norte: El Caso de Reynosa.* Mexico, 1986.

Maril, Robert Lee. *Poorest of Americans: The Mexican Americans of the Lower Rio Grande Valley of Texas.* Notre Dame, Indiana, 1980.

Martínez, Oscar J. *Border Boomtown: Ciudad Juárez Since 1848.* Austin, Texas, 1975.

_____. *Troublesome Border.* Tucson, Arizona, 1988.

Martínez, Oscar J., ed. *U.S.-Mexico Borderlands: Historical and Contemporary Perspectives.* Wilmington, 1996.

Mascareñas, José Manuel, and Michael R. Moses, eds. *Juárez, Milagro del Norte.* El Paso, Texas, 1991.

Millán Peraza, Miguel Angel. *A Tijuana (Nosotras las Gringas).* Tijuana, 1992.

Miller, Michael V. *Economic Growth and Change Along the U.S.-Mexico Border: The Case of Brownsville, Texas.* San Antonio, Texas, 1981.

Miller, Tom. *On the Border: Portraits of America's Southwestern Frontier.* New York, 1981.

Montejano, David. *Anglos and Mexicans in the Making of Texas, 1836–1986.* Austin, Texas, 1987.

Murrieta, Mayo, and Alberto Hernández. *Puente México (La Vecindad de Tijuana con California).* Tijuana, 1991.

Ojeda, Mario, ed. *Administración del Desarrollo de la Frontera Norte.* Mexico, 1982.

Paredes, Américo. *Folklore and Culture on the Texas-Mexican Border.* Austin, Texas, 1993.

_____. *With a Pistol in His Hand: A Border Ballad and Its Hero.* Austin, Texas, 1958.

Peña, Devon G. *The Terror Machine: Technology, Work, Gender, and Ecology on the U.S.-Mexico Border.* Austin, Texas, 1997.

Peña, Manuel H. *The Texas-Mexican Conjunto: A History of a Working-Class Music.* Austin, Texas, 1985.

Pérez, Ramón "Tianguis." *Diary of an Undocumented Immigrant.* Houston, 1989.

Piñera Ramírez, David, ed. *Historia de Tijuana: Semblanza General.* Tijuana, 1985.

Polkinhorn, Harry, Gabriel Trujillo Muñoz, and Rogelio Reyes. *La Linea: Ensayos Sobre Literatura Fronteriza México-Norteamericana.* Tijuana, 1988.

Poppa, Terrence E. *Drug Lord: The Life and Death of a Mexican Kingpin.* New York, 1990.

Price, Carol Ann. *Early El Paso Artists.* El Paso, Texas, 1983.

Price, John A. *Tijuana: Urbanization in a Border Culture.* Notre Dame, 1973.

Price, Thomas J. *Standoff at the Border: A Failure of Microdiplomacy.* El Paso, Texas, 1989.

Reed, John. *Insurgent Mexico.* New York, 1969.

Restrepo, Iván, ed. *Agua, Salud, y Derechos Humanos.* Mexico, 1995.

Roca, Hernán de la. *Tijuana In.* Mexico, 1990.

Rodríguez, Francisco M. *Baco y Birján: Una Historia Sangrienta y Dolorosa de lo Que Fué y lo Que Es Tijuana.* Mexico, 1968.

_____. *Trinchera Obrera.* Tijuana, 1977.

Rosa, Martín de la. *Marginalidad en Tijuana.* Tijuana, 1985.

Ruiz, Vicky L., and Susan, Tiano, eds. *Women on the U.S.-Mexico Border: Responses to Change.* Boston, 1987.

Sada, Daniel. *Lampa Vida.* Mexico, 1980.

Sánchez, Mario L. *A Shared Experience: A History, Architecture, and Historic Designations of the Lower Rio Grande Heritage Corridor.* Austin, Texas, 1994.

Santibañez Romellón, Jorge, ed. *La Migración Nacional e Internacional de los Oaxaqueños.* Mexico, 1995.

Saravia Quiroz, Leobardo, ed. *En la Linea del Fuego: Relatos Policiacos de Frontera.* Mexico, 1990.

Simon, Joel. *Endangered Mexico: An Environment on the Edge.* San Francisco, 1997.

Sklair, Leslie. *Assembling for Development: The Maquila Industry in Mexico and the United States.* Boston, 1989.

Smith, Peter, ed. *Drug Policy in the Americas.* San Francisco, 1992.

Sonnichsen, C. L. *Pass on the North: Four Centuries on the Rio Grande.* 2 vols. El Paso, Texas, 1968–1980.

Steinhart, Peter. *Two Eagles. Dos Aguilas.* Berkeley and Los Angeles, 1994.

Stoddard, Ellwyn. *Patterns of Poverty Along the US-Mexican Border.* El Paso, Texas, 1978.

Szekely, Gabriel, ed. *Manufacturing Across Borders and Oceans.* San Diego, 1991.

Timmons, W. H. *El Paso: A Borderlands History.* El Paso, Texas, 1990.

Ugalde, Antonio. *The Urbanization Process of a Poor Mexican Neighborhood.* Austin, Texas, 1974.

Urrea, Luis Alberto. *Across the Wire: Life and Hard Times on the Mexican Border.* New York, 1993.

U.S. Department of Commerce. Economics and Statistics Administration. Bureau of the Census. *Census 1990. Brownsville-Harlington, Texas.* Washington, D.C., 1993.

Valenzuela Arce, José Manuel, ed. *Decadencia y Auge de las Identidades.* Tijuana, 1992.

Vélez-Ibañez, Carlos G. *Border Visions: Mexican Cultures of the Southwest United States.* Tucson, Arizona, 1996.

Weisman, Alan. *La Frontera: The United States Border with Mexico.* New York, 1984.

Zamora, Emilio. *The World of the Mexican Worker in Texas.* College Station, Texas, 1993.

Articles and Pamphlets

Aguilar Melantzón, Ricardo, and Fernando García Núñez. "La Frontera México-USA: Novela, Cuento y Chiste." Center for Inter-American and Border Studies, *Border Perspectives*, May 1990. University of Texas, El Paso.

Aguilera Mora, Manuel. "Barbarie Imperialista y Respuesta Popular en la Frontera Norte." *Cuadernos del Norte*, April 1993.

American Friends Service Committee. *Sealing Our Borders: The Human Toll.* Philadelphia, 1992.

_____. *The Global Economy: Positive Alternatives for Those Left Out.* Philadelphia, 1993.

Americas Watch. *Brutality Unchecked: Human Rights Abuses Along the U.S. Border with Mexico.* New York, May 1992.

_____. *United States Frontier Justice: Human Rights Abuses Along the U.S. Border with Mexico Persist Amid Climate of Impunity.* New York, May 1993.

Applegate, Howard G. "Air Quality Issues: El Paso/Cd. Juárez." Center for Inter-American and Border Studies, *Border Issues and Public Policy*, September 1982. University of Texas, El Paso.

Bath, Richard C. "The Emerging Environmental Crisis Along the United States-Mexico Border." In Lawrence A. Herzog, ed., *Changing Boundaries in the Americas.* Center for United States-Mexican Studies, University of California, San Diego, 1992.

Binder, Norman E. "Attitudes Toward Language Use: A Multi-Group Analysis." In Dennis J. Bixler-Márquez, Jacob L. Ornstein-Galicia, and George K. Green, *Mexican-American Spanish in Its Societal and Cultural Context*. El Paso, Texas, 1989.

Brecher, Jeremy. "Global Village or Global Pillage." *Nation*, December 6, 1993.

Center for Global Studies. *Uniting the Basin/Uniendo la Cuenca*. The Woodlands, Texas, 1994.

Centro de Estudios Regionales y Comunicación Alternativa. "Impacto de la Maquiladora en el Medio Ambiente de Ciudad Juárez." *Noesis*, January-December 1991.

Corona Rentería, Alfonso. "Polarización Internacional y Desarrollo de las Regiones Fronterizas del Norte de México." In Lay James Gibson and Alfonso Corona Rentería, *Regional Impacts of United States Mexico Economic Relations*. Mexico, 1984.

Fix, Michael, and Jeffrey S. Passel. *Immigration and Immigrants: Setting the Record Straight*. Washington, D.C., 1994.

Flores Benavides, Liliana. "Medioambiente y Política en México: Análisis y Propuesta." Center for Inter-American and Border Studies, *Border Issues and Public Policy*, May 1994. University of Texas, El Paso.

George, Edward Y. *Sales Taxes on Mexican National's Purchases*. El Paso, Texas, 1982.

Ham Chande, Roberto. "Etnicidad y Estructuras de Población en la Frontera de Estados Unidos con México." *Frontera Norte*, January-June 1991.

Herrera, Eva Lucrecia. "El Quehacer Cultural en el Norte." *Cuadernos del Norte*, May-June 1991.

Herzog, Lawrence A. "Regional Factors as Explanations of Political Change in Baja California." *Frontera Norte*, January-June 1991.

Jordan, Terry C. "A Century and a Half of Ethnic Change in Texas, 1836–1986." *Southwestern Historical Quarterly*, April 1986.

Kamel, Rachael. *The Global Factory: Analysis and Action for a New Economic Era*. Philadelphia, c. 1990.

Kochan, Leslie. *The Maquiladora and Toxics: The Hidden Costs of Production South of the Border*. AFL-CIO, Washington, D.C., 1989.

Lutton, Wayne. "Study: Illegal Immigrants Cost San Diego Millions." *Social Contract*, Fall 1992.

McNamara, Patrick H. "Prostitution Along the U.S.-Mexican Border: A Survey." In Ellwyn R. Stoddard, ed., *Prostitution and Illicit Drug Traffic on the U.S.-Mexico Border*. El Paso, Texas, 1971.

Morales, Rebeca, and Jesus Tamayo Sánchez. "Urbanization and Development of the United States-Mexico Border." In Lawrence A. Herzog, ed., *Changing Boundaries in the Americas*. Center for United States-Mexican Studies, University of California, San Diego, 1992.

Moser, Andrea. "Two Cities, One Economy." *UCSD Perspectives*, Summer 1993.

Nathan, Debbie. "El Paso Under the Blockade." *Nation*, February 28, 1994.

National Commission for Human Rights. *Report on Human Rights Violations of Mexican Migratory Workers on Route to the Northern Border, Crossing the Border and upon Entering the Southern United States Border Strip*. Mexico, 1992.

Piñera Ramírez, David, and Antonio Padilla Corona. "Impacto de la Ley Seca en las Fronteras Canadienses y Mexicana." *Meyibo*, January-June 1991.

Reding, Andrew. "Narco-Politics in Mexico." *Nation*, July 10, 1995.

Ruiz Marrujo, Olivia. "A Tijuana: Las Visitas Transfronterizas Como Estrategias Femeninas de Reproducción Social." In Soledad González, Olivia Ruiz Marrujo, Laura Velasco, and Ofelia Woo, *Mujeres, Migración, y Maquila en la Frontera Norte*. Mexico, 1995.

_____. "Visitando la Patria: Los Cruces Transfronterizos de la Población de Ascendencia Mexicana de la Frontera Californiana." *Frontera Norte*, January-June 1992.

Saint-Germain, Michelle A. "Public Managers on the U.S. Mexico Border." Center for Inter-American and Border Studies, *Border Issues and Public Policy*, July 1994. University of Texas, El Paso.

Santamaría Gómez, Arturo. "The Porous US-Mexico Border." *Nation*, October 25, 1993.

Schmidt, Samuel. "Planning a U.S.-Mexican Bi-National Metropolis: El Paso, Texas–Ciudad Juárez, Chihuahua." Center for Inter-American and Border Studies, *Profmex: Serie de Estudios Urbanos*, University of Texas, El Paso, 1994.

Schmidt, Samuel, Jorge Gil, and Jorge Castro. "El Desarrollo Urbano en la Frontera México-Estados Unidos." Center for Inter-American and Border Studies, *Estudio Delphi en Ocho Ciudades Fronterizas*. University of Texas, El Paso, 1994.

Simon, Joel. "NAFTA—The View from Tijuana." *Nation*, November 30, 1992.

Sklair, Leslie. "The Maquila Industry and the Creation of a Transnational Capitalist Class in the United States-Mexico Border Region." In Lawrence A. Herzog, ed., *Changing Boundaries in the Americas*. Center for United States-Mexican Studies, University of California, San Diego, 1992.

Southeast Network for Economic Justice. *From Global Pillage to Global Village*. Chicago, 1992.

Stoddard, Ellwyn. "Patterns of Poverty Along the US-Mexico Border." El Paso, 1978.

Tabuenca, María Socorro. "Apuntar el Silencio." *Puente Libre*, January-March 1994.

Trujillo, Gabriel. "Crónicas de Mexicali." *Cuadernos del Norte*, May-June 1991.

Wilson, Patricia A. "Maquiladoras and Their Transaction Patterns." *Frontera Norte*, January-June 1991.

Witness for Peace. *Newsletter*. Summer 1992.

Manuscripts

Aguirre, Eleas A. "The Urban Form of El Paso del Norte: A Cluster Analysis." M.A. thesis, University of Texas, El Paso, 1993.

Baca, Vincent Z. C. "Moral Renovation of the Californias: Tijuana's Political and Economic Role in American-Mexican Relations, 1920–1935." Ph.D. diss., University of California, San Diego, 1991.

Bustamante, Jorge, and Marcela Martínez del Castro de la Lama. "Los Derechos Humanos y la Migración de Mexicanos a Estados Unidos." Colegio de la Frontera Norte, Tijuana, 1994.

Dillman, Charles D. "The Functions of Brownsville, Texas, and Matamoros, Tamaulipas: Twin Cities of the Lower Rio Grande." Ph.D. diss., University of Michigan, Ann Arbor, 1968.

Guillén López, Tonatiuh. "La Crisis de la Vivienda en Tijuana." El Colegio de la Frontera Norte, Tijuana, 1992.

Hidalgo, Margarita Guadalupe. "Language Use and Language Attitudes in Juárez, Mexico." Ph.D. diss., University of New Mexico, Albuquerque, 1983.

Rungling, Brian S. "The Impact of the Mexican Alien Commuter on the Apparel Industry of El Paso, Texas (A Case Study)." Ph.D. diss., University of Kentucky, Lexington, 1969.

Tabuenca Córdoba, María Socorro. "Identidad Cultural y Comunidades Imaginadas en Dos Textos de Rosina Conde y Rosario Sanmiguel." Ciudad Juárez, 1996.

Urquidi, Victor L. "Los Problemas del Medio Ambiente en las Relaciones México-Estados Unidos, Presentada en el Coloquio Sociedad y Política: México-Estados Unidos." Colegio de la Frontera Norte, 1996.

Vila, Pablo. "Being Proud of Mexican Heritage: The Mexican and Chicano Version." Colegio de la Frontera Norte, Tijuana, Ciudad Juárez, 1993.

_____. "Ethnic Identity and the Invention of Heritage." Colegio de la Frontera Norte, Ciudad Juárez, 1993.

_____. "Regional Identity, Young Immigrants, and the History of the Future," El Colegio de la Frontera Norte, Ciudad Juárez, 1993.

_____, "Visiones a Través de la Frontera: El Paso–Ciudad Juárez. Identidades Sociales en la Frontera México-Americana. Un Informe Preliminar." Colegio de la Frontera Norte, Ciudad Juárez, 1993.

Wilcox, Jessica. "Impact of Maquiladoras on the Female Mexican Worker in the Border Region." Colegio de la Frontera Norte, Tijuana, 1992.

Index